Why People Join, Leave, and Stay With Health/Fitness Clubs

The Ultimate Handbook of Member Retention

Stephen J. Tharrett, M.S.
Paul Bedford, Ph.D.

HEALTHY LEARNING
www.healthylearning.com

ISBN: 978-1-60679-216-2
Library of Congress Control Number: 2012934628
Cover design: Roger W. Rybkowski
Book layout: Roger W. Rybkowski
Front cover photo: iStockphoto/Thinkstock
Photo of Stephen Tharrett (back cover): Alyssa Tharrett

Healthy Learning
P.O. Box 1828
Monterey, CA 93942
www.healthylearning.com

Dedication

The authors would like to dedicate this book to the memory of Robert H. Dedman, the founder and former chairman of ClubCorp, who passed away in 2002. Robert Dedman founded ClubCorp on the core belief that a club should be a home away from home, a place were like-spirited people of all races, genders, clans, and creeds could gather to together to have fun, befriend each other, and enrich their lives.

Robert was an advocate of treating each member and guest as a *king,* of greeting every member by name, of building trusting relationships with members, and literally of bringing the private club experience to the world. His indomitable spirit and strength of character has influenced and continues to influence thousands of professionals in the health/fitness club business to embrace the mantra of building relationships and enriching lives.

Robert's spirit lives on, not only in the company he founded, but in every facility that has at its helm a former ClubCorp employee partner. Robert understood what was at the heart of membership retention and member loyalty, and his approach exemplified a quote by Lord Burleigh, which says, "Win peoples' hearts, and you have their hands and purses."

In his honor, we have included as part of this dedication Robert's poem, entitled "A Club," so that those individuals who have never had the chance to contemplate the true meaning of a club may do so.

A Club

"A club is a haven of refuge and accord in a world torn by strife and discord.

A club is a place where kindred spirits gather to have fun and make friends.

A club is a place of courtesy, good breeding, and good manners.

A club is a place expressly for camaraderie, merriment,
good will, and good cheer.

It humbles the mighty, draws out the timid, and casts out the soreheads.

A club is one of the noblest inventions of mankind."

—Robert H. Dedman

Acknowledgments

I would first like to acknowledge my parents, for giving me the opportunity to pursue my passion. Second, I want to thank my wife and best friend of 35 years, Denise, for encouraging me, supporting me, and coaching me to be a better person, a better professional, a better husband, and a better father, as well as for hanging in when it seemed I was a ship without a rudder. I want to thank my children, Alyssa and Travis, for enriching my life with their love and incredible energy.

On a more professional note, I also want to thank the people who have inspired me, encouraged me, and educated me about the health/fitness club industry. Numerous individuals should be thanked for their contributions to my personal and professional growth, such as all the great employees who shared the journey with me at ClubCorp, the wonderful and passionate team at the Russian Fitness Group, and the incredible leaders whom I have been blessed to meet and know through my involvement in IHRSA, ACSM, and the health/fitness club industry. I feel truly blessed by the enormity of the exceptional people who have shared a part of themselves with me over the past 30 plus years in the fitness industry.

—S.T.

Case Study Contributors

The following industry professionals and club operators have contributed the case studies and stories which the authors have used in this book to provide real-world examples and insights into membership retention:

Gigliola Aycardi, Executive Vice President, BodyTech, Lima, Peru

Vincent C. Bradley, general manager, Oase Health & Sports Club, Bochum, Germany

Clive Caldwell, President, Cambridge Group of Clubs, Montreal and Toronto, Canada

Amber Cekerevac, owner, Body Care Health Club, Albany, Australia

Jamie Hayes, owner, Body Express, Sydney, Australia

Ryan Johnston, owner, First Place Fitness, Hamilton, New Zealand

Dr. Ralf Kriegel, owner, body + soul, Munich, Germany

Irina Kutina, COO World Class, Moscow, Russia

Bill McBride, President & COO, Club One, San Francisco, California

Joe Rossie, manager, Eastbank Club, Chicago, Illionois

Justin Tamsett, Managing Director, Active Management, Beecroft, Australia

Guillermo Velez, Publisher, Mercado Fitness, Buenos Aires, Argentina

Contents

SECTION III: CONSUMER AND MEMBER BEHAVIOR: FACTORS DRIVING EXERCISE AND HEALTH/FITNESS CLUB MEMBERSHIP

SECTION IV: STRATEGIES FOR ENHANCING MEMBER RETENTION

Preface

Since its inception, the health/fitness club industry has been about members—initially attracting and then, holding on to them. Without members, or as some in the industry might refer to them as customers and clients, the industry would simply cease to exist. At my former employer, ClubCorp, members were fondly referred to as the "lifeblood" of the organization. They represented the essence of what the club business was about. In fact, ClubCorp's chairman would regularly comment that without members, we would be unemployed. As a result, it behooved the staff to do everything in its power to create an environment that appealed to our members.

At the inception of the fitness "club" or gymnasium industry in the mid-1800s, owners and operators understood that in order to be successful, they not only had to attract clients, they also had to retain them. An early proponent of placing equal emphasis on retention and sales was Hippolyte Triatt, who in 1848, opened a gymnasium in Paris, which, at the time, was the grandest such facility on the world stage. Triatt was one of the first club operators to realize that retaining his clients and making them feel as comfortable as they did at home (he was adamant about establishing a "home away from home" atmosphere for his members) was as important as enrolling new clients. What the early pioneers of fitness, such as Triatt, Desbonnet, and Attilla, understood and what today's successful club operators are fully aware of is that retaining members is absolutely essential to the profitability of a club.

At the inception of the modern era of fitness in the mid-1940s, the industry started to shift its focus from membership sales and retention to primarily membership sales. Over the next several decades, leading health/fitness club operators became known for their ability to sell memberships at any cost, with the resulting philosophy being to sell more memberships than a club could accommodate and to have members not use the club. This shift in the industry's approach to membership resulted in retention taking a back seat to sales. As John McCarthy indicated in the preface to *IHRSA's Guide to Membership Retention,* a landmark text that was published in 2007, membership retention has become the industry's Achilles heel. As recently as 2007, the health/fitness club industry had more former health/fitness club members than existing members, a testament to the industry's inability to capture the commitment of its members.

Over the past 20 years, the industry's annual retention rates have ranged from 60 to 75 percent, with many of the largest club chains experiencing retention levels closer to 50 to 60 percent. Over the past five years, the industry has experienced rather stagnant membership growth, particularly in mature western markets (e.g., U.S., Western Europe). This trend can, in large part, be attributed to the industry's recent history of "clear cutting" the market (skimming all the low hanging fruit), while concurrently failing to plant the seeds of retention.

While the authors do not propose an absolute answer to this perplexing and century's old issue, we detail several plausible theories concerning why the health/fitness club industry continually struggles with the retention of its clients. One such theory involves the industry's obsession with sales, often to the exclusion of service, an obsession best summarized by the following quote from David Toomar, which states that "Sales without customer service is like stuffing money into a pocket full of holes."

Another possible argument may entail the fact that over the past several decades, the industry has moved from a "club" model that emphasized camaraderie, social interaction, and common beliefs around the pursuit of physical excellence to a gym or exercise model that places more emphasis on the pursuit of exercise behavior. As the industry has evolved to an exercise model, its ability to retain its members becomes more reliant on people's attitudes and beliefs about exercise and their ability to adopt the exercise "habit," rather than on the earlier model's emphasis on a strong social support network.

Yet another equally plausible theory regarding the challenge that the industry faces to rein in member attrition may be attributed to the separation between what customers expect (e.g., lose weight, get more fit, etc.) and the time they are actually willing to allocate to such expectations, and their ability to achieve a viable solution.

A fourth and no less plausible theory for the retention problem may be related to the fact that while most club professionals are passionate about fitness and sport, they are unable to "culturally" connect to the average citizen whose passions lie elsewhere.

Not withstanding the hypothetical and factual reasons why retention continues to be a challenge to the health/fitness club industry, the reality is that no matter what a club's retention level is (e.g., 50, 65, 80, or 90 percent), it can always benefit from improving its rate of membership retention. Research conducted in other industries shows that a 5 percent reduction in the attrition of customers can lead to as much as a 25 to 125 percent improvement in profitability. As a result, from a business perspective, regardless of whether a club is marginally profitable or incredibly profitable, finding a means to improve membership retention remains essential to enhancing its profitability.

In a *New York Times* article from the 1960s, a writer shared a quote from the desk of Vic Tanny management, which paraphrased said, *"If you fail to make the sale, take a gun out of your desk and shoot yourself."* In the current market, the more appropriate quote might be, "If you fail to focus everyone's efforts on retaining members, then you are cutting off the hand that feeds you."

Introduction

As the preface of this book indicates, driving membership retention is essential to the short-term and long-term profitability of a club. Our objective in writing this book is several-fold. First, we want to share the story of some of the experiences of our industry regarding membership growth and retention. We believe this undertaking will provide a perspective on the challenge that the industry faces, as well as the cultural barriers that must be overcome when dealing with it. Second, we want to provide an in-depth look at the facts about membership retention, a consequence of which we hope is creating a greater sense of urgency among club operators to focus on the issue. Third, we want to share information on the attitudes, beliefs, and behaviors of people regarding exercise, and how these factors impact the ability of the health/fitness club industry to improve member retention. Fourth, we want to explore the reasons consumers give for joining a club, remaining a club member, and lastly, terminating their membership experience. Lastly, through the use of case studies and detailed descriptions, we want to share business models and strategies with members of the industry that can significantly enhance a club's ability to retain its members.

To enhance the usefulness of this book as a resource for club owners and operators, it has been divided into four primary sections, comprised of 13 chapters. The four major sections of the book include:

- *The state of customer and member retention.* This section has one chapter that defines the real value of a member and how this value impacts the success of the industry.
- *A global perspective on industry membership.* This section has two chapters. The first chapter provides an overview of the industry's recent experiences with membership growth, membership retention, and several related factors. The second chapter offers a profile of the "typical" club member, both globally and in the U.S.
- *Consumer behavior around exercise and joining a club.* This section has four chapters, beginning with a chapter on consumer attitudes toward exercise and the club experience. The second chapter delves more deeply into why consumers actually join a club or gym, and how these factors influence their behavior as a club member. The third chapter in this section takes a look at member retention and member participation, and reviews the connection between the two. The final chapter in this section addresses member loyalty and customer service and discusses how the two factors intertwine to drive membership retention.
- *Strategies for enhancing member retention.* This section is divided into five distinct chapters, each of which is dedicated to a different element of member retention—engaging the new member, getting members involved in the club, scripting an exceptional member experience through outstanding member service, designing a club to drive retention, and finally a chapter of case studies that leverage the various strategies. Each chapter provides a blend of case studies, data, insights, and step-by-step strategies.

The Appendix of the book provides several sample materials (i.e., supplemental forms) that clubs can utilize to develop their own unique retention system.

*It should be noted that a significant difference exists concerning how retention figures are determined in the United Kingdom vs. the United States. As such, the following descriptions illustrate the major differences between the two countries:

- U.K.—Retention numbers in the U.K. represent the percentage of members who retain their membership after a 12-month period of time. For example, if a U.K. club with an average monthly membership count of 2,000 members has 70 percent retention, it means that 70 percent of the members who join that particular club maintain their membership for a period of 12 months. This measurement is a very realistic measure of how well a club performs at retaining the memberships it sells.
- U.S.—Retention numbers in the U.S. are typically calculated by taking the average membership count for the year (average from the end of each month) and dividing by the number of memberships that were terminated. The resulting number is then subtracted from 100 percent. For example, if a U.S. club with an average monthly membership count of 2,000 has 70 percent retention, it means that during the course of the year, they had 600 memberships terminate. This measurement does not take into account the tenure of membership. As a result, it fails to take into account whether new members or tenured members are resigning.

MEMBERSHIP RETENTION: UNDERSTANDING THE BASICS

© Wavebreak Media/Thinkstock

Section One

1

The Value of Membership Retention

Before the factors that influence retention can be addressed, which occurs in later chapters, it is first necessary to understand what membership retention is and is not. It is also essential to know how to quantify (calculate) membership retention. In addition, it is important to be aware of how membership retention can contribute to the value proposition of the health/fitness club industry. Once those understandings are clear, the attitudes and behaviors of members that impact retention, as well as the strategies that clubs can take to enhance their facility's level of member retention performance, can be more thoughtfully discussed.

What Are Membership Attrition and Retention?

Standard Industry Definition of Member Retention

Membership retention is a term that describes the business outcome of a club holding on to, or keeping, members after the initial membership sale, by subsequently renewing their membership or signing up for a new contractual term. As in any successful business, the objective in this instance is to retain the highest possible number of customers for the longest possible period of time. In the health/fitness club business, retaining members is as important, or even more so, than retaining clients is for other businesses, given that members represent the "lifeblood" of clubs. The health/fitness club business represents a form of "closed economic model" in which facilities are dependent on their ability to drive ongoing business from a relatively restricted or limited market of customers (e.g., members). As a result, retention becomes a key driver of long-term profitability. As such, the majority of clubs measure retention on an annual basis.

In the health/fitness club business, retaining members is as important, or even more so, than retaining clients is for other businesses, given that members represent the "lifeblood" of clubs.

Alternate Definitions of Member Retention

In their groundbreaking studies on membership retention in the United Kingdom, renowned researchers Melvyn Hillsdon, Ph.D., and Paul Bedford,

Ph.D., defined retention as the proportion of members who remain a member for a predetermined period of time (e.g., three months, six months, 12 months, 18 months, etc.). This definition takes into account the variable of a member's tenure. The researchers' rationale for tying membership tenure into the retention equation lies in the understanding that the longer members remain with a club, the more likely they are to spend money in the club. According to Bedford, one way of looking at retention is to equate it to miles per gallon or the measure of distance, or in the case of membership, a measure of time. In essence, retention defines not only whether a person remains a member, but more importantly, how long that individual remains a member.

Clarifying Who It Is We Want and Need to Retain

One of the most profound issues attendant to member retention is defining what it is that the club really wants to retain. Some individuals in the health/fitness club industry believe that the end game is retaining the body or the dues-paying entity, somewhat similar to retaining a possession which may or may not be valued, other than for its existence. For example, many clubs follow what some individuals might define as the "Bally Principle" (authors' terminology based on the approach of Bally to generating memberships back in the 1980s and 1990s).

One of the most profound issues attendant to member retention is defining what it is that the club really wants to retain.

The Bally Principle states that if a club's dues rate is low enough, members will not terminate their membership, either because they do not want to give up such a "great" deal, or because the dues amount is so small that they do not notice it on their bank or credit card statement. In the 80s and 90s, Bally sold membership contracts that allowed members to keep their membership for as little as seven dollars a month once their initial contract expired. At the turn of the 21st century, Bally, according to the authors' sources, was reported to have over three million members on their roster, some of whom were paying as little as seven dollars a month.

The Bally Principle is also the underlying basis behind the current trend of low-price, high-volume clubs, in which members pay relatively little on a monthly basis (under $20 in the U.S. and under 20 euros in Europe). When the monthly membership charge is that low, a number of individuals will either ignore it altogether on their statement, or see it as a deal that is too good to give up. As such, many of the "budget" club operators in Europe appear to have retention levels approaching 70 percent, a situation that, if true, lends support to the aforementioned "Bally Principle."

The second proposition put forth by many industry professionals adheres to the precept that member retention goes beyond retaining the actual body of the individual. Rather, it involves engaging and retaining the emotions of the member, or as Lord Burleigh so eloquently once stated, "Capture the heart, and you win hands and purses." This approach to retention encompasses viewing the member as an individual, rather than just a dues-paying entity. The primary focus of those facilities that subscribe to this philosophy is to fully engage members in the club experience. Not only does this strategy enrich the life of each member, it also generates a constantly increasing stream of revenue from a loyal member base. All factors considered, depending upon which approach a facility adopts, these two divergent attitudes toward member retention will dictate how a club pursues its retention strategies.

Standard Industry Definition of Member Attrition

Membership attrition, which is a measure of member behavior, is the opposite of retention, representing the departure of clients and members from a club. Attrition of clients, like death and taxes, is inevitable for any business, but like the other two, the objective is to minimize and delay it as long as possible. In the case of the health/fitness club industry, when facilities are able to delay, and more importantly prevent, the attrition of their members, their bottom line financial performance will benefit substantially. Every time a member leaves a club, a valuable source of income is lost. All factors considered, the expense involved in replacing that member costs far more than it does to provide an environment that encourages the member to remain.

While the majority of health/fitness clubs measure attrition on an annual basis, some facilities in the industry monitor it on a monthly basis. The operators of these facilities believe that monitoring monthly attrition provides an additional perspective with regard to the seasonality of the health/fitness club business. For example, publicly held companies, such as Lifetime Fitness and Town Sports International, often report their monthly attrition figures as part of their monthly calls with investors.

While the majority of health/fitness clubs measure attrition on an annual basis, some facilities in the industry monitor it on a monthly basis.

Alternate Definition of Member Attrition

In their groundbreaking research on membership retention in the United Kingdom, the aforementioned researchers Hillsdon and Bedford defined member attrition as the rate of member churn (i.e., turnover) per 1,000 members. These investigators believe that attrition is best measured not as a percentage of the total membership, but rather as a turnover rate, based on an objective and comparable metric. According to Bedford, one way of looking at attrition is to equate it to miles per hour, or the speed at which someone terminates their membership experience. Their recommended methodology allows a club to objectively measure its attrition at any point in time. For example, Figure 1-1 presents a hypothetical club that starts the year with 1,000 members, loses 100 members each month, and then concludes the year with 1,000 members. Based on this chart, the overall churn rate of the hypothetical facility is 120 percent. Figure 1-2 illustrates that clubs with similar attrition rates, based on IHRSA's methodology for calculating member attrition, can have different churn rates when calculated using the approach of Hillsdon and Bedford. All factors considered, the churn rates based on Hillsdon and Bedford's method provide a more predictive approach to the requirements for replacement sales.

Start 1000
Members Jan 1st

Finish 1000
Members Dec 31st

Jan	Feb	Mar	Apr	May	Jun	Jul	Aug	Sep	Oct	Nov	Dec
+100	+100	+100	+100	+100	+100	+100	+100	+100	+100	+100	+100
-100	-100	-100	-100	-100	-100	-100	-100	-100	-100	-100	-100

1200 Members Joined

1200 Members Joined

83% Attrition

Figure 1-1. Hypothetical example of a club's retention level

Club	Average Monthly Membership	Annual Members Terminated	Annual Attrition Rate (IHRSA)	Turnover or Churn Rate
A	2,000	700	35%	350
B	3,000	1,000	33%	340
C	6,000	1,700	34%	330

Figure 1-2. An illustration of the fact that clubs with similar attrition rates can have different churn rates

Calculating Member Attrition and Retention

How does a club calculate the attrition or retention of its members?

Retention Measurement Approach Recommended by IHRSA

The statistical methodology recommended by IHRSA and commonly used in the United States involves the following five-step procedure:

- Begin by calculating the number of members at the end of each month.
- Take the number of members at the end of each month, then add them together, and divide by 12 (e.g., the number of months in the year). This calculation will give a club its average member count for the year.
- Calculate the total number of members who resigned for the year.
- Divide the average member count by the total number of members who terminated their membership during the year in order to determine the facility's annual attrition rate.
- Subtract the annual attrition percentage from the integer "one" in order to calculate the club's annual retention rate.

Figure 1-3 provides an example of calculating a club's annual attrition and retention levels, using IHRSA's recommended approach.

Month	Members at the End of the Month	Number of Members Who Resigned	Monthly Rate of Attrition
January	3,200	60	1.8%
February	3,250	80	2.5%
March	3,300	90	2.7%
April	3,350	85	2.5%
May	3,350	90	2.7%
June	3,325	100	3.0%
July	3,275	105	3.2%
August	3,250	120	3.7%
September	3,275	95	2.9%
October	3,350	85	2.5%
November	3,350	90	2.7%
December	3,300	100	3.0%
Year-End Average	3,298	1,100	
Annual attrition level			33.3%
Annual retention level			66.7%

Figure 1-3. Calculating a facility's annual attrition and retention levels, using IHRSA's recommended method

It should be noted that the methodology put forth by IHRSA is not a statistical approach. As a result, its validity as a true measure of a club's ability to retain members is somewhat flawed. In other words, using this methodology to measure attrition and retention may not provide the proper data to make good business decisions as it pertains to combatting a club's membership attrition and retention challenges.

Retention and Attrition Measurement Approach Recommended by Bedford and Hillsdon in the United Kingdom

Hillsdon and Bedford recommend using a form of "survival analysis" for accurately measuring retention, an approach in which the calculation takes into account the time between events, as well as the proportion of individuals who remain members of the club at specific points in time. It could be argued that this approach provides a more accurate reflection of member retention, given that it takes into account both the proportion of involvement and the tenure of the relationship.

Figure 1-4 presents a visual comparison of three clubs. If only the standard definition of retention is considered, then each of these clubs had the same retention level at the 14th month. On the other hand, Hillsdon and Bedford's alternate definition of retention, which takes into account membership tenure is employed to calculate retention level, it can be seen that in the eighth month in the example, club A's retention is 60 percent, and club B's is 40 percent, while club C is at 90 percent. As a result, while all three clubs have the same retention level after 14 months, six months earlier, club C had a significantly higher retention level.

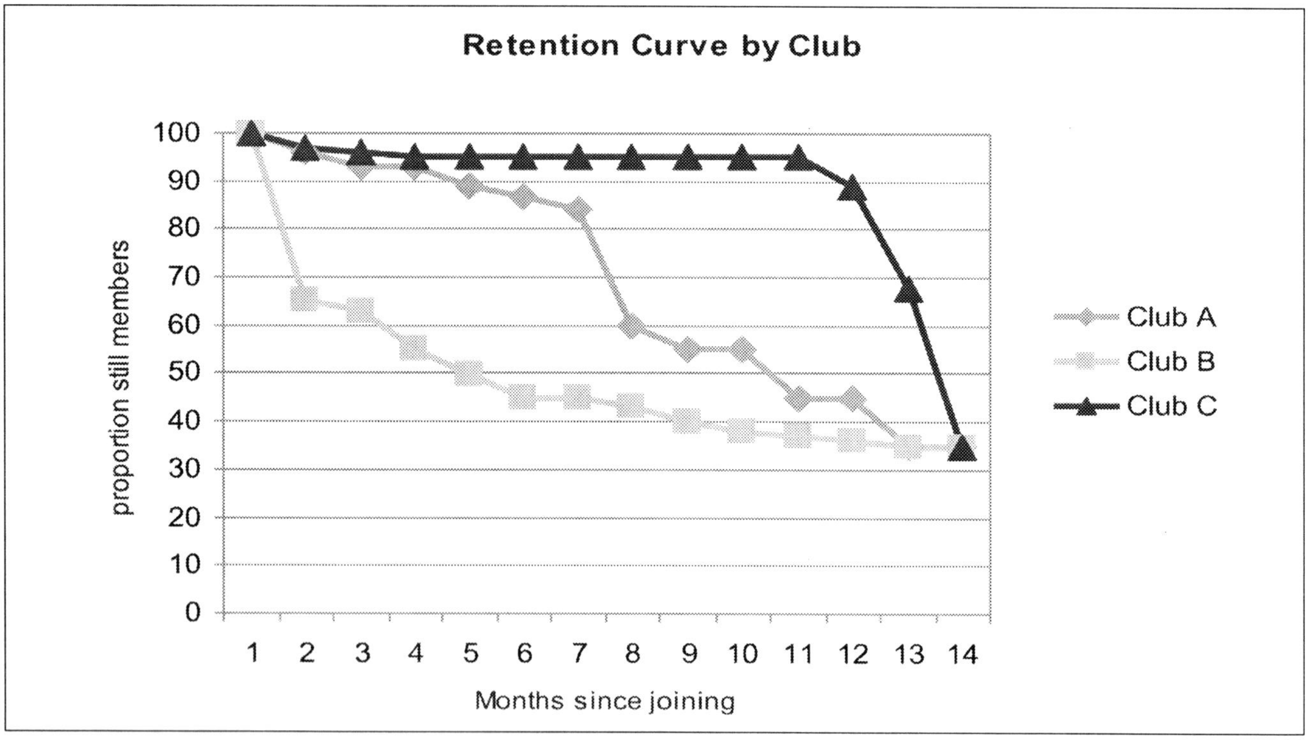

Figure 1-4. Retention curve by club

The Business Value of Driving Membership Retention

What is the real value to of driving retention for a club and the industry, and why is it so important? Brian Tracy, a well-recognized business leader and presenter, has been quoted as saying, *"The purpose of business is to create and keep customers. If you successfully create and keep customers in a cost effective way, your business will make a profit."* Furthermore, according to Dun & Bradstreet, the primary reason most businesses fail is that they either lack sales and/or fail to retain their existing customers. In the health/fitness club business, the value of retaining a customer, or member as that individual is referred to in the industry, is even more critical than in many other businesses, given the fact that facilities do not have a limitless supply of new customers for their business offerings.

According to Dun & Bradstreet, the primary reason most businesses fail is that they either lack sales and/or fail to retain their existing customers.

The following statistics on member pricing, member spending, and membership retention from IHRSA's *2010 Profiles of Success* can help provide a more insightful understanding of the "real dollar" value of a typical health/fitness club member (note: the statistics are based on the average of the facilities included in the IHRSA survey):

Example based on average club statistics

• Average initiation/enrollment fee for an individual:	$95
• Average monthly dues for an individual:	$60
• Average annual dues:	$720
• Average percentage of revenue from non-dues:	30%
• Average annual non-dues revenue:	$308
• Total annual revenue per member:	$1,028
• Average attrition rate:	29%
• Average lifespan of a member:	3.3 years (based on attrition)

Based on IHRSA's 2010 statistics, the average club member spends $1,123 in the individual's first year of membership. Furthermore, if the net present value of the dollar is not factored in, that member will, on average, be worth approximately $1,023 annually for the tenure of the individual's membership. As such, if the tenure of an average member is 3.3 years, then the total dollar value of an average club member over the tenure of that person's membership is approximately $3,487.

More compelling, based on the IHRSA 2010 statistic that indicated that the average club lost 601 members in 2009, it would mean that the average club lost over $2,095,000 in revenues that year alone. On the other hand, if a facility could reduce its attrition rate by just five percent, thereby retaining an additional 30 members, it would achieve an annual savings of approximately $104,600. It should also be noted that the aforementioned scenario does not factor in either the impact of member referrals and the value those referrals can bring to the bottom line, or the fact that the longer an individual remains a member of a club the more incremental spending that occurs. By any reasonable measure, however, it is quite obvious that when a member leaves a club, especially the earlier a member leaves a facility, the situation can have a negative impact on the club's level of profitability.

Example from an actual club company

- Average revenue per member: $2,500
- Average attrition rate: 37%
- Average length of a membership: 2.5 years

Based on the statistics from this company, each member is worth $2,500 annually, or over the duration of that individual's membership, $6,250. In 2009, the company's portfolio of clubs (20 in total) saw 17,760 members terminate their membership, which means that $111 million in future revenue left the business. As such, if this particular company were able to reduce its attrition by just five percentage points (32% vs. 37%), thereby retaining an additional 888 members, it would save $5.5 million.

The value equation of retaining a member becomes even more important during periods of economic volatility, such as during recessionary periods or times when the economy experiences financial bubbles.

The value equation of retaining a member becomes even more important during periods of economic volatility, such as during recessionary periods or times when the economy experiences financial bubbles. All factors considered, when people are less secure about their financial position, most are less likely to spend money on a new purchase, but more likely to stay with existing investments. As experienced during the most recent economic turmoil of 2008 and 2009, existing members who had already invested in a club membership tended to use their club more frequently. As a consequence, these individuals were less likely to surrender their membership.

On the flip side, during the most recent recessionary period, new membership sales in health/fitness clubs experienced a significant downturn. As a consequence, when the economic environment is less than ideal, member retention becomes even more critical to the profitability of a club.

A GLOBAL PERSPECTIVE ON CLUB MEMBERSHIPS: GROWTH, PENETRATION, AND RETENTION

© Creatas

Section Two

While the health/ fitness club facility industry had its infancy in the early 1800s, the modern era can earmark its beginnings to the late 1940s, when Vic Tanny introduced America, and later Europe, to the modern fitness center.

While the health/fitness club facility industry had its infancy in the early 1800s, the modern era can earmark its beginnings to the late 1940s, when Vic Tanny introduced America, and later Europe, to the modern fitness center. Since that time, the industry has emerged as an essential element of both the U.S. and the global consumers' lifestyle. As a global industry, health/fitness clubs currently serve over 120 million people in over 50 countries, and generate an estimated 70 billion dollars in revenues annually.

The industry is unique in its product offering, providing both current and future members with a setting in which they can pursue exercise and related lifestyle options that have been shown to benefit the quality of a person's life. Despite the enormous strides made by the industry over the past 60 years, it currently faces a tipping point that will ultimately determine its future potential both as a global investment opportunity and as a resource for global citizens to improve the quality of their lives. This tipping point involves the industry's ability to retain members. This situation not only is a business imperative with regard to increasing revenues and sustainable profitability, but also as it relates to exposing a larger global audience to the benefits of exercise and healthy lifestyle practices.

Section II includes two chapters—the first chapter addresses the current state of membership, both in the U.S. and globally, by looking at trends in membership growth, membership participation, and membership retention, while the second chapter details a demographic and psychographic profile of club members, both in the U.S. and globally.

2

The State of Membership in the Health/Fitness Club Industry

The U.S. Market Trends

Membership Growth in the U.S. Over the Past 20 Years

As of December 31, 2009, an estimated 45 million Americans were members of health/fitness clubs. In fact, over the past 20 years, the number of Americans involved as members of health/fitness facilities has more than doubled, going from an estimated 20.7 million members in 1990 to over 45 million by the end of 2009 (Figure 2-1). During that same 20-year time period, the percentage

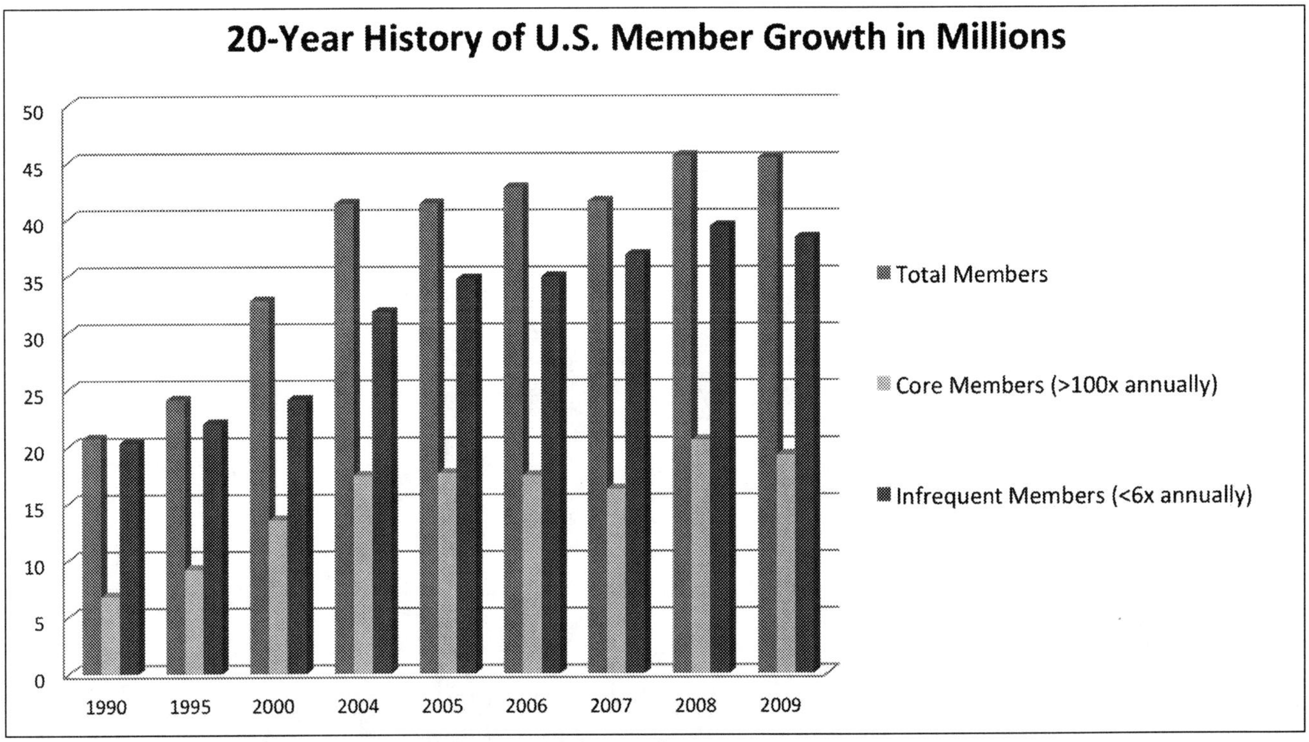

Figure 2-1. Twenty-year history of U.S. member growth in millions

of Americans who have made membership in a health/fitness club an integral part of their life has risen from 7 percent to approximately 16 percent (Figure 2-2). At the present time, nearly one in six Americans holds a membership in a health/fitness club. In fact, in some U.S. markets, one in four adults are club members. Despite these glowing statistics, the most insightful perspective of the level of success currently experienced by the health/fitness club industry, and more importantly of the opportunities that exist for the industry going forward, can be seen in the trends of the past five years.

During the most recent five-year period, the total number of U.S.-based health/fitness club members has remained relatively stagnant. In 2004, 41.3 million individuals were members of health/fitness clubs. In fact, over the succeeding three-year period, that number remained virtually the same. Only in 2008 and 2009 did the number increase, reaching 45 million in each year respectfully. It should be noted that the bump from slightly over 41 million to 45 million club members between 2007 and 2008 can be partially attributed to a change in the way data was collected and analyzed, rather than entirely to an actual increase in the number of club members. In reality, the percentage of Americans who hold a club membership has remained at approximately 16 percent for the past five years, indicating that collectively the industry has failed to reach a larger audience of Americans.

What does the future hold for U.S. club membership going forward? If the assumption is made that past behavior is the best predictor of future behavior, then the industry is faced with a significant challenge. That challenge is two-fold. First, can the industry be recharged and the public sufficiently educated so that the industry can penetrate a larger segment of the U.S. population?

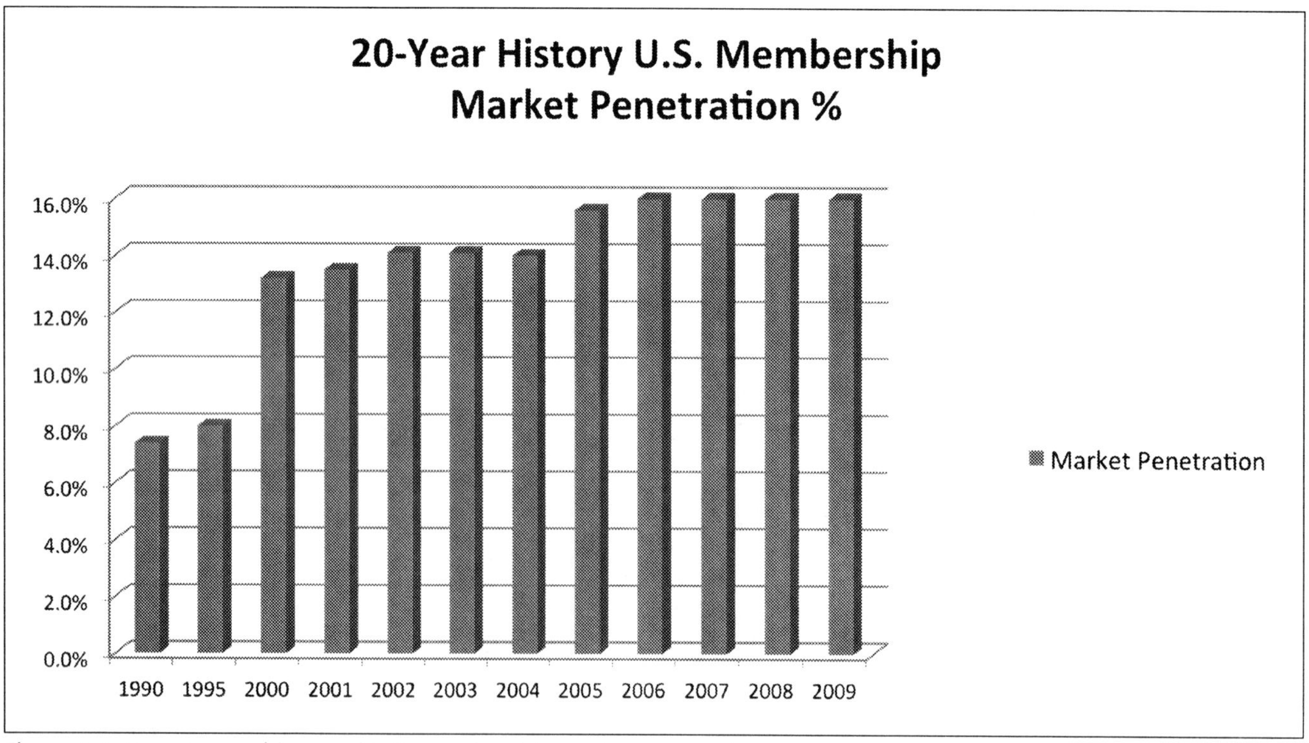

Figure 2-2. Twenty-year history of U.S. membership market penetration percentage

Second, can clubs retain a larger base of their existing members so that industry membership growth can be increased to higher levels?

How Frequently Do American Members Use Their Clubs?

While membership growth has more than doubled in the past 20 years, over the past five years, it has remained relatively flat. This situation has not experienced a comparable response in how members actually use their clubs.

According to statistics compiled in 2010 by the International Health Racquet and Sportclub Association (IHRSA) in its annual *Profiles of Success: The Annual Industry Survey of the Health and Fitness Club Industry,* health/fitness club members use their club 102 times a year on average. In its recently released 2011 *Profiles of Success,* it indicates that members use their club on average approximately 90 times a year, similar to what was reflected by industry statistics prior to 2008 and 2009. In fact, over the past 20 years for which data has been collected an analyzed, the average number of visits credited to club members has increased from just under 80 visits annually in 1990 to 102 visits in 2009 (Figure 2-3). This statistic indicates that over the past 20 years, the "typical" American club member visits their club 30 percent more frequently than they did approximately two decades ago.

Figure 2-3. Twenty-year history of U.S. membership average member visits annually

On one hand, the aforementioned date would seem to represent a significant improvement in usage and therefore be reflective of members doing a better job leveraging their membership investment. On the other hand, if a closer look is taken at the data, it can be seen that from 1995 to 2007, the average number of visits by an individual to their club remained relative flat at 89 to 92 visits annually (7.4 to 7.6 visits a month). Only in 2008 and 2009, did the average usage increase, a factor that can be partially or entirely attributed to statistical methodology. As a result, at least on average, club members are currently no more likely than individuals of 20 years ago to frequent their club.

Looking beyond the "average" member, studying the trends involving the "core" members of the industry (i.e., individuals who use their club more than 100 times on an annual basis) can be helpful. As of 2009, the number of core members in U.S. health/fitness clubs represented 42 percent of the membership base or 19.2 million members. Over the past 20 years, that number has grown from 33 percent in 1990 (Figure 2-4).

During the most recent five-year period, the percentage of core members in a facility has remained flat, paralleling the trends seen in overall membership growth and average annual member visits. What might be the most telling statistic in usage is the number of members who visit their club at least six times annually, which as of 2009 was 84 percent of the total membership base, down from 89 percent in 1990, and relatively flat with the usage patterns that existed in 2005. In fact, these statistics indicate that overall, members

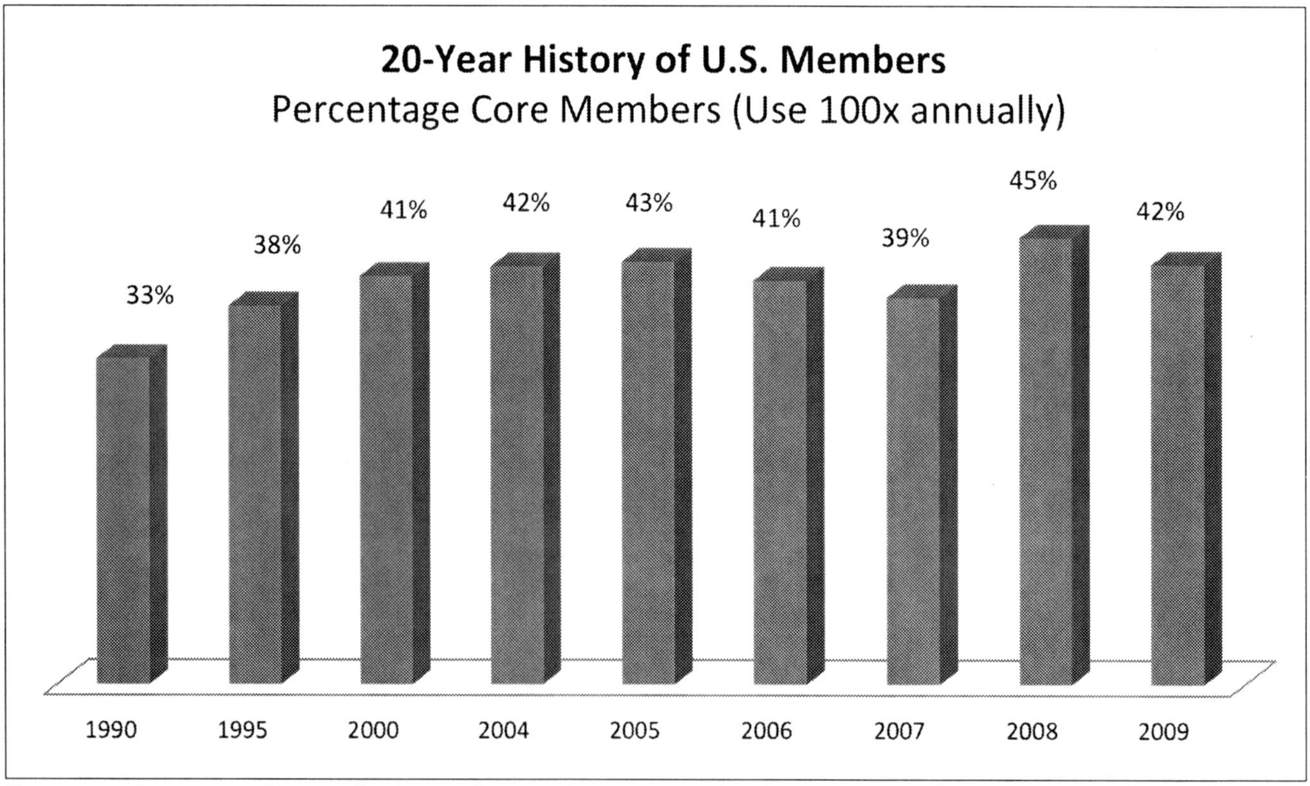

Figure 2-4. Twenty-year history of U.S. members percentage core members

may actually visit their clubs less frequently than they did in the past. Even accounting for statistical error, this data suggests that membership practices in 2009 have not changed significantly over the past 20 years.

U.S. Membership Retention Trends

According to IHRSA's 2010 Profiles of Success, the average retention rate for U.S. clubs in 2009 was 71 percent. Ten years ago, the U.S. club industry's retention rate was 65 percent, which indicates that over the past decade, the industry has made strides in its ability to retain members (Figure 2-5). Most of that gain was achieved over the first five years of the 21st century, going from 65 percent in 2000 to 71 percent in 2005. During the next five years, it has remained at 71 percent, on average.

The important takeaway from the aforementioned statistics is that the industry was able to improve its overall level of retention performance during the first half of the decade, and over the last half of the decade, has been able to sustain that performance. From a retention perspective, that factor is good news.

It is of interest to note that some of the largest players in the health/fitness club industry have been unable to duplicate these industry-wide retention levels. For example, according to recent public filings by Lifetime Fitness, its retention rates from 2006 to 2011 have floated between 58 and 65 percent, and during its most recent financial year it stood at approximately 65 percent.

Figure 2-5. Ten-year history of U.S. membership trends in monthly dues and fees

In turn, Equinox, one of the premier operators of quality clubs in the United Stated has indicated (off the record) that its retention rates tend to fluctuate around 65 percent.

According to IHRSA's survey data, the average number of membership terminations a club experiences has declined steadily over the past decade (Figure 2-6), going from an average of 1,300 in 2000 to an average of 750 in 2009. On an absolute basis, this statistic is a significant improvement in the average club's ability to retain its members. Over the past five years, the average number of member resignations has remained relatively flat at around 725 to 750, with only two aberrations—one occurring in 2007 and the other in 2008.

According to the aforementioned data on the average number of new memberships sold and the average number of memberships cancelled, the average U.S. club experienced more membership terminations in 2009 than sales. This scenario is the first time in the 10-year history that this average has been kept, that membership terminations have been greater than new member sales. Again, the data would seem to reflect that the U.S. industry was able to make inroads into member attrition during the first part of the decade, and, since then, has been able to maintain those achievements. Unfortunately, as new member sales continues to struggle, retention efforts will need to intensify, if indeed the industry wants to grow over the next decade.

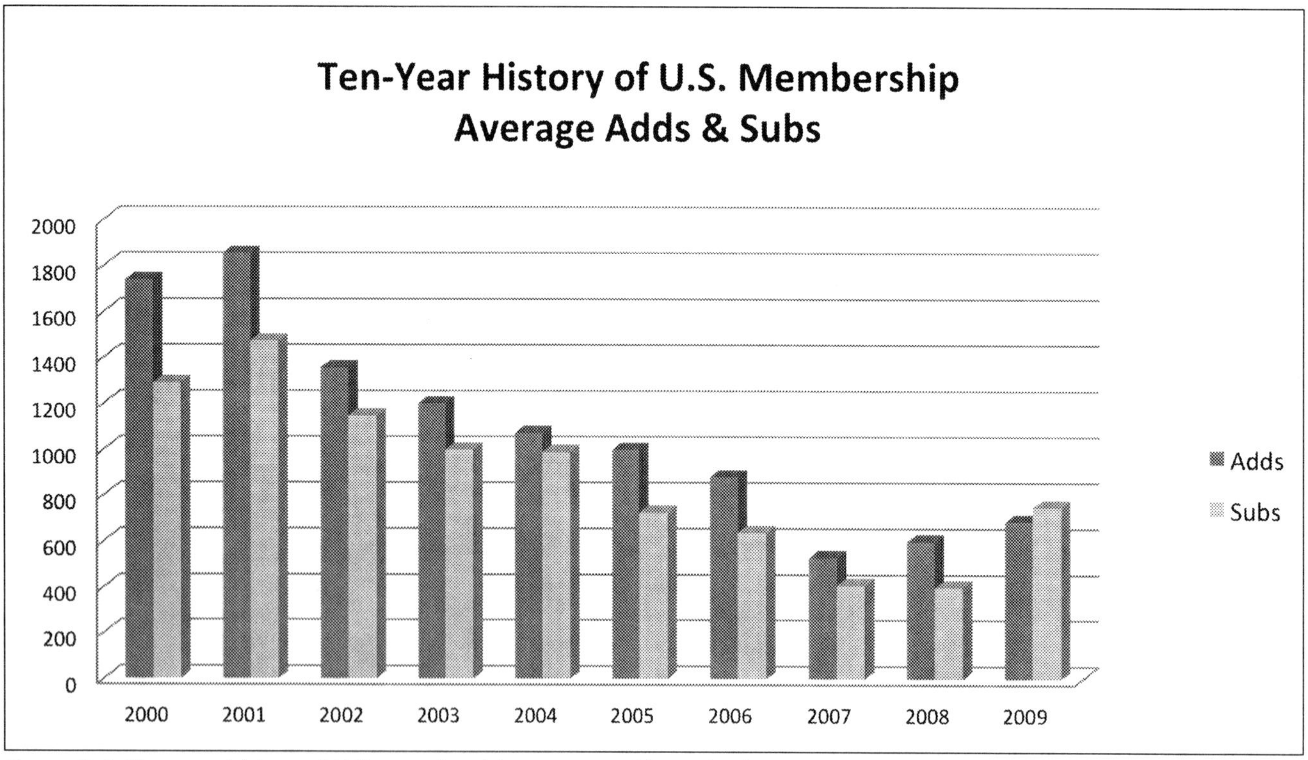

Figure 2-6. Ten-year history of U.S. membership average adds and subs

U.S. Trends in Membership Pricing

Pricing of club memberships, both monthly dues and initial enrollment fees, is a critical variable in the success of the health/fitness club industry. It could logically be expected that pricing would increase on an annual basis due to global and domestic economic pressures, with some of those increases being softened by the heightened level of competition in the marketplace, a factor that often exerts downward pressures on pricing.

In 2009, according to data detailed in IHRSA's annual industry survey, the average monthly dues for all clubs was $60, which is the highest average monthly dues the industry has experienced in the past decade. Over the past decade, the average monthly dues, as measured by IHRSA, has grown from $52 to $60, an increase of 15 percent. Until 2009, the average monthly dues price had remained flat, ranging from $50 to $54 monthly every year (Figure 2-7). In turn, during this same time period, the average enrollment fee (e.g., initiation fee, joining fee, induction fee, etc.) for all clubs dropped from an average of $150 to $95, a decrease of 36 percent.

Taking into account the net present value of money (i.e., the impact of inflation and other factors on the dollar), the average 2009 monthly dues of $60 would be equivalent to approximately $48 in 2000, which means that the average monthly dues over the past decade has declined by 7.6 percent. If the same principle is applied to the average enrollment fee, then the average enrollment fee of $95 at the present time would be the same as $77 in 2000, which indicates that over the past decade, the net value of initiation fees has also declined substantially.

Figure 2-7. Ten-year history of U.S. membership trends in monthly dues and fees

It would seem that from a purely pricing perspective, that in current dollars, both membership dues and fees have declined over the past decade. The primary reasons for this situation are most likely the increase in marketplace competition and the introduction of new lower-priced business models.

Global Market Trends

Global Membership Growth

At the end of 2009, health/fitness clubs around the world had nearly 120 million members. Since 2006, the number of global health/fitness club members has increased by approximately 17 million, or 16.5 percent (Figure 2-8). This statistic is significantly different than the trends in the number of club members in the U.S., which have shown no relative change in the past five years. During the last five years, the continents that have shown the greatest level of growth in overall membership have been Europe and Asia, both of which increased their number of club members by approximately 4 million each.

From a global perspective, the U.S. market still represents 37.5 percent of the total global membership base, down from over 50 percent in the early part of the 21st century. In 2009, Europe and the U.S. had nearly the same number of club members, with an estimated 43 to 45 million, respectively. On an individual nation basis, after the U.S. at nearly 45 million, Spain ranks second with 7.5 million members (6.25 percent), the U.K. third with 7.3 million members (6.2 percent), and Germany fourth with 7.1 (6.2 percent) million

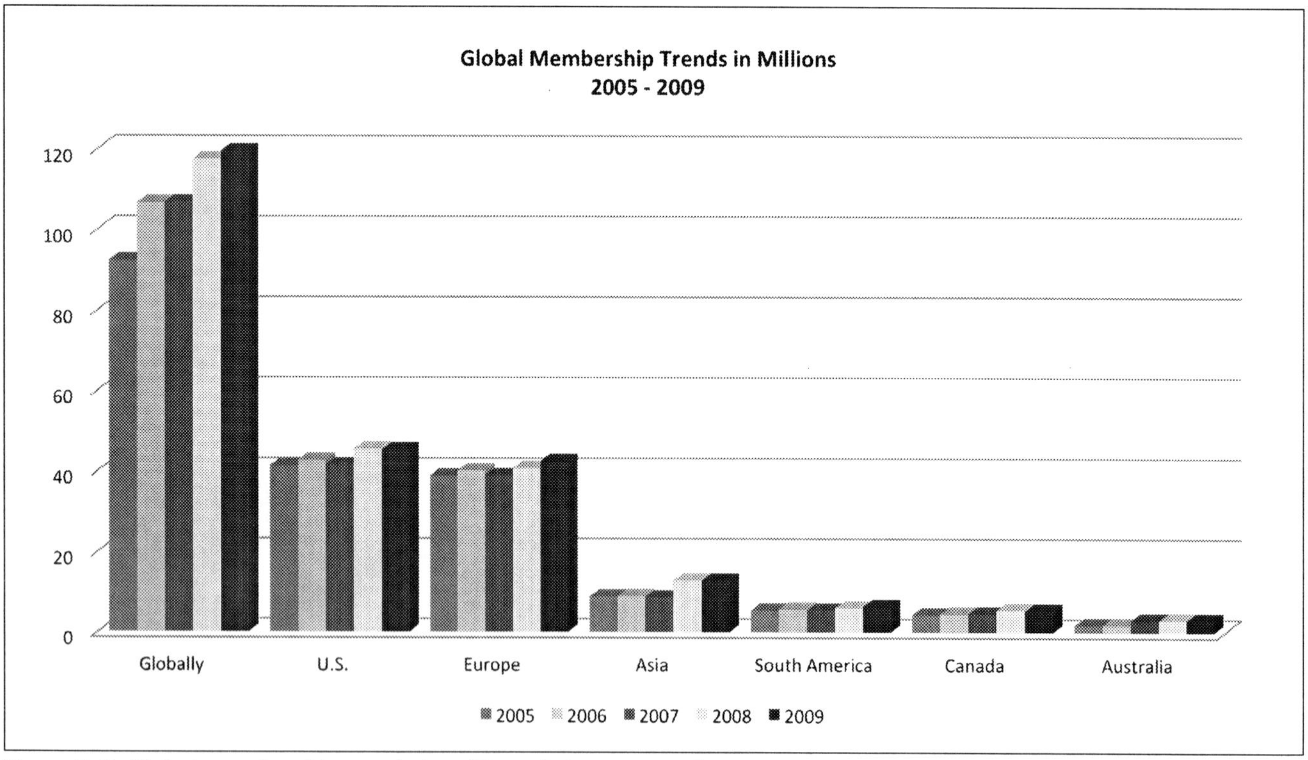

Figure 2-8. Global membership trends in millions (2005 – 2009)

members. The fastest expanding markets are currently in Asia, where China, India, and Korea are experiencing excellent growth.

From the perspective of market penetration, no actual global percentage exists that could be shared with any degree of certainty. In terms of national penetration rates, a few nations as of 2009, such as Canada (16.2 percent), the Netherlands (16.7 percent), and Spain (19.7 percent) have achieved levels of market penetration that exceed the 16 percent level of the U.S (Figure 2-9). Over the past three years, while the U.S. penetration percentage has remained flat, several nations, such as Australia, China, Germany, India, Netherlands, New Zealand, and Spain, have all experienced increased levels of market penetration. Concurrently, some mature markets, such as France, Italy, and the U.K., have actually experienced declining levels of market penetration over the past three years. In fact, countries of the BRIC (Brazil, Russia, India, and China), which for most of the 21st century represented the pinnacle of global economic development, have market penetration levels of under 3 percent. On a more positive note, when compared to other more mature economies, these countries have an opportunity to significantly increase their level of club memberships.

Global Trends in Membership Pricing

Similar to the U.S. market, membership pricing is critical to supporting the value proposition of the business, not to mention helping bolster long-term revenue and profitability growth. Globally, clubs price themselves in accordance with local market forces, just as in the U.S. One of the primary differences

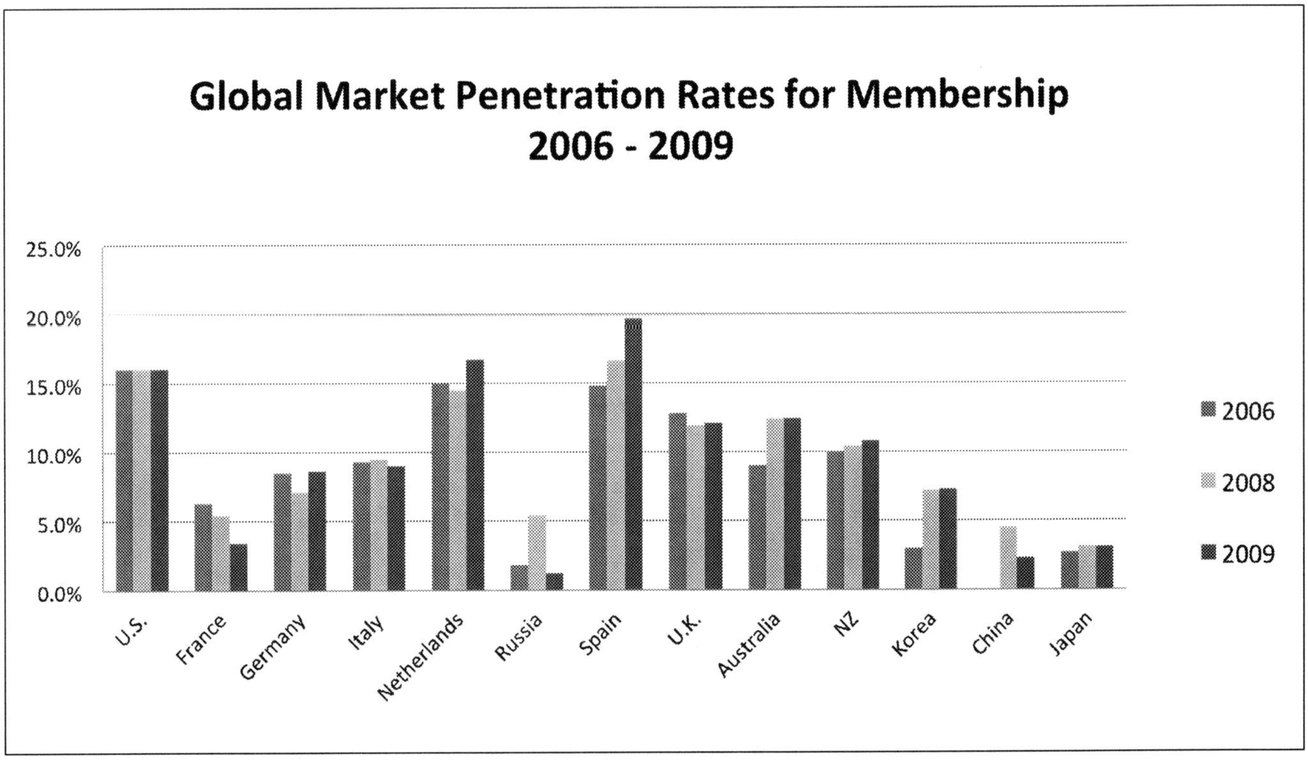

Figure 2-9. Global market penetration rates for membership (2006 – 2009)

between the global and U.S. markets may be in the way dues are priced and memberships sold, since many markets sell annual memberships or even bi-monthly memberships instead of monthly options (a practice that is often the result of market conditions and national laws).

Nonetheless, in 2009, it is amazing how closely the pricing across nations aligns. For example, in 2009, the U.S. the average monthly dues was $60, while in Europe, the majority of national dues averages fell between 40 and 45 Euro a month, which inclusive of VAT (value added tax) is the equivalent of $56 to $63 a month. In fact, when the inclusion of VAT is accounted for, then the monthly dues averages across Europe were nearly the same, or slightly lower than existed in the U.S.

In Asia, dues rates fluctuate, with emerging markets, such as China and India, having averages dues of under $35 a month. In Japan, the cost of dues is nearly identical to the U.S market, with an average of $60 a month. The most expensive market in the world is Russia, where the average monthly dues are slightly over 60 Euro or the equivalent of $85 U.S. dollars, with the VAT included. As reflected in Figure 2-10, the trend globally over the last three years has been for the average monthly dues in nearly every nation for which statistics are available to decline, with the possible exception of Australia. When taking into account inflationary pressures, the real value of dues in 2009 has declined in every market when compared to 2005.

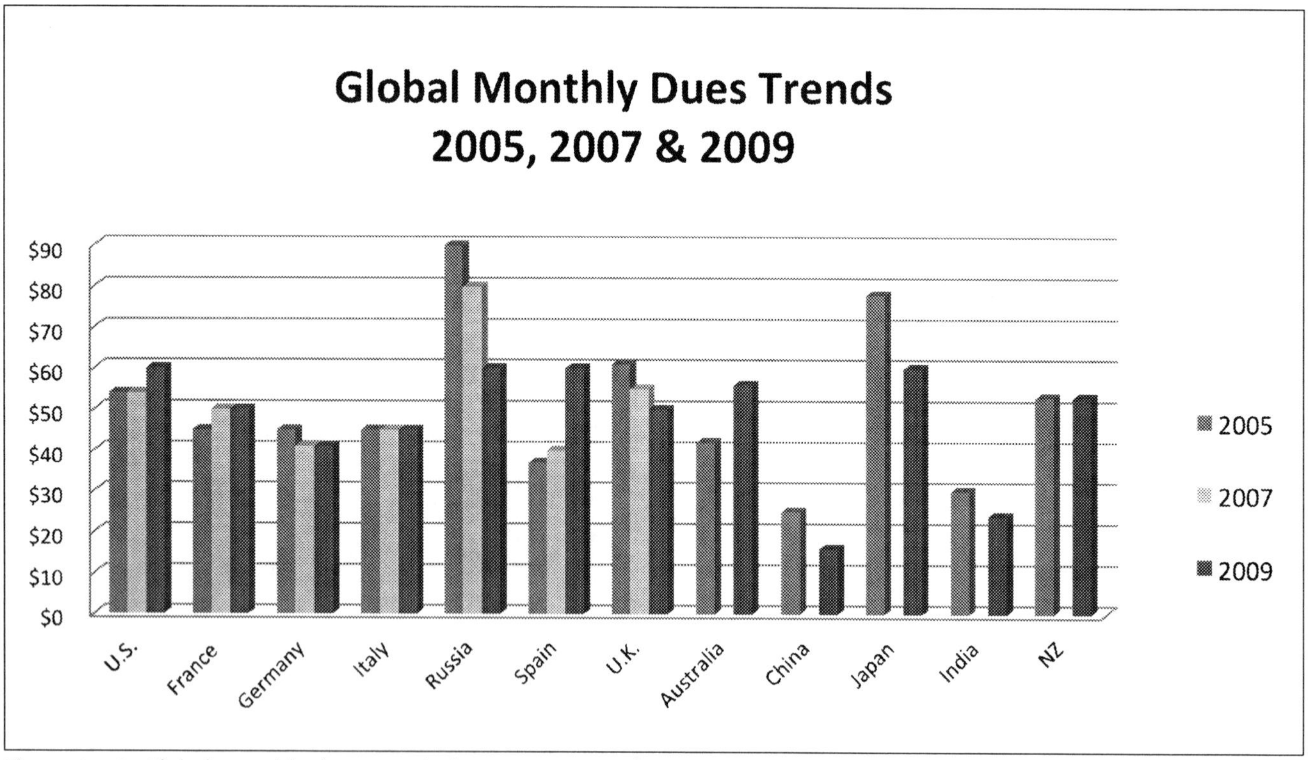

Figure 2-10. Global monthly dues trends (2005, 2007, and 2009)

Reflections on the Data—What Might It Mean?

The data presented in this chapter suggest several important trends concerning both global and U.S. membership retention and the overall health of the global health/fitness industry from a membership growth perspective, including the following:

- The global industry is still experiencing net membership growth, which is mostly due to expansion in emerging markets, such as Asia, Eastern Europe, and South America. In mature markets, such as the U.S., Canada, Western Europe, and Japan, membership growth has either stalled or is expanding insignificantly.

- The global industry has garnered a mixed bag of results with regard to membership penetration of the respective national markets. In mature markets, such as the U.S. and Western Europe, market penetration rates have remained relatively flat over the past few years, while in Asia and Eastern Europe they have increased.

  It seems apparent that not all nations can expect to achieve similar market penetration rates as the result of economic, cultural, and environmental conditions. On the other hand, it is relatively clear that the higher a nation's average per capita income, the more capable the industry in that country is of capturing a higher percentage of the market for membership.

  The real question is, "What is the potential market capture rate in the respective markets?" Frankly, an accurate means for predicting this measure may not exist. On the other hand, an argument could be made that based on global statistics, a national penetration rate of 20 percent might be the peak the health/fitness club industry can expect, while on a local level (country or city), that penetration cap might be closer to 30 percent.

The higher a nation's average per capita income, the more capable the industry in that country is of capturing a higher percentage of the market for membership.

- Membership retention, at least in the U.S., has stabilized over the past five years after experiencing improvements over the previous five-year period. With the U.S. average hovering around 70 percent, but with some clubs reporting percentages in the range of 80 to 90 percent, it is possible that the industry, as a whole, can improve its overall retention levels another five percent points or so in the next decade.

  Globally, retention percentages are similar to the U.S. market, with ranges from 40 to 70 percent. In Russia, for example, the leading operator of premium clubs has an average annual retention rate of approximately 65 percent, with clubs ranging from 50 to 80 percent. In a 2001 U.K. study sponsored by the Fitness Industry Association and Leisure Industry, club retention levels in the U.K were reported to range from 39 to 89.5 percent, with the 50th percentile falling at 58.5 percent. Globally, with the recent growth in high-volume, low-price clubs and low-price franchise clubs, market pressures seem to exist that drive overall industry retention lower. As a consequence, more focus is required from everyone in the industry to find new approaches to enhancing retention if these pressures are to be countered.

- Membership pricing, both in the U.S. and globally, continues to show a decline. Over the past five years, the average cost of joining a club, as well as the cost of using the club on a monthly basis, has either remained flat or decreased. When accounting for the net present value of currency, nearly all markets are offering their health/fitness club product at a lower price point than they did five years ago.

Over the past five years, the average cost of joining a club, as well as the cost of using the club on a monthly basis, has either remained flat or decreased.

  This lower pricing can be attributed, in large part, to the influx of lower-priced operators, such as Planet Fitness in the U.S., the Gym Group in the U.K., and McFit in Germany, as well as many of the club franchise operators, such as Anytime Fitness. As these low-priced business models have emerged, the situation has caused other industry players to discount their pricing in an effort to compete (whether real or imaginary). As a result an overall drop in the average cost of being a club member across the globe has occurred. In China, price pressure has become so intense, with the average monthly dues for many clubs now being offered for under $10 U.S. a month, that industry survival has become an issue. More importantly, since research clearly shows (refer to Chapter 6 for details) that retention levels typically decrease as the membership price point drops, it becomes essential that the industry evaluate its value proposition so that a membership price point is not established that exasperates the attrition factor and makes retention an even greater challenge.

- In the U.S., data shows that, as a whole, the health/fitness club industry has not made significant inroads into increasing existing member participation. Research shows that retention levels improve as participation levels increase (refer to Chapter 7 for details). As a result, unless the industry can dramatically increase overall member participation in its clubs, it will continue to face a challenge in improving retention levels. A reasonable assumption can be made from the data that most clubs engage between 40 and 50 percent of their members (e.g., core members) on a frequent-enough basis to retain them. On the other hand, the balance of a club's members are not using the facility frequently enough to generate a value proposition that will entice them to remain members. As such, the challenge of member participation may be the industry's #1 opportunity for enhancing retention.

In conclusion it is obvious that on a global basis, the industry has demonstrated outstanding growth over the past decade. It is also apparent that certain factors, including strong pressure on market penetration, existing member usage, and product pricing, have the real potential to impact retention levels and, as such, need to be addressed. The benefits of an enhanced retention rate are substantial. Improving member retention creates greater demand, which allows pricing to be increased. It also results in the need for fewer new memberships to be sold in order to increase or maintain market penetration. More importantly, it will ultimately increase incremental spending by the members and overall revenue generation for the club.

3

The Profile of a Health/ Fitness Club Member

In any business, having a clear understanding of the customer is vital. Positioning, selling and then delivering the business offering all require a clear and comprehendible understanding of who the prospective customers are. In the health/fitness club industry, understanding the particulars of the customer can help insure that the facility's brand offers the right products and services for its targeted audience. In addition, by understanding the demographic and psychographic profile of their customers (in the case of the health/ fitness club industry, their members), businesses can more effectively engage their customers' emotions, and, in turn, their resulting behavior. One of the consequences of this knowledge is an enhanced ability to attract and retain members.

By understanding the demographic and psychographic profile of their customers (in the case of the health/ fitness club industry, their members), businesses can more effectively engage their customers' emotions, and, in turn, their resulting behavior.

This chapter focuses on the core demographic and psychographic characteristics of the typical health/fitness club consumer. Most of the research cited in this section is based on the U.S. market. On the other hand, in those instances where global data on health/club fitness members is available, it is included as well.

A Demographic Profile of Members

Men and Women—Does a Distinct Lean Exist in the Industry?

According to the most recent data shared by IHRSA in its *2010 Profiles of Success,* 51 percent of U.S. club members were men and 49 percent were women. This finding represents the second consecutive year in which the U.S. market trended more toward a male influence. Previously, from 2000 to 2007, women represented the majority of club members in the U.S. In fact, as recently as 2005, women represented a significant majority (i.e., 57 percent) of club members (Figure 3-1) of the total club membership. As shown in Figure 3-1, over the past 10 years, women have comprised between 52 and 57 percent of the market in the U.S.

Based on the limited data available regarding the gender composition of European and Asian health/fitness clubs, it is difficult to provide an accurate year-on-year comparison between foreign countries and the U.S. In 2001, according to research sponsored by the Fitness Industry Association (FIA) and facilitated in part by The Leisure Database Company of the United Kingdom (U.K.), clubs in the U.K. were comprised of 55 percent women and 45 percent men. During that same year in the U.S., the percentage of club members who were women was 52 percent, while men represented 48 percent of the membership. Assuming that the U.K. market has trended in similar fashion to the U.S. over the past decade, it could be concluded that the U.K. market attracts a slightly larger market share of women compared to men than the U.S. market does, although not to the degree that would be defined as having a statistically significant gender difference in market share.

Data from other European nations concerning the composition of men and women in health/fitness clubs is more qualitative than quantitative. As such, most of the information in this area is based essentially on general discussions with operators. This qualitative feedback indicates that in Germany, men encompass a larger segment of club membership than women. On the other hand, in France, Italy, and Spain, women compose a larger segment of club membership. In Russia, based on a limited sampling of 13,000 club members, the gender breakdown of clubs was 65 percent women and 35 percent men.

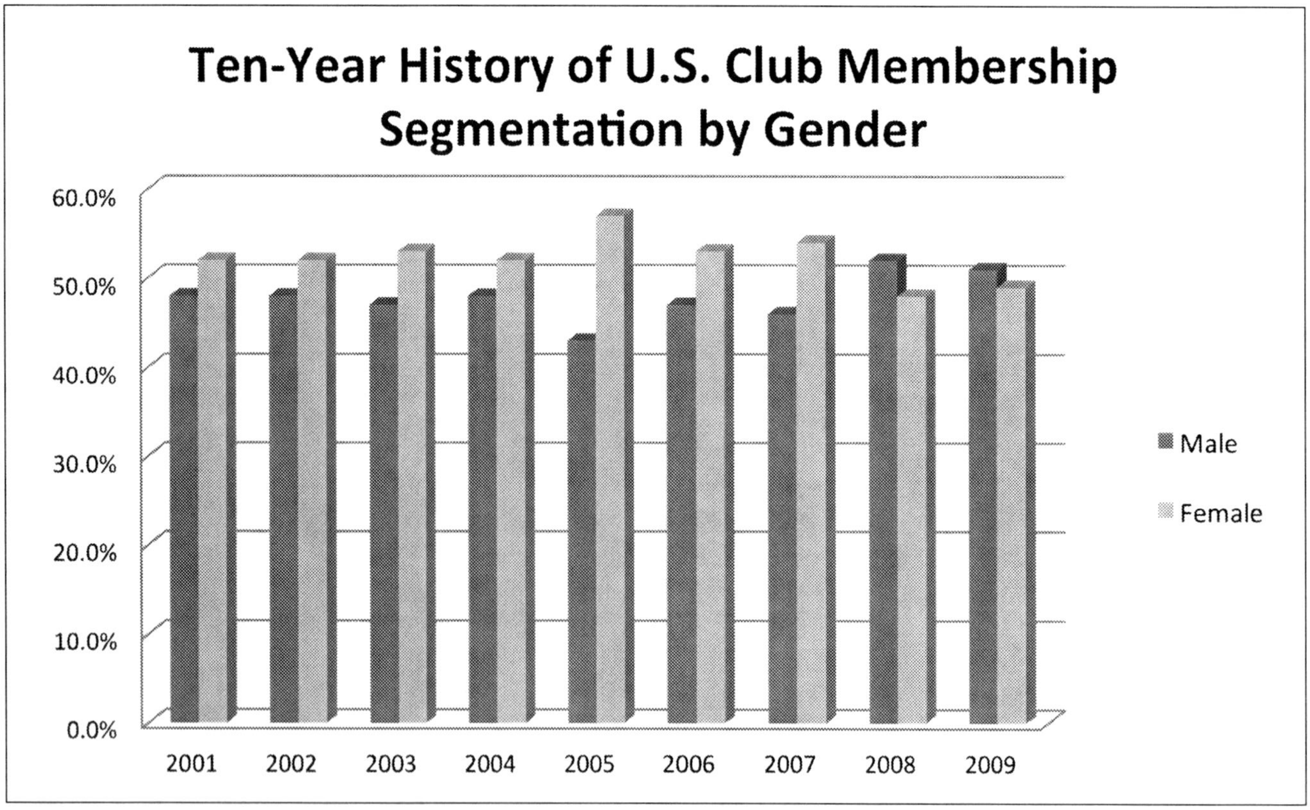

Figure 3-1. Ten-year history of U.S. club membership segmentation by gender

According to data on the U.S. market, when the mix of men and women among the general membership base is compared to those individuals who are defined as core members of a club (members who use the facility at least 100x annually), it appears that men comprise a slightly larger percentage of the core member base than the general member base (Figure 3-2). Chapter 4 includes a breakdown of the differences in the attitudes of men and women regarding both exercise and health/fitness clubs, opinions that ultimately impact how the club experience should be delivered to these two distinct audiences.

Age and Its Impact on Membership

According to the most recent data provided by IHRSA on the U.S. market, the largest segment of members (36 percent) falls between the ages of 35 and 54 (baby boomers and generation X), while a close second are those members between the ages of 18 and 34 (31 percent) denoting generation Y (millennial generation). Those individuals who are over age 55 (primarily baby boomers) represent approximately 23 percent of the market. According to IHRSA's U.S.-based research, over the past decade, the percentage of club members involving the 55 and over group has increased slightly, while those members between the ages of 18 and 34 has declined slightly (Figure 3-3). Over the next 10 years, the 55 plus population will continue to occupy a larger percentage of the "typical" U.S. club's membership base. Population demographics for the U.S. also indicate that over the next five years, a growing number of the under-35 population can be expected to comprise a larger segment of the club membership population.

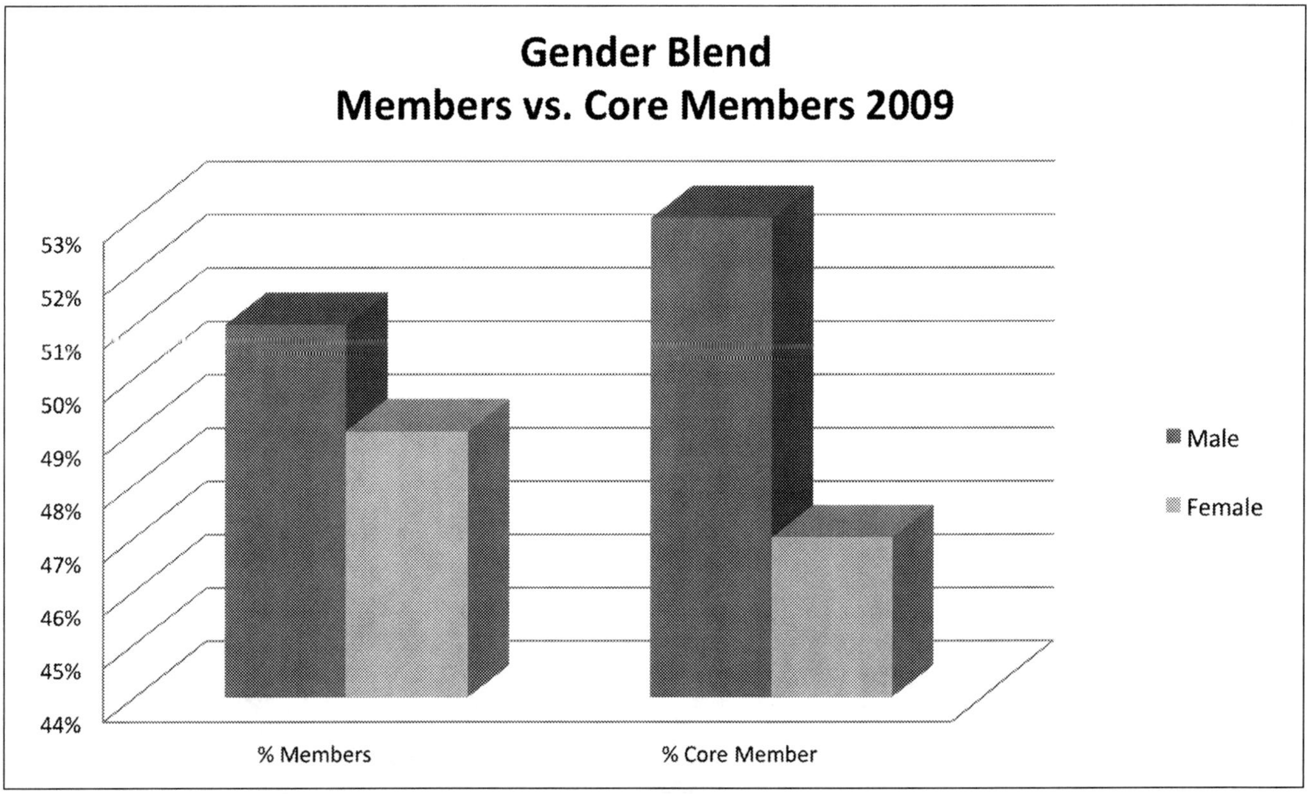

Figure 3-2. Gender blend of members vs. core members (2009)

Furthermore, when the various age groups represented among the general membership is compared to those individuals who are classified as core club members, individuals between the ages of 45 and 54 comprise the largest portion of core members (i.e., over 20 percent). The second largest segment of core members, by percentage, are individuals between the ages of 25 and 34—nearly 20 percent (Figure 3-4). When data reflecting the average annual usage of members is assessed, three age brackets are nearly identical at close to 109 visits annually—the 35 to 44, 45 to 54, and 55 to 64 age group segments (Figure 3-5). Overall, in at least the U.S. market, the older age demographic (45 and over) seems to comprise the largest segment of club memberships, as well as encompasses the largest portion of active members.

The data pertaining to age segmentation in the European market is still somewhat elusive. What data that is available is based on information contained in IHRSA's *2007 European Market Report.* That report indicated that based on general data from six select European markets (France, Germany, Italy, Netherlands, Spain, and United Kingdom), the largest demographic segment of membership was over the age of 35 (39 percent of the membership base was 35 to 54), while the second largest demographic group were those individuals between 18 and 34 (36.5 percent). A breakdown of age segmentation, by nation, is shown in Figure 3-6.

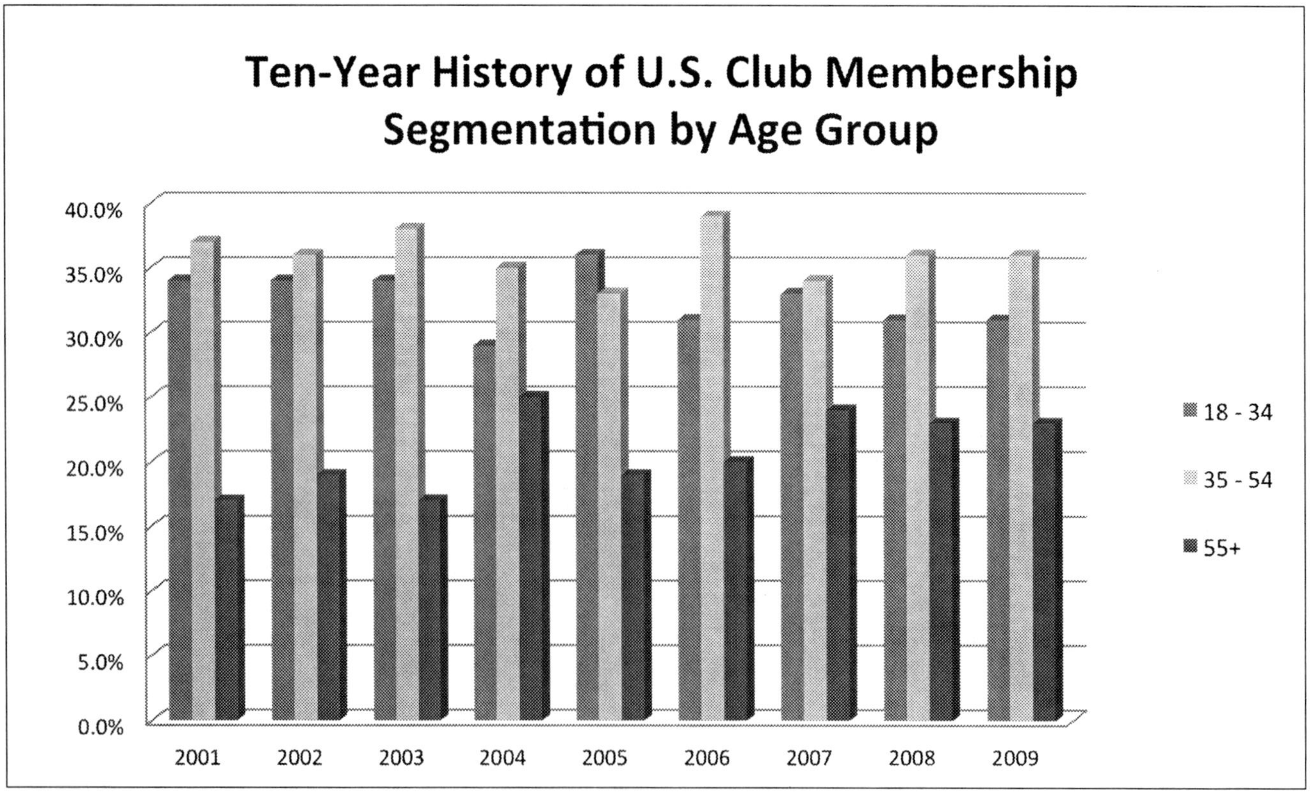

Figure 3-3. Ten-year history of U.S. club membership segmentation by age group

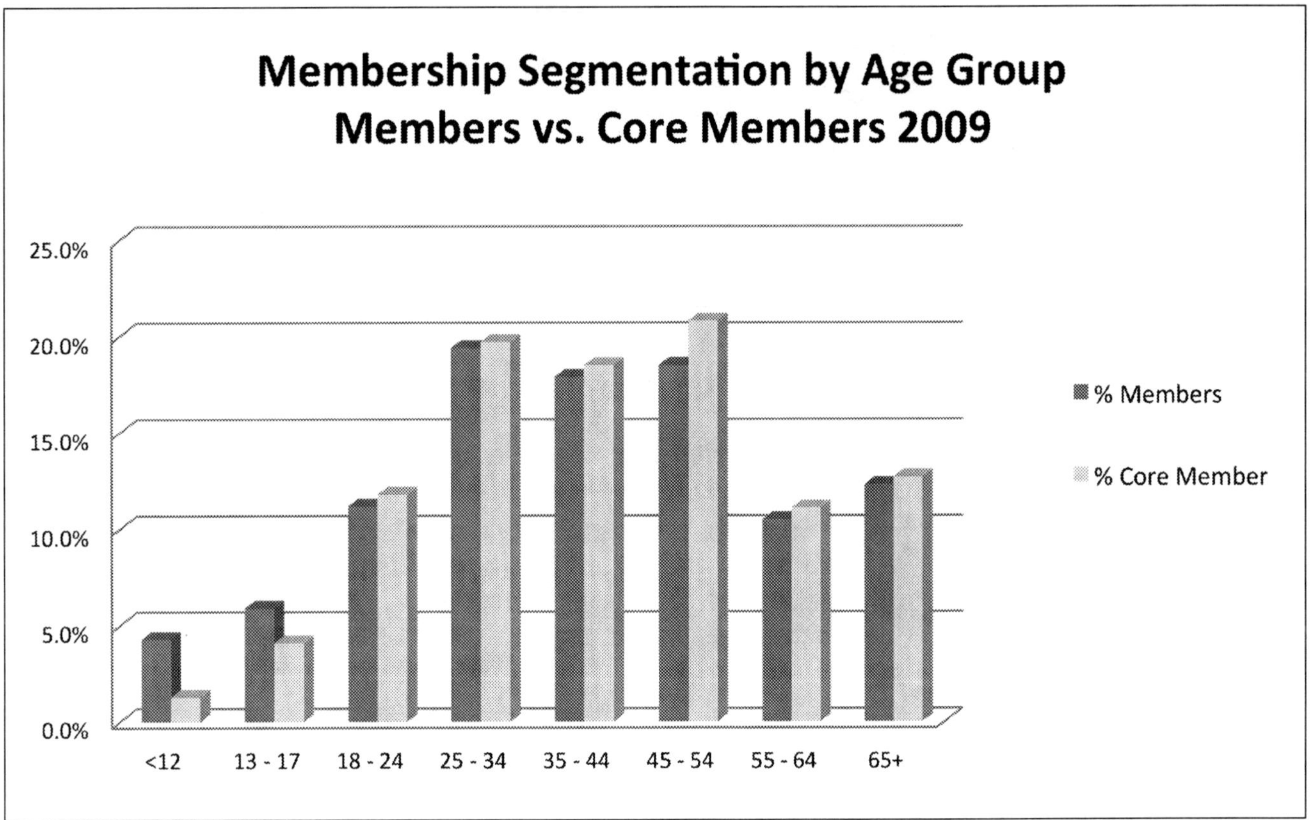

Figure 3-4. Membership segmentation by age group—members vs. core members (2009)

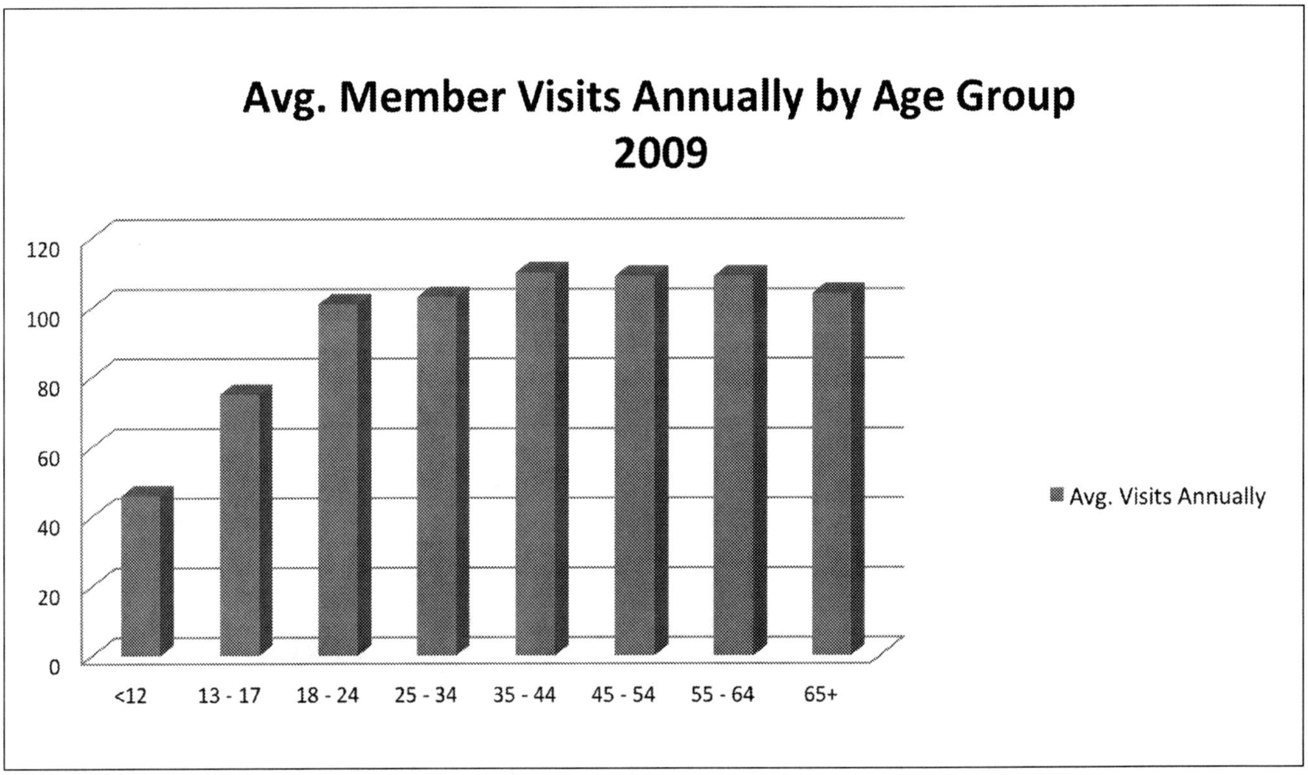

Figure 3-5. Average member visits annually by age group (2009)

Nation	<16	16 – 34	35 – 54	55+
France	7%	38%	33%	22%
Germany	4%	53%	20%	23%
Italy	7%	11%	54%	28%
Netherlands	8%	36%	29%	17%
Spain	9%	38%	33%	20%
U.K.	5%	36%	38%	21%

Figure 3-6. A breakdown of age segmentation, by nation

Several key factors regarding the age composition of membership in the U.S. and Europe can be observed, including the following:

- As a whole, Europe and the U.S. have similar population demographics (based on data from 2007), especially in the 35 to 54 age bracket where the percentage of the total membership is nearly identical at 39 percent. In Europe, clubs attract a larger portion of members in the 18 to 34 age group than facilities in the U.S. (36.5 to 33 percent).
- In nearly all of the European markets reported in the IHRSA study, the percentage of members who are 55 or older is comparable to the U.S. market, with the exception of Italy where those individuals over the age of 55 comprise nearly 5 percent more of the membership base than in the U.S. or other European zones.

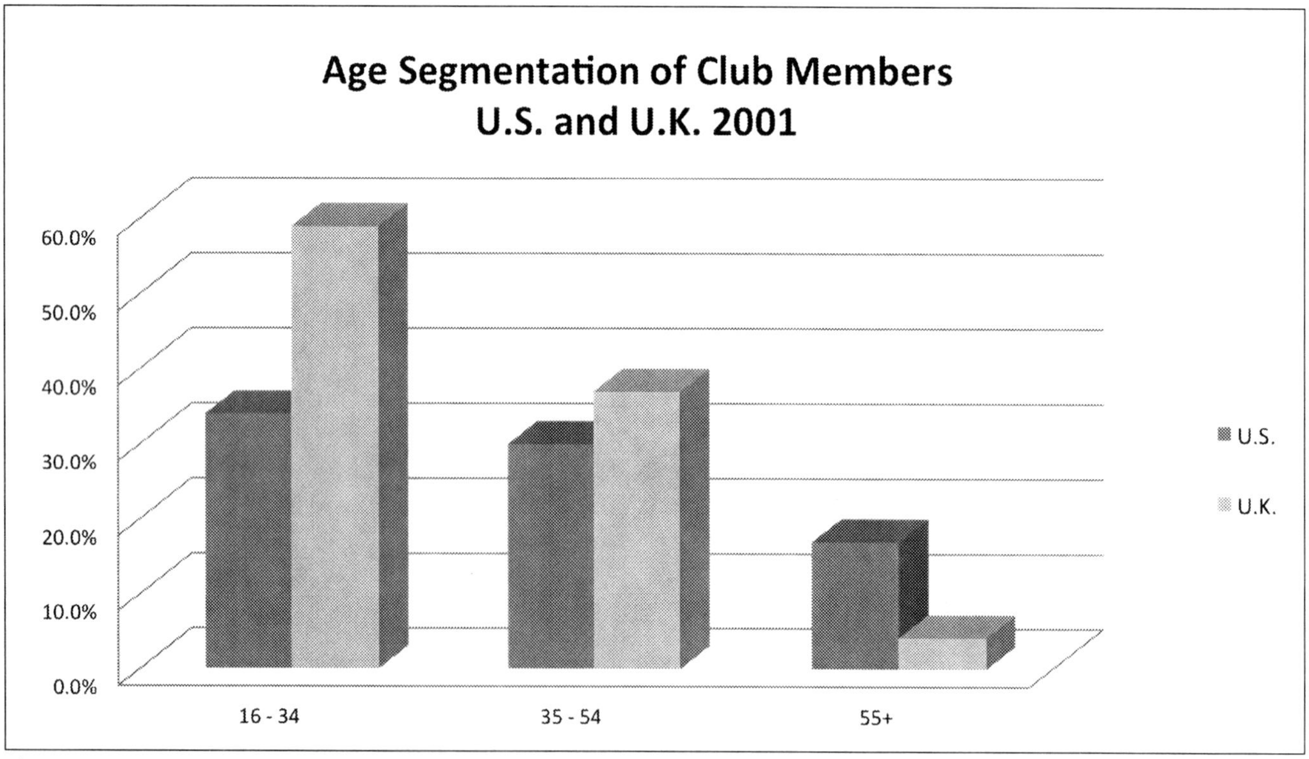

Figure 3-7. Age segmentation of club members U.S. and U.K. (2001)

- In the 18 to 34 age bracket, which represents the next generation of club members, Germany, with over 53 percent of its member base coming from this group, has a distinctly larger population of younger members than other Western European nations and the U.S. Concurrently, very few of the members of clubs in Italy are drawn from the 18 to 34 age group (11 percent), a statistic that could have a material impact on how the industry evolves over the next 10 years. Figure 3-7 provides a comparison of the U.S. and the U.K. club markets by age.

Education Level and Its Impact on Membership

In the U.S., education level is a strong determinant of membership viability. According to the most recent data, approximately 59 percent of club members in the U.S. have either a college degree or a graduate-level diploma, while another 29 percent have received some post-secondary education (Figure 3-8). Over the past decade, the trend has been for an ever-increasing portion of the club membership base to be derived from the group of individuals with college and post-graduate educations. As is detailed in Chapters 4 and 5, audiences with post-secondary and higher-education degrees exert a notable influence on consumer and member behavior that skews in a positive way toward exercise and health/fitness club memberships.

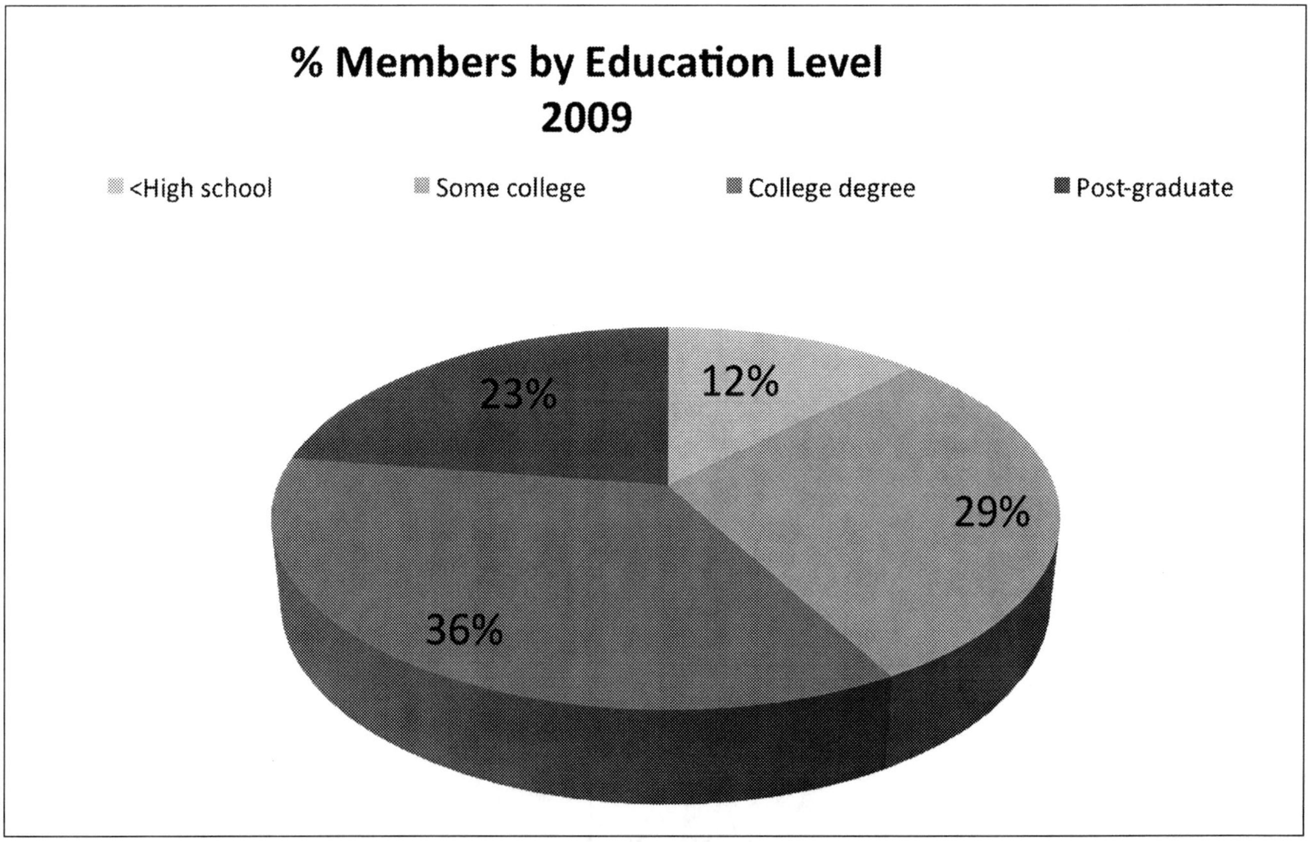

Figure 3-8. Percentage of members by education level (2009)

When club participation levels (i.e., visits per year) are compared across the various education segments, it can be seen that as the level of education increases, the level of participation also increases (Figure 3-9). For example, those individuals with a post-graduate degree use their memberships 20 percent more frequently than individuals with a high school education or less, 15 percent more than the average health/fitness club member, and 10 percent more than members with a college education. As such, in the U.S., a post-secondary education (especially a college degree or higher) is often a strong determinant of both club membership and club participation levels.

Based on the limited data available on the European market, it would seem that obtaining a higher education is not nearly as strong a factor affecting membership make-up as it is in the U.S. Figure 3-10 provides a comparison of membership composition, based on education levels, in select European nations. The data is derived from IHRSA's *2007 European Market Report.*

Nation	Secondary Education	Post-Secondary	University Degree
France	24%	27%	32%
Germany	42%	18%	13%
Italy	25%	5%	17%
Spain	27%	15%	
U.K.	28%	33%	

Figure 3-10. A comparison of membership composition, based on education levels, in select European nations

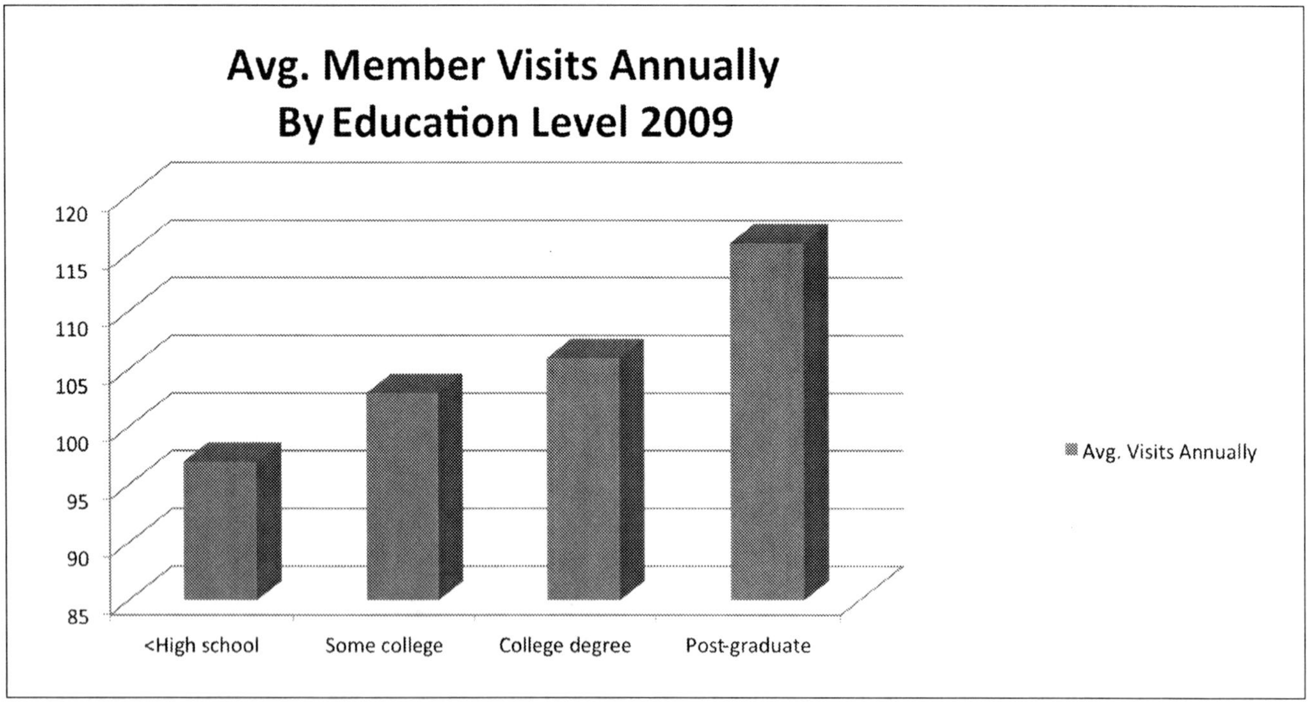

Figure 3-9. Average member visits annually by education level (2009)

Several observations regarding the importance of education level when it comes to the overall make-up of the U.S. and European markets can be made, including the following:

- The U.S. market has a significantly higher percentage of club members with college and post college educations than the markets in Europe. The U.K. is the only European market where a college or university degree seems to be an influencing demographic for membership.
- In Germany, data would seem to indicate that a university degree is not a significant factor in determining membership suitability, at least when compared to the U.S market.
- Given that research indicates that education level has a significant influence on membership retention (refer to Chapter 7), with the higher the education level the higher the retention rate, it could be argued that the educational demographics of the European market lend themselves to higher attrition rates than in the U.S. market.

Household Income and Its Significance to Membership

Household (HH) income, similar to educational attainment, has a strong influence on membership viability, particularly in the U.S. In 2009, 36 percent of all U.S. club members reported household incomes in excess of $100,000 annually, while approximately 53 percent reported HH incomes of over $75,000 annually. Correspondingly, an estimated 27 percent of members reported HH incomes of under $50,000 annually. Over the past five years (Figure 3-11), the percentage of U.S. members that reported HH incomes of

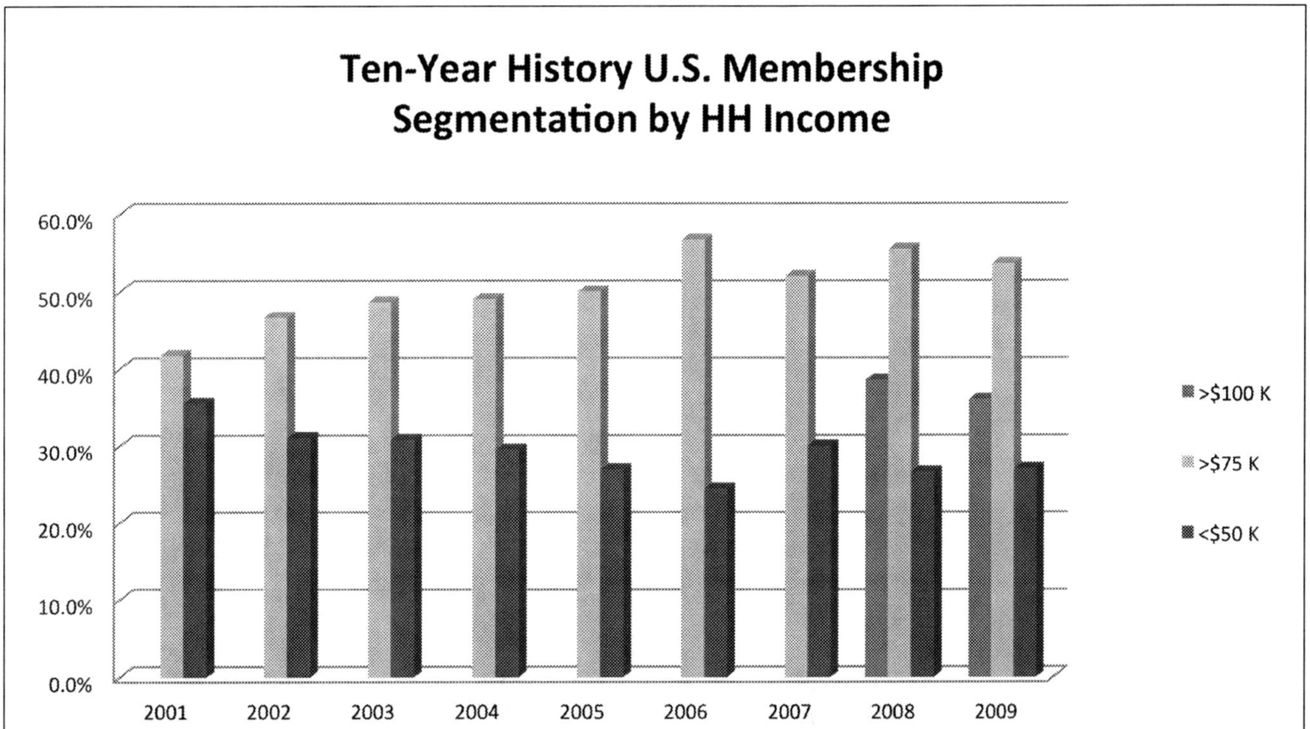

Figure 3-11. Ten-year history of U.S. membership segmentation by household income

over $75,000 annually has remained relatively stable, while the percentage of members reporting HH incomes under $50,000 has also remained flat (27 percent of membership). Interestingly, it seems that the "big" shift in member composition, based on HH income, arose on or about 2003, when members reporting HH income of over $75,000 annually comprised under 50 percent of the membership, and those individuals reporting incomes of under $50,000 annually encompassed close to 35 percent of the membership.

When the various HH income segments among the general membership and core members are compared, it can be seen that the two highest HH income segments ($75,000 to $99,999 and over $100,000 annually) comprise a larger percentage of the core members than the general membership (Figure 3-12). For example, if 35 percent of all members report HH income of over $100,000 annually, then those individuals who are core members comprise more than 37 percent of the member population. While not a significant variance, the data indicates that a smaller percentage of core members come from households in the lower-income brackets. Furthermore, when the data pertaining to the average number of visits by members in each of the HH income segments (Figure 3-13) is looked at, it can be observed that affluent members use their club more frequently than the average member, and nearly 6 percent more frequently than those members earning less than $50,000 annually.

Household income also plays an important role in club membership in Russia. While no industry-wide data is available for Russia, in a sample study group of 13,000 members from one of Russia's leading club operators, the data showed that approximately 30 percent of that organization's membership base was derived from households earning in excess of 220,000 rubles a month (approximately $95,000 annually at the time). It is interesting to note that the average Russian, based on Federation statistics for per capita income and the data from the aforementioned study group, spends between 4 and 8 percent of their annual earnings on membership, compared to less than 2 percent in most Western nations.

Reflections on the Data—What Might It Mean?

The global health/fitness club industry appeals relatively equally to men and women, with only minor gender-related differences occurring in the last 10 years.

In assessing the data included in this chapter, several important trends stand out that relate to the demographic profile of the average U.S. and global health/fitness club member, including the following:

- The global health/fitness club industry appeals relatively equally to men and women, with only minor gender-related differences occurring in the last 10 years. Over the past decade in the U.S., the make-up of the industry, from a gender-perspective, has become more heavily weighted toward men when compared to the previous five-year period (currently 51 percent male versus 43 percent male).

  On a global basis, from what data is available regarding European markets, it would seem that health/fitness clubs attract a greater proportion of women then men, a factor that may be related to the demographics of

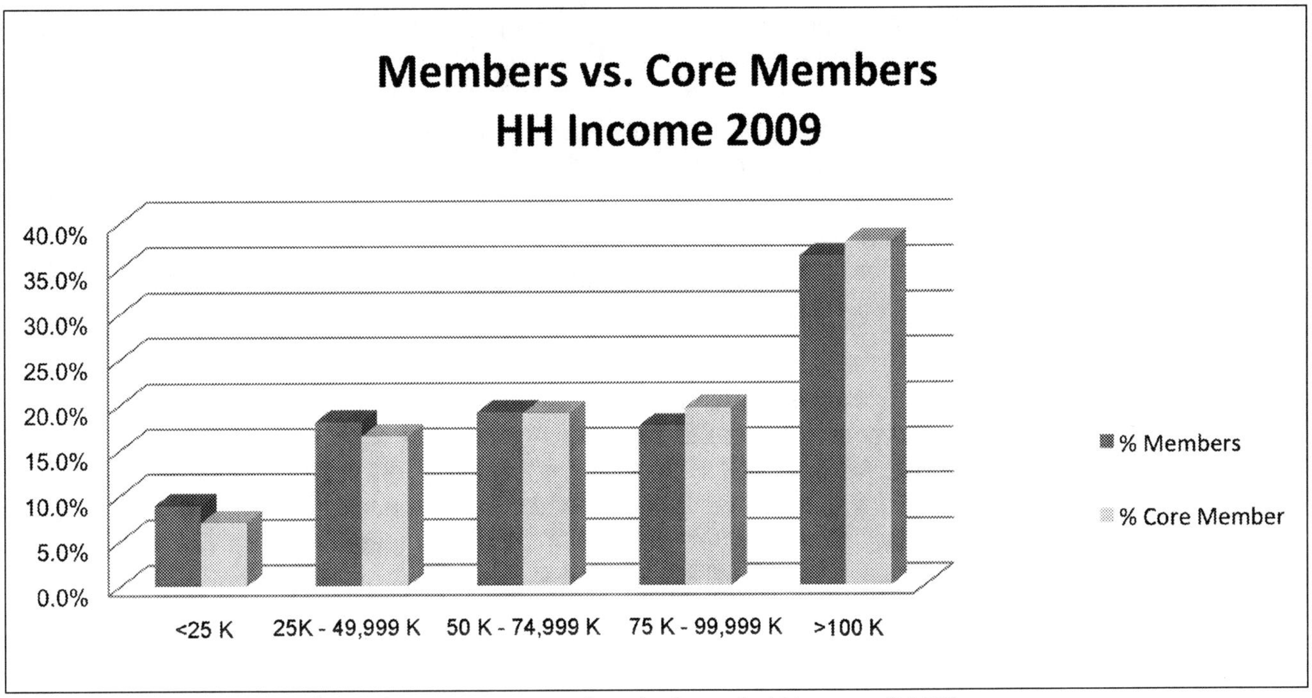

Figure 3-12. A comparison of members vs. core members by household income (2009)

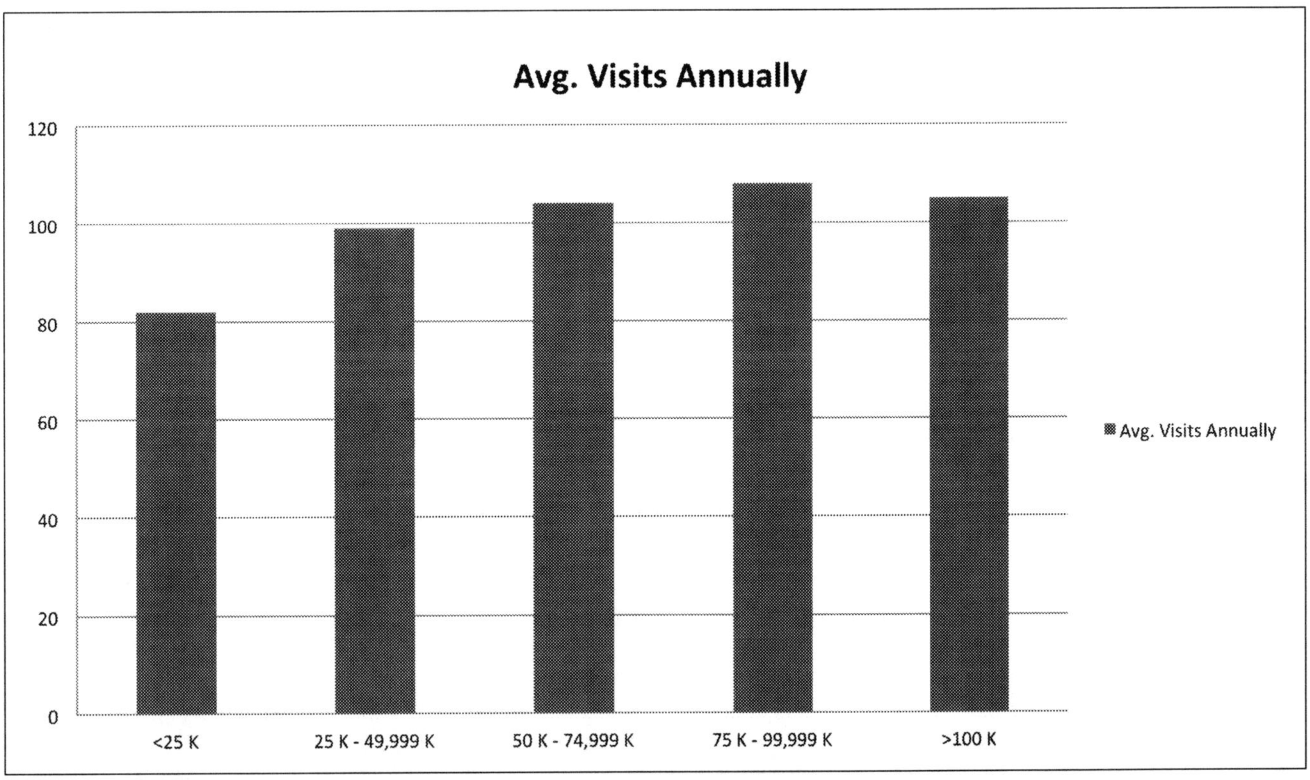

Figure 3-13. A comparison of average number of visits by household income (2009)

the general population. Since men and women have considerably different rationales in many cases for exercising, as well as for joining a club (refer to Chapters 4 to 6 for additional information on this subject), this proportional mix of male and female members can have a significant impact on clubs. For example, it would be in the best interest of clubs to regularly monitor the gender balances in their facilities. Such information could be used to identify, develop, and offer a diversity of services and programs that would appeal to the specific needs of these two distinct audiences. To a great degree, their ability to effectively manage and control their retention levels will depend on it.

In the U.S., education level is a far greater determinant of who is likely to be a club member than it is in Europe.

- In the U.S., education level is a far greater determinant of who is likely to be a club member than it is in Europe. Furthermore, not only does educational attainment seem to be a much greater predictor in the U.S. of membership acquisition, it also affects member activity and retention more than it does in Europe. In the U.S., the higher the educational achievement of the individual, the more likely the person will be a club member, and the more likely that individual will actively use the facility.

A possible theoretical explanation for this situation could be advanced that individuals with a higher education level may have a more comprehensive understanding of the benefits of exercise and the value of a healthy lifestyle. As a result, these individuals are able to make a more informed decision regarding club membership and the types of activities to pursue. This demographic data indicates that club operators who desire to improve membership retention should consider positioning their club so it appeals to a more educated audience.

- In the U.S., HH income, like educational attainment, is an important predictor of both membership activity and exercise participation. The industry, whether it wants to believe it or not, has become an enterprise that has positioned itself to appeal primarily to an upper middle class and affluent population. While this situation is not necessarily a bad thing, it seems counter to the trends that have been transpiring in membership pricing.

Over the past decade, the industry has engaged a larger audience of higher income households, while at the same time lowering its price points. From a purely economic perspective, the average annual dues in the health/fitness club industry in the U.S. in 2009 were $720, a statistic that represents 1.8 percent of the average per capita income of an American. In contrast, a decade earlier, annual club dues in the U.S. represented 2.1 percent of per capita income. In essence, over the past decade, the industry has asked its members to pay a smaller percentage of their HH income for membership. At the same time, the industry has made a concerted effort to communicate the importance of exercise to the public. Based on the HH income ranges of members in 2009, the average U.S. club's dues represent approximately 1 percent of HH income.

The lower expenditure on dues may ultimately be impacting industry retention levels, since it may suggest that the American consumer does not place enough value on the health/fitness club industry's offering. In Russia, the average annual dues for a health/fitness club represent approximately 6.8 percent of the per capita income. Data from a private company shows that many club members in Russia often invest one month of their earnings into membership, as opposed to 3.1 percent of per capita income in Spain, and 2.1 percent of per capita income in Germany.

It could be argued that the health/fitness club industry has evolved to serve a more educated and affluent consumer over the last two decades.

It is apparent in other nations that citizens are ready and willing to invest a larger portion of their annual income in club membership. For club operators, this data indicates the importance of targeting their business toward a higher economic demographic if they want to have a more active membership, as well as a membership base that is ready to retain their membership for a longer period of time.

In conclusion, it could be argued that the health/fitness club industry has evolved to serve a more educated and affluent consumer over the last two decades. The by-product of this situation is that the industry has a prospective membership base that has an extensive understanding about exercise and knows what to expect when they join a club. Furthermore, the circumstances lead to members who are also better prepared to pay for a membership that not only gives them what they need, but also what they want.

CONSUMER AND MEMBER BEHAVIOR: FACTORS DRIVING EXERCISE AND HEALTH/FITNESS CLUB MEMBERSHIP

© Hemera/Thinkstock

Section Three

The health/fitness club industry offers a product and service that are truly unique in the global marketplace. While most businesses can classify themselves as a product business, a service business, or an experience business, the health/fitness club industry crosses the boundaries of several segments of the commercial arena, while also depending, in large part, on supporting people in adopting a new lifestyle behavior. From a business perspective, the health/fitness club industry could be classified as being in one of several business segments including the following:

- *Hospitality business.* Similar to hotels and resorts, health/fitness clubs offer their customers a true hospitality experience. People visit them for a variety of reasons—to unwind, to be pampered, to be motivated, to be treated as an honored guest, and most importantly, to achieve one of their lifestyle dreams.
- *Leisure and recreational business.* Health/fitness clubs are somewhat similar to bowling, golf, sports leagues, and gaming centers. People visit them to pursue and engage in their preferred leisure and recreational activities.
- *Service business.* Health/fitness clubs are like many current businesses in that they offer their members a service that depends on delivering an experience that is rewarding and enriching, and which is highly dependent on people, as well as the relationships that they form with their customers.
- *Healthcare business.* Health/fitness clubs provide their members with the opportunity to exercise, which has been shown to enhance the overall health of individuals, as well as play a documental role in both preventative and rehabilitative medicine.

All factors considered, since the health/fitness club industry crosses the boundaries of various business offerings, it can lead to a greater variety of member attitudes, rationales, and needs—all of which can drive consumer decision-making and behavior adoption.

As indicated previously, the health/fitness club industry also has another major influencer that compounds the challenges set forth by the multidisciplinary aspect of the business model—exercise adoption. Adopting exercise is like switching to other lifestyle behaviors (e.g., eating healthier, losing weight, quitting smoking, kicking a drug habit, etc.)—it is difficult. Truth be known, many individuals never truly adopt the new lifestyle behavior. Studies from the U.S. indicate that up to 50 percent of individuals who begin an exercise program drop out by the sixth month. Data from the United Kingdom shows that only 66 percent of those who begin an exercise program remain with it for a period of one year.

Studies from the U.S. indicate that up to 50 percent of individuals who begin an exercise program drop out by the sixth month.

As such, if the industry builds its business model, in particular its retention model, on the basis of getting people to accept and adopt exercise, then it is virtually dooming itself to failure. Accordingly, the industry must look beyond exercise and focus on other more relevant factors, such as the total product offering, the service delivery process, and ultimately the complete "experience" that it can provide to its members.

The initial step in developing a successful business model for enhancing retention involves understanding the attitudes, beliefs, and actions that support exercise behavior, and next, to understand the attitudes, beliefs, and behaviors that support an individual's desire to become and remain a member of a health/fitness club.

This section addresses both factors. Chapter 4 delves into exercise behavior and the process by which people choose to begin, accept, adopt, and then stay with exercise. Chapter 5 looks at what drives people to seek out a health/fitness club and remain a member. Chapter 6 reviews why people terminate their membership in a club and how that action relates to their initial attitudes and beliefs about joining and remaining a member of a club. Chapter 7 details how general demographic characteristics drive retention. Finally, Chapter 8 discusses member satisfaction and member loyalty and addresses how these two factors influence member retention.

The initial step in developing a successful business model for enhancing retention involves understanding the attitudes, beliefs, and actions that support exercise behavior.

4

The Exercise Habit: Making Exercise a Part of Life

Exercise Theories and Strategies to Leverage Their Principles

Exercise—some people look at it as a four-letter word. Others consider it torture. A number of individuals love the feeling and adrenaline rush that they get from exercise. Finally, some are "true believers" who couldn't live without it. What other behavior brings forth such a polar array of emotions?

Theories of Exercise Behavior

As a result of this gambit of emotions, some driven by the thought of exercising and others by the actual act of exercising, health/fitness professionals and industry experts have derived several theories, over the decades, concerning what is required to get people to start and stay with exercise. Understanding these theories and how they can be manipulated can go a long way toward helping clubs influence member and prospect exercise behavior. Among these theories are the following:

- *Concern for health.* The basis for this theory is that people will begin and adopt exercise in their lives to the degree that they believe exercise will benefit their health and longevity. For some individuals, this reasoning might actually apply. On the other hand, most experts in exercise behavior find this theory to explain exercise behavior of limited value in actually getting people to exercise.
- *Belief in one's self (social learning theory).* The underlying foundation of this theory is the principle of self-efficacy that states that a person's own belief in their ability to regularly exercise is what drives adherence. Self-efficacy depends on a process of small steps in which the individual masters a step, and as a result of the confidence obtained, moves on to the next step. Self-efficacy, as espoused by this theory, presumes that the individual places a value on the expected outcome and their perceived ability to actually master the behavior. In this theory, mastery of each element is critical and is often influenced by one of the following four approaches:

Health/fitness professionals and industry experts have derived several theories, over the decades, concerning what is required to get people to start and stay with exercise.

- ✓ Performance mastery. This approach involves an individual mastering a behavior by actually performing it themselves. Often, this undertaking is performed by taking on small steps so that each stage is mastered before moving on to the next. In the case of exercise, this procedure would require that individuals be allowed to perform an exercise or several exercises with professional guidance and support until they master the movements.
- ✓ Vicarious experience. In this manner, an individual learns by observing someone who is considered competent at the behavior. In the case of exercise, this approach would involve an individual closely observing a skilled professional perform the exercises before they could proceed to master it themselves. Truth be known, this factor may have considerable application to both group exercise and personal training.
- ✓ Verbal persuasion. This measure involves both technique instruction and positive reinforcement. In exercise, this approach would require that a competent instructor provide detailed instruction and monitoring of the exercise movements and offering honest feedback and praise when the exercise is done correctly.
- ✓ Emotional arousal. This approach involves providing an individual with information that supports the benefits of a behavior, followed by the strengthening of the individual's belief in their performance through continued practice and visible results.

The aforementioned theories of exercise behavior adoption and maintenance have significant application in the health/fitness club industry. If given the importance of self-efficacy and the approaches outlined in this chapter, it is apparent that clubs need to be open to a multitude of approaches for helping new members make exercise an integral part of their lifestyle and existing members to sustain their exercise pattern.

- *Reasonable person.* This theory, which has applications in other areas, states that a reasonable person will make assumptions, analyze them, and act accordingly based on those assumptions if they're supported by analysis. In other words, this theory involves the precept that people will consider the implications of a specific behavior, such as exercise, before moving forward.

The underlying analysis an individual undertakes concerning whether to initiate an exercise regimen will often differ from an analysis that same person undertakes concerning whether to remain with an exercise program.

This theory presumes that individuals will weigh the risks and benefits of their potential action before acting. Accordingly, individuals will weight their attitudes toward exercise and health, their existing health condition, the proven benefits of exercise, and the perceived barriers to exercising before applying a rational analysis that will dictate their final actions. While this theory has been proven in research settings, its application to the real world, especially one in which barriers exist that need to be considered, is likely less applicable than the other theories. It is also important to understand that the underlying analysis an individual undertakes concerning whether to initiate an exercise regimen will often differ from an analysis that same person undertakes concerning whether to remain with an exercise program.

- *Behavioral skills.* This theory ascribes to the belief that exercise, like many other initiatives that people undertake, is a behavior, and therefore, is controlled by the core principles of behavioral science. A hypothetical example of the underlying premise behind this model might be to consider "a dog and training it to behave."
- *Ecological model.* This theory embraces the concept that undertaking a new behavior, such as exercise, is influenced by both social/cultural factors and environmental conditions. It supposes that an individual's success in embracing the so-called exercise "habit" is strongly influenced by a multitude of environmental factors, which can collectively intertwine with each other, resulting in a matrix of influences.

  The major elements that play a role in the ecological model include personal influences, social influences, community-based influences, political influences, and institutional influences. How these various influences create opportunities or barriers can have an impact on exercise adoption. If clubs subscribe to this theory of exercise adoption and maintenance, then it becomes extremely important for them to understand the various environmental conditions that influence each member of their club. In other words, in essence, one size does not fit all.
- *Transtheoretical model—stages of change.* This theory seems to have the broadest support among health/fitness professionals and industry experts, though not in all circles. This model relates to the process of getting started and staying with exercise. As a consequence, it has strong implications to the realities inherent in exercise adoption. This model states that every individual either moves through each of the stages of change or gets stuck at one stage, and as a result, does not move on to the next.

The action phase can last for six months, and is the time when exercise either becomes a habit or becomes another lost cause.

The first stage of the transtheoretical model is called precontemplation, a stage at which the individual is not even thinking of exercise. To go beyond this stage, individuals have to receive enough pertinent information so that they can begin to form an opinion about exercise (authentic and trustworthy information is essential at this juncture).

The second stage is called contemplation, which is the juncture when an individual seriously considers exercise (information on the benefits and costs of exercising is really helpful at this point, as are personal testimonials). At this stage, the individual typically performs a personal SWOT analysis of the benefits and risks associated with exercising.

The third stage is preparation, a time when some form of action is taken, such as purchasing a piece of home equipment or purchasing a club membership (trial memberships can be very effective at this point).

The fourth stage is referred to as the action phase, which is the point at which an individual actually starts to exercise. The action phase can last for six months, and is the time when exercise either becomes a habit or becomes another lost cause. Since this stage usually lasts six months or longer, individuals will need recognition and support throughout this phase.

The final stage is termed maintenance. At this point, exercise becomes a part of an individual's lifestyle. Even during this phase, recognition and support are critical. Unfortunately, an individual can regress from exercising on a regular basis, which does happen far too often. Each of the aforementioned theoretical models has some application to how people adopt exercise.

Club operators need to understand that they probably will have to reach beyond the four walls of their facility to be successful.

A Strategy for Leveraging the Transtheoretical Exercise Adoption Theory

From a club operator's perspective, the transtheoretical model is a reasonable alternative to consider, though by no means is it the only option that can be incorporated into the club's business practices. If each of the transtheoretical stages is considered, it is evident that a club operator can use resources to help individuals through each stage.

What it does require on the part of club operators is to understand that they probably will have to reach beyond the four walls of their facility to be successful. The following example illustrates what a club operator might consider doing on a community and club level to facilitate each stage of the transtheoretical model for their club members and members of the community:

- Precontemplation. Clubs could serve as the community "expert" on fitness and exercise. They can offer information on their website, Facebook page, etc. that provides information about exercise and healthy living. Clubs could also host educational sessions at various community sites. The endgame goal for them is to be viewed as the community expert and resource.
- Contemplation. Clubs could consider providing not just information, but also testimonials from both members and individuals from the community, each of whom could share what they have achieved as the result of exercising. The key would be to give people tools to help them assess the actual benefits and risks of exercising.
- Preparation. Clubs should afford both prospects and members of the community the opportunity to get started in an exercise regimen. This step could involve offering complimentary trial memberships or trial package programs that allow individuals to "test the waters." Another approach could be to form a community trust that provides funds toward purchasing exercise equipment for those would-be exercisers who can only work out at home. Finally, facilities could develop a club-based, smart-phone application for monitoring exercise that community members could download.
- Action. During the first six months that an individual engages in an exercise program, clubs need to develop tools that can provide their members with guidance, social support, and recognition. For example, clubs might consider special-orientation programs, social-support events, and special-recognition programs for new exercisers.
- Maintenance. After six months, while new exercisers are beginning to adopt a more positive lifestyle, they still need support and feedback. In that regard, clubs might consider special-recognition programs tied to ongoing activity or a special application on their website so their members can continue to receive feedback and recognition.

A Strategy for Leveraging the Social Learning or Self Efficacy Theory for Exercise Adoption

From a club operator's perspective, the social learning or self-efficacy model is another acceptable option to consider when developing an internal approach to helping members adopt exercise behavior. Given this theory states that an individual is more likely to adopt exercise if they first master it in stages, clubs need to be prepared to assist members in mastering these stages. Furthermore, since the learning required to master the steps often takes one of several forms, clubs must also be flexible enough to support these various learning approaches. The following example illustrates what a club operator might consider doing to leverage this particular theory of exercise-behavior adoption:

- Performance mastery. Since this approach to learning is based on an individual learning through practice, the club might consider making sure that new members receive the necessary support and guidance to reinforce their performing the exercise correctly. This measure often involves breaking an exercise program down to specific phases (warming up, upper-body exercises, core exercises, lower-body exercises, cooling down, etc.), and then taking each phase and making sure that the individual understands and properly performs each movement within each of those stages. This approach to learning requires more than a single induction session, since no person could reasonably be expected to master an entire program by performing it once.
- Vicarious experience. This approach involves an individual learning by observing someone else who is considered competent at the behavior. Under this learning style, a club should try to provide members with the opportunity to observe professional instructors demonstrating each exercise. This strategy could involve large classes, on-line video tapes, or small-group instruction demonstrated by a professional.
- Verbal persuasion. This approach involves both technique instruction and positive reinforcement. This undertaking requires that the club's instructors not only provide instruction in technique, but also offer encouragement and reinforcement when the technique is performed correctly. As a rule, this approach can require more than one step or stage.
- Emotional arousal. This approach involves providing an individual with information that supports the benefits of engaging in exercise (e.g., a particular positive behavior), followed by the strengthening of that individual's belief in their performance through continued practice and visible results. As such, a club should make sure it provides sufficient information about the benefits of exercise and how to perform it. One example of undertaking this approach could be through the use of technology, such as the web-based system used by McFit in Germany. At McFit, members receive information about exercise, instruction and feedback through a comprehensive web-based program, and in-club support materials.

From a club operator's perspective, the social learning or self-efficacy model is another acceptable option to consider when developing an internal approach to helping members adopt exercise behavior.

What People Really Think About Exercise

Where Do People Really Stand on Exercise and Fitness?

Researchers have identified four general categories to define the attitudes that most Americans hold toward fitness and exercise.

Researchers have identified four general categories (Figure 4-1) to define the attitudes that most Americans hold toward fitness and exercise. In this regard, these broad categories help to establish a framework for determining the factors that drive the behaviors of individuals towards exercise. These four categories are as follows:

- Non-believers (estimated 2% of the population). This group is staunch in their belief that exercise is not important. To them, exercise is not something that they or anyone else needs. This group could be defined as the atheists of exercise.
- Indifferent (estimated 17% of the population). This segment of the population sees exercise as having some value. On the other hand, for them, there are lifestyle choices that are far move favorable. While this group does not feel exercise is for them because there are better uses of their time, they can see how it may have value for others.
- Uninitiated believers (estimated 64% of the population). This group of people understand the importance of exercise, and generally speaking, don't mind exercising. If personally asked, they would say, "I really need to exercise more than I do." To some degree, they represent people who are treading water at the action phase of the transtheoretical model of exercise adoption. Back in the late 1990s, the health/fitness club industry viewed this segment as the untapped market for membership. All factors considered, while they can be a great source for sales (they have great intentions), they are a horrible candidate for retention, since they are not likely to perceive value in their membership due to their level of activity.

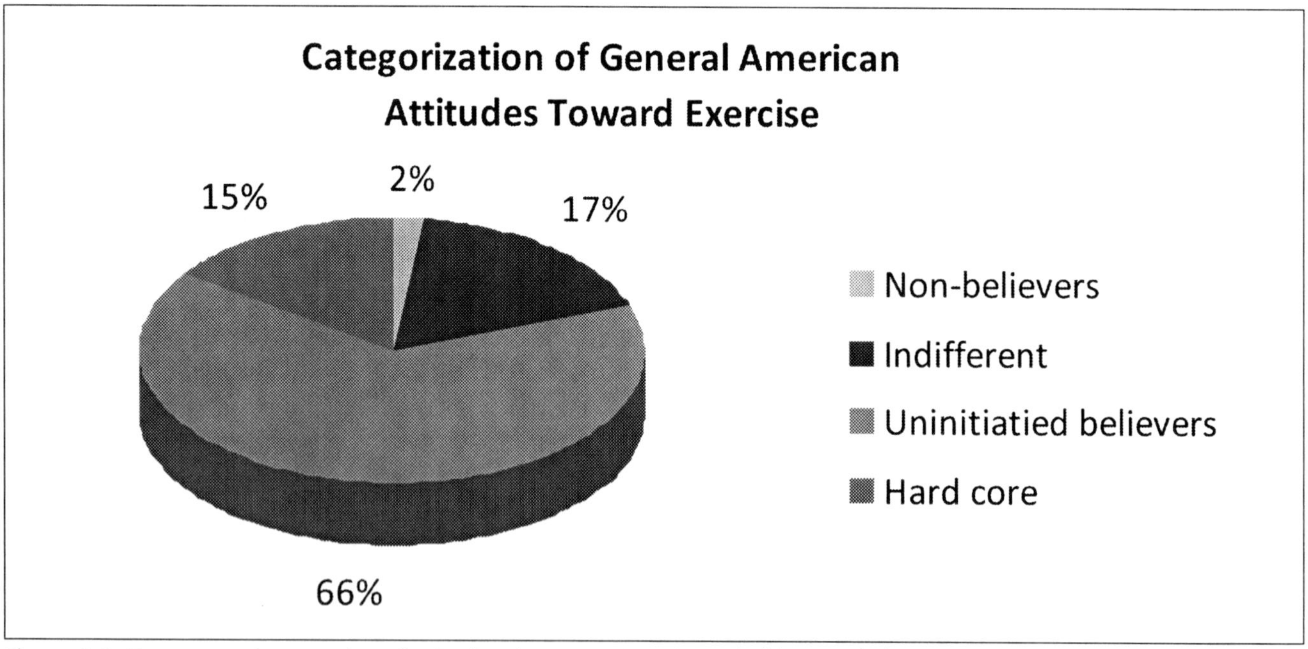

Figure 4-1. Four general categories of attitudes that most Americans hold towards fitness and exercise

- Hard core (estimated 15% of the population). These individuals believe that exercise is very important. As might be surmised, the majority of club members fall into this category, as do many of those individuals who exercise either outdoors or at home.

With regard to the aforementioned, club operators have done an outstanding job in selling and retaining those individuals who would most likely be considered hard core exercisers. To a degree, they have also done a reasonably good job of promoting their product to the uninitiated (given that 16% of the U.S. population are club members, and in some markets, as many as 25% of the population are members). On the other hand, they do a terrible job in holding on to these individuals as members (a potential influencer of the lower retention rates in pure fitness facilities and gyms). As such, an opportunity exists for the health/fitness club industry is to find a way move these individuals from the uninitiated to the hard core category. In fact, doing so may be essential to the ability of the industry to expand its penetration of the market.

What Do People Believe About Those Individuals Who Exercise?

To understand why people start and stay with exercise, it is also important to comprehend the general public's perceptions about people who do exercise. Since society often exhibits a "keeping up with the Jones's mentality," it is imperative to be aware of how the public perceives those individuals who exercise, since those perceptions can play an important role in whether non-exercisers enter the preparation stage and action stages of exercise.

The top five beliefs that Americans have about those individuals who exercise, based on research conducted in the late 1990s by American Sports Data, (Figure 4-2), include the following:

- Prolongs life. Eighty-five percent of Americans polled believe that exercise will contribute to a longer life.
- Leads to a happier life. Seventy-three percent of people polled believe that those individuals who exercise are generally happier than those people who don't.
- Are more attractive. Seventy-one percent indicated that they believe those individuals who exercise are generally more physically attractive.
- Need to know more about it. Fifty-five percent of those individuals polled replied that they needed more information about exercise before they could really render a judgment.
- No discipline and no time. Over 65% of the population who participated in the study indicated that they have neither the time nor the self-discipline to exercise.
- The magic pill. A total of 46% of respondents replied that if a magic pill existed that could do what exercise does, they would take it.

To understand why people start and stay with exercise, it is also important to comprehend the general public's perceptions about people who do exercise.

So, what do people really believe? It appears that they are convinced that exercise helps people be happier, more physically attractive, and allows them to live longer. Looking at these responses, it would seem that exercise is perceived as the real deal, the fountain of youth, the magic pill for happiness and the elixir for physical appeal. On the downside, while Americans believe that exercise is like the magic foundation of youth and happiness, they also strongly believe they don't have either the time or the discipline to undertake the effort needed to garner all of the perceived benefits. What all the aforementioned indicates is that at least for the majority of Americans, the perceived barriers to exercise are strong enough to counter the actual proven benefits of exercise. In other words, the contrasting beliefs that Americans hold about exercise indicate that Americans' words are not as strong as their actions.

What Those Individuals Who Started to Exercise Say Got Them Over the Hump

In the middle part of the 1990s, IHRSA sponsored research that would lead to a better understanding of why people exercise. One study conducted at the University of Michigan, under the leadership of Christine Brooks, Ph.D., examined the drivers that would give people the impetus to begin exercising. A second study conducted a year later looked at why people actually exercise. In 2001 IHRSA, commissioned another study that investigated exercise behavior.

The first research report by Brooks, Understanding Exercise Adoption Behavior, released in 1994, looked at the rationales and beliefs of Americans as it pertained to exercise. Among the key understandings that arose out of Brooks' work were the following:

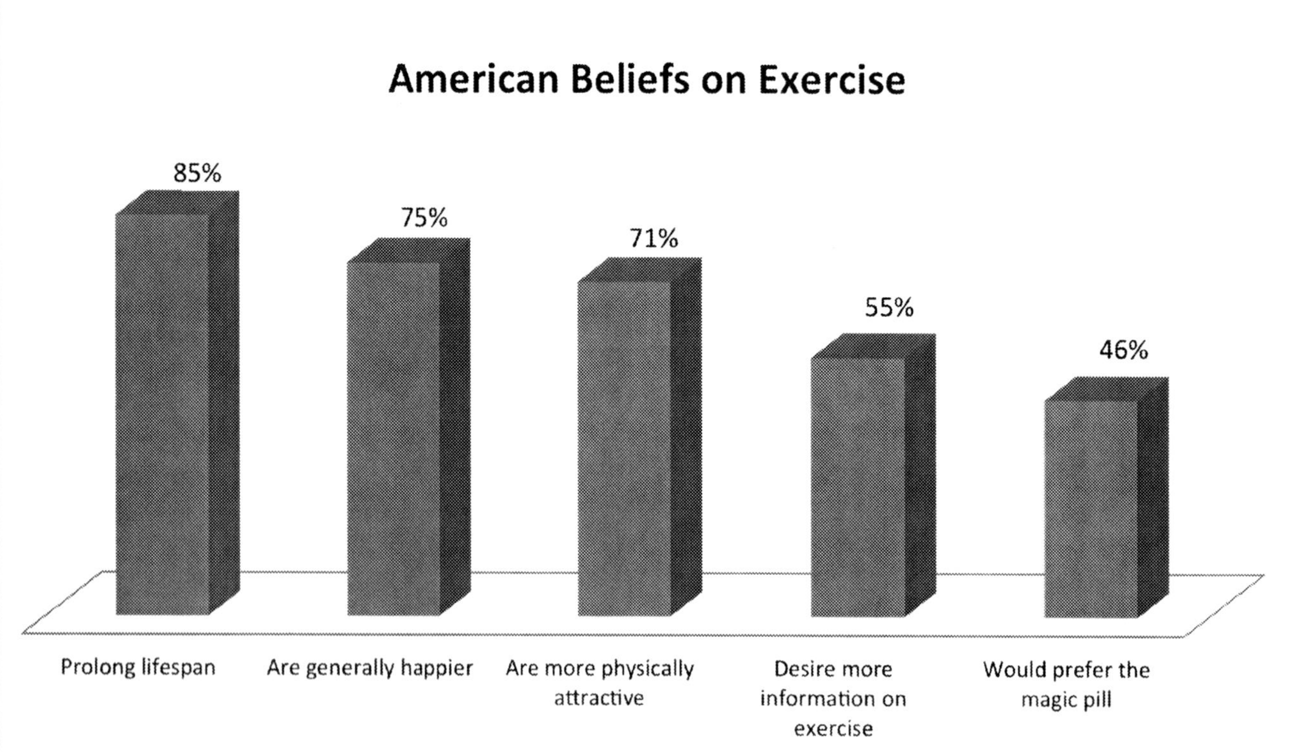

Figure 4-2. The top beliefs that Americans have about those individuals who exercise

- The majority of Americans believed that exercise was good for their health and wellbeing.
- Americans who lived a sedentary lifestyle indicated the two primary reasons they were not active were, the fact that their family and friends did not exercise and that they had were more important priorities in their life, and as a result, they did not have time in their schedule to exercise.
- On a more personal level, the respondents indicated that the top three reasons they remained sedentary and did not exercise were that they were self conscious about their bodies; that they did not feel they had the skills or experience to properly use exercise equipment; and that they felt other individuals who did exercise would be judging them in a negative manner.

In addition to studying the beliefs people had about exercise, Brooks also looked at the primary reasons that people who exercised gave for exercising. On that regard the top three motives were:

- *To improve appearance.* Forty-eight percent of the respondents indicated that improving their appearance was their top reason for exercising. In this regard, losing weight was indicated nearly three times as often as bulking up and improving muscle tone.
- *To improve health.* Twenty-six percent of those individuals who answered the survey indicated that they started exercise to improve their overall health. As such, by a margin of two to one, these respondents indicated that getting in shape rather than overcoming a specific health problem was important to them.
- *Feeling good.* Fifteen percent of those individuals who were surveyed replied that the most important reason behind exercising was to feel good about themself. Responses in this category included enhancing self image, feeling better about one's self, and having the energy to do more with their life.

The second study reported in 1995 and 1996, entitled *Why People Exercise,* looked at why people exercised, whether it was in a club setting or in another setting. In addition, the study looked at some of the differences concerning why men and women exercise. Among the key findings from this work were the following:

- The top five reasons that people gave for exercising were: weight control (85% of respondents); obtain more energy for daily life (84.7% of respondents); improve muscle tone (84.4% of respondents); feel good (84.4% of respondents) and; improve cardiovascular condition (81.5% of respondents).
- The leading reasons that women provided for exercising were: weight control (88% answered affirmative vs. 82% for men); feel good about self (87% answered affirmative vs. 82% for men); and improve energy level (86% of women answered affirmative vs. 83% of men).
- Among the leading reasons that men listed for exercising were: improving muscle tone (88% of men answered affirmative vs. 84% of women); improve energy level (83% of men, a viewpoint that was below the level of importance expressed by women); and improve cardiovascular condition (82% answered affirmatively, vs. 81% for women).

Fifteen percent of those individuals who were surveyed replied that the most important reason behind exercising was to feel good about themself.

- For adults over the age of 45, the most important reasons behind exercising were to improve both cardiovascular conditioning and energy levels. For those adults under the age of 34, the leading reasons for exercising were to improve muscle tone and to maintain their weight.
- The three most significant reasons for exercising (Figure 4-3) were to improve appearance (54% of respondents), improve health (29% of individuals) and feel better (17% of people surveyed).

The third report, *Fitness American Style,* which was released in 2001, looked closely at the motivators of exercise behavior. Among the most valuable insight to come out of this report were the following:

- Approximately 97% of Americans indicated that maintaining their health was their most important priority in life, even more important than a fulfilling relationship with their family (95%), their emotional well being (94%), having good friends (89%), or having lots of money (68%).
- Sixty percent of Americans indicate that they are somewhat satisfied with their health, while another 13% say they are completely satisfied with their health. When asked about their level of satisfaction with their physical appearance, nearly the same percentage of Americans responded as they did to the question about health.
- The majority of Americans feel that exercise contributes to higher levels of mental and physical energy, better health, and a greater sense of self-image.

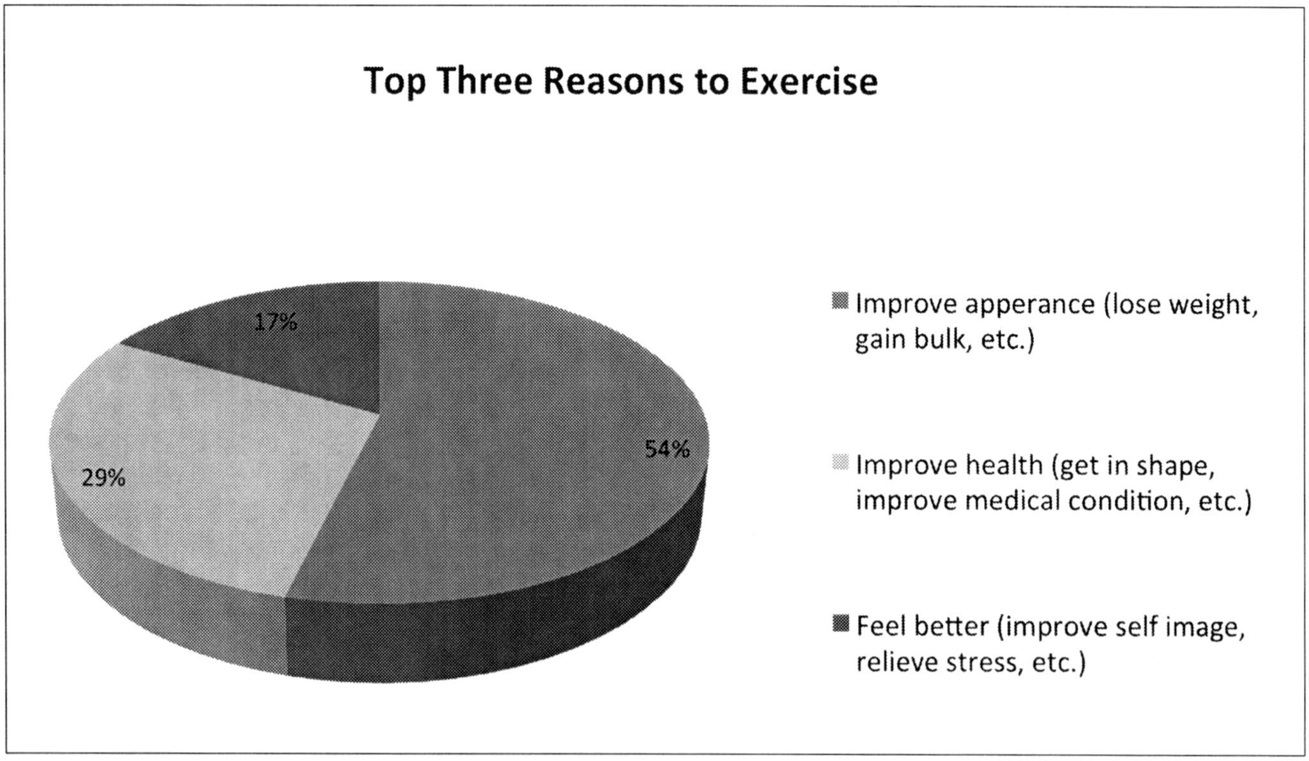

Figure 4-3. The three most significant reasons that Americans give for exercising

- Over 97% of Americans state that exercise is essential or very important to maintaining good health, while 91% indicated the same point with regard to keeping up their physical appearance.
- Women are more prone than men to believe that exercise is essential to good health and physical appearance, while men are more inclined to reference exercise as important for participating in sporting activities or building muscle.
- The top five reasons women share for exercising are becoming physically fit (70%), losing weight (54%), having fun (44%), preventing health problems (42%), and dealing with a current medical condition (33%).
- The top four reasons men give for exercising are becoming physically fit (63%), having fun (56%), challenging self (29%), and competing (27%).

In turn, when they were asked why they stopped exercising, the six leading reasons (Figure 4-4) were as follows: I am not motivated, I don't have enough time, I don't like to exercise, I am already healthy, I am not encouraged, or I have not achieved my goals.

Can People Really Be Classified by Their Exercise Preferences?

The resolute answer to this question is probably no. Nonetheless, researchers have made an effort to categorize people by their exercise-and-lifestyle attitudes and behaviors. The underlying premise behind this effort is that by categorizing behavior, a person's suitability to that categorization can be more

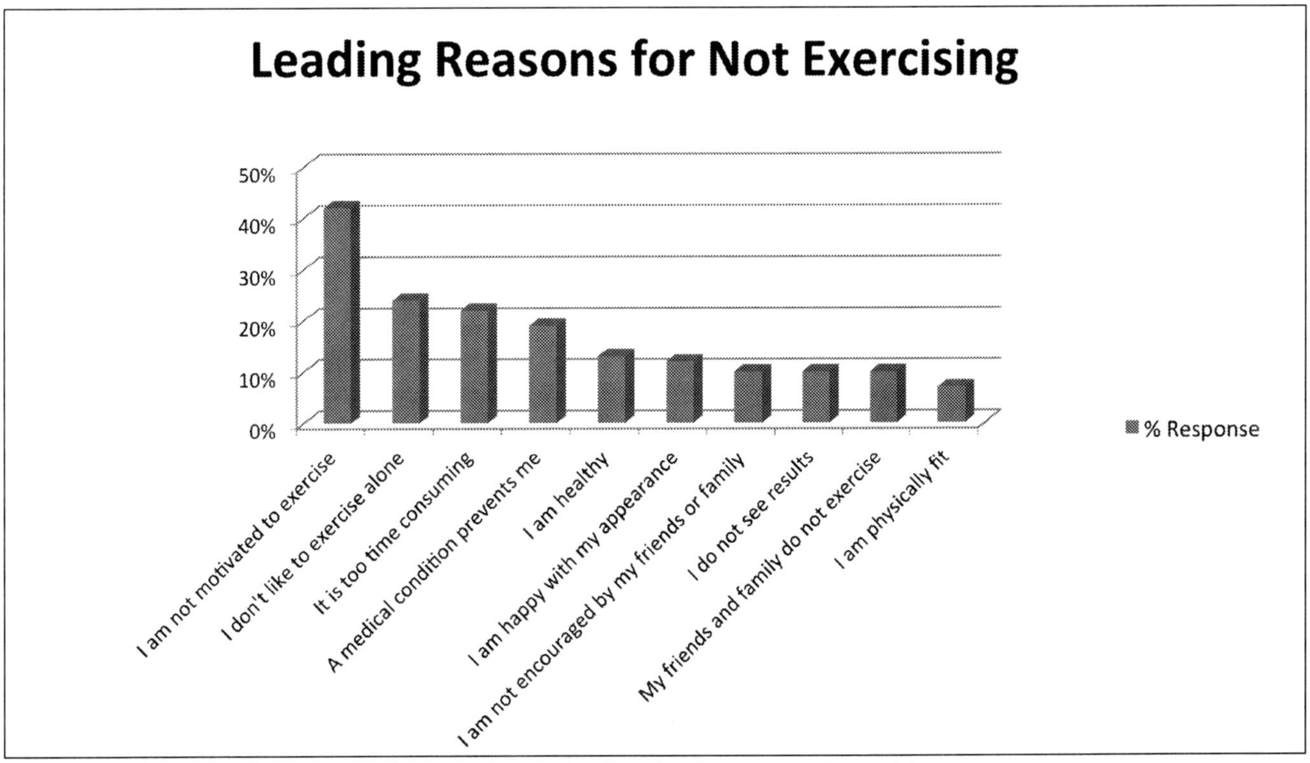

Figure 4-4. The six leading reasons that Americans give for why they stopped exercising

easily identified and in turn, an appropriate intervention selected. One such nomenclature system was proposed by Christine Brooks in the mid-1990s, as the result of her work in the area of exercise. Brook's identified the following six categories of active-lifestyle participants:

- *Mind & body purifiers.* These exercisers supposedly have a "love affair" with exercise, based on a belief that exercise provides a means to purify and fortify the mind and body. These individuals tend to be more fanatical exercisers (as a rule, they're easily identified in clubs). This category actually aligns with a form of exercise that developed in the early 1800s entitled Swedish Pedagogical Gymnastics and later called Swedish Medical Gymnastics. This form of exercise had four core principles, one of which was termed pedagogy that related to the connection of mind and body and another, termed aesthetics, that also connected the mind to exercise.
- *Practical folk.* These exercisers see good value in exercising and connect effort to accomplishments. These exercisers are focused on health and reasonable outcomes. They believe that exercise is not about trends, but rather about connecting their efforts to reasonable outcomes. Women tend to fall into this category, since it relates to specific outcomes, such as improved health and well-being. In Swedish Gymnastics in the early 1800s, this was referred to as the medical principle.
- *Experiences.* These exercisers are in it for the overall experience. They tend to be exercisers who prefer sports-oriented activities for their exercise.
- *Easy does it.* These exercisers are aware of the value of exercise but prefer low-intensity, social-oriented exercise. These individuals are not likely to break a sweat or adhere to the "no pain, no gain" philosophy. Instead, they want to enrich the exercise experience by enjoying the activity, while sharing it with others.
- *Combatants.* These exercisers like to compete, either against themselves or others. More often than not, folks will measure their heart rate and level of perceived exertion, will try to outdo their most recent performance each time out, and will basically treat the gym as a Roman coliseum. In Swedish Gymnastics of the 1800s, this attitude would have been part of the core principle of martial.

Adopting the exercise habit can be difficult and fraught with numerous barriers.

Reflections and Insights

To this point, this chapter has reviewed theories about exercise, specifically the attitudes, beliefs, and reasons behind why people do or don't exercise. As such, ten valuable takeaways can be recognized:

- Adopting the exercise habit can be difficult and fraught with numerous barriers. While some people "fall into exercise," most people must go through a series of stages, starting with precontemplation and progressing through preparation, action, and maintenance. At each stage, triggers for moving forward and barriers that stop people in their tracks exist. Ultimately, only a handful of people complete all the stages on their own. In reality, only with the help of others, can these individuals expect a high degree of success in completing their journey.

- No one "perfect" theory exists concerning how and why people adopt exercise. As a result, health/fitness professionals need to understand the various theories underlying exercise behavior and identify practical solutions, based on the current psychological, emotional, social, and environmental conditions. Clubs should keep in mind that exercise is definitely not one size fits all. In turn, clubs should not assume that one approach will be the magic bullet to success with regard to getting individuals to exercise.
- Americans may talk a good game, but their words speak far louder than their actions in this regard. As noted previously, Americans' indicate that maintaining health and exercising are as important to them and possibly more important than family, money, and friends. Furthermore, Americans state unequivocally that they believe that exercise is essential to having good health, achieving a positive self-image, and being physically attractive. Finally, Americans clearly believe that exercise can resolve many of life's problematic issues, including reducing stress, feeling better, losing weight, and enhancing energy levels. Overall, if only these beliefs and attitudes were considered, it could easily be argued that exercise is truly the magic elixir to treat the great physical and mental challenges in life. On the other hand, clubs should realize that what prospective members profess to believe should not be taken as the final word in what will be required to engage them in exercise.
- Americans clearly understand the positive implications of exercise. They have received the information, and as such, the majority of Americans buy into the "exercise is good for you" narrative.
- Americans have a tendency to find excuses why they should not exercise. Their resulting excuses tend to be far more powerful than the positive beliefs they have about exercise. Time seems to be their big barrier. In other words, these individuals don't believe that they have the time to exercise, or possibly simply they don't understand the time that is actually necessary to reap the benefits of being physically active. In addition to time, a lack of social support from friends and family (e.g., social acceptance and reinforcement) is also a barrier to initiating an exercise regimen. As such, it is imperative that club operators identify and implement viable approaches to help their members overcome these barriers and challenges.
- Americans also don't exercise, in large part, because while they feel it will benefit their health and appearance, the majority of them believe that they are already healthy and have a good appearance. As a result, their logic is why pursue exercise if they already have achieved the end point. In reality, it could be argued that many individuals don't really understand what good health is, and possibly don't understand the principle of physical entropy, which entails that as people age, their health and appearance tend to deteriorate. It could also mean that in general, the principle often referred to in American culture as, "Do what I say, not what I do," applies. In other words, these individuals believe exercise is important for everyone, but themselves. As such, club operators must bring clarity on this topic to their members, but do it in a professional, not personal fashion.

Americans also don't exercise, in large part, because while they feel it will benefit their health and appearance, the majority of them believe that they are already healthy and have a good appearance.

- Men and women exercise for similar, but somewhat different, reasons. Women are more rational; they value exercise for its ability to improve health, treat medical conditions, lose and control their weight and provide an avenue for enhancing emotional and mental health. Women also value the social and fun aspect of exercising more than men. Men, in turn, view exercise as means to improve their improvement in sports, get stronger and more muscular, and control their weight. Men also pursue exercise from a more competitive perspective then women, who are more likely to prefer a social-exercise experience. Clubs need to take these factors into consideration when tailoring their offerings.
- The age of a member impacts the outcomes that people seek from exercise, as well as the barriers concerning exercise that they perceive, and finally the factors that motivate them. Older adults are focused more on improving the quality of their life, preventing health problems, and overcoming existing health conditions. Younger adults, on the other hand, tend to pursue goals that are related to their appearance (maintain weight, build muscle, improve physical appearance, etc.). Older adults also prefer guidance from an educated fitness professional, a factor that carries less significance for a younger adult.
- The reasons that people drop their exercise program tend to be grouped into three important categories. The first involves the failure to achieve results. The second is a lack of a support network, whether family or friends, and a lack of encouragement from others. The third is a lack of motivation and a general displeasure with working out in the first place. Collectively, these factors indicate that a club must provide a social-support network, along with finding a way to help members establish realistic and achievable expectations.
- Club operators, if they are serious about retention, must first understand the attitudes and beliefs attendant to exercise. Once a club appreciates these member attitudes and beliefs, they can effectively implement targeted strategies to assist every new and existing member to adopt exercise as a way of life. In this regard, among the tips that can be identified, based on what has been detailed in this chapter, are the following:
  - ✓ When an individual enrolls, clubs should collect information about the new member's fitness goals (e.g., 30 days, 90 days and one year), their past exercise experiences, their success in achieving their healthy-lifestyle goals in the past, their perceived barriers to working out and achieving expressed goals, their preferences for social and/or competitive opportunities, and their preferred form of communication (phone, text, email, etc.). As such, clubs should build a profile of each member that will help them guide their members into the appropriate activity program and elements of club life.
  - ✓ When individuals enroll, clubs should collect information about the health and current physical condition of their members. Clubs should keep in mind hat because consumers tend to believe that they are already healthy and in reasonable shape, obtaining and sharing information that can help educate members about their health and fitness status is essential.

The age of a member impacts the outcomes that people seek from exercise, as well as the barriers concerning exercise that they perceive, and finally the factors that motivate them.

✓ Clubs should establish an orientation program that can help guide members through their first 180 days of exercise. This effort can include initial training sessions, weekly or monthly follow-up and coaching appointments, on-line monitoring, and a feedback program, etc.

✓ Clubs should tailor the orientation program to the member. In reality, not everyone wants personal training. The orientation might revolve around a number of factors including group exercise, court sports, etc. To the degree possible the orientation effort should be made personally relevant to the member.

In reality, not everyone wants personal training.

✓ Clubs should create recognition programs that are linked to both the achievement of outcome goals (e.g., losing a desired amount of weight, performing so many repetitions of a particular exercise/lift, gaining a certain amount of muscle, etc.) and process goals (e.g., exercising twice a week, visiting the club ten times the first month, visiting the club twenty-four times in the first quarter, etc.). Although recognition programs can take many forms, it's important that they are relevant to the individual.

5

Why Consumers Join Health/Fitness Clubs

To the general consumer, the perception of a fitness club, fitness center, and gym are all identical.

The previous chapter addressed the attitudes and beliefs that impact an individual's decision to embark on an exercise program, as well as the attitudes and beliefs that affect an individual's ability to either temporarily or permanently adopt exercise. This chapter moves beyond the exercise arena and explores the attitudes, beliefs, and reasons that consumers indicate influence their decision to join a health/fitness club. As part of the discussion surrounding consumer attitudes about clubs, in particular joining a health/fitness club, the commercial differences between a health/fitness club and a gym/fitness center are detailed.

Understanding the Difference Between a Health/Fitness Club and Gym/Fitness Center

To the general consumer, the perception of a fitness club, fitness center, and gym are all identical. Once individuals become a member though, they begin to see the difference, and as a result, the reasons they had for joining begin to separate themselves from the reasons they remain a member.

A fitness center, or gym as it is referred to in Europe and Asia, is a facility that provides consumers with the tools to pursue their fitness and/or exercise objectives. These tools of the trade for fitness centers and gyms encompass several items, including the equipment with which people need to exercise (e.g., treadmills, elliptical trainers, resistance machines, weights, etc.); the programs that provide the appropriate environment for personal exercise adherence (e.g., group exercise, personal training, etc.), and the staff that provide the requisite guidance and instruction (instructors, trainers, counselors, etc.). Among the global examples of fitness centers/gym are 24 Hour Fitness, U.S.; Fitness First, U.K.; McFit, Germany; and LA Fitness, U.S.

A club is a different animal all together. The original definition of a club states that a club is an environment where people of similar interests and social standing gather together to network, socialize, and pursue their personal goals. As such, a club implies that the participants have similar interests and backgrounds, are present to network and socialize, and are pursuing their respective goals. Accordingly, a health/fitness club would be an environment that provides the tools for individuals to pursue their fitness goals, but also is an entity that allows its members to interact, network, socialize, and engage with other members whose backgrounds are somewhat similar. Examples of global health/fitness clubs include David Lloyd Leisure, U.K.; Eastbank Club, U.S.; Houstonian, U.S.; Hillside City Club, Istanbul, Turkey; Oase Health & Sport, Germany; and New York Athletic Club, U.S. These facilities not only provide an environment for the pursuit of a person's fitness goals, they also accommodate the social expectations that members have.

The reasons why people join a health/fitness club vs. a gym/fitness center tend to closely parallel each other, but the reasons members remain at each type of facility differ drastically.

In the modern marketplace, the health/fitness club industry has done relatively little to help consumers differentiate between these two offerings. Clubs tend to have higher retention rates than gym/fitness centers because the experience members have depends not only on the outcome of their exercise achievements, but also on the development of interpersonal relationships. The reasons why people join a health/fitness club vs. a gym/fitness center tend to closely parallel each other, but the reasons members remain at each type of facility differ drastically.

What Do Consumers Really Think About Health/Fitness Clubs?

Before the reasons why people join a club can be discussed, it is necessary to understand the perceptions the general public has about clubs. In that regard, in *Fitness American Style,* a study conducted in 2001 by Roper Starch on behalf of IHRSA, the public was asked to share their perceptions of clubs. Among the most interesting insights that were derived from this research were the following:

- Americans, in general, hold a positive view of health/fitness clubs.
- Approximately 66% of those individuals polled believe that a club membership is usually worth the money if a person makes good use of the membership. In other words, consumers perceive the value of a club membership is closely correlated to how the member uses the club.
- Six in ten consumers indicated that a club offers the member more knowledge and expertise on exercise and fitness then they could obtain on their own. It would be interesting to know if this belief was as strong currently as it was ten years ago, since information on exercise and fitness is rampant on the internet.
- Approximately 56% of those individuals polled indicated that they thought health/fitness clubs were fun. On the other hand, when the differences between former members and non-club members are examined, the fun element is not as prevalent a perception among non-members.
- Nearly half (48%) of those individuals polled indicated they thought health/fitness clubs were only for people who are fit—the basic perception being that if you are not fit and want to get fit, don't go to a fitness club.

- Forty-five percent of those individuals polled believe that clubs are for young people. In 2011, that perception might be somewhat different since a large segment of individuals over the age of 45 are currently members of clubs, at least in the U.S.
- Thirty-one percent believe that clubs are a place a person goes to pick up someone (a perception originally espoused in the movie *Perfect* in the late 1980s).
- The biggest negative perception was that clubs are overcrowded (62% of non-members and 73% of members). The fact that such a significant majority of respondents perceive clubs as being crowded, especially former members, is problematic (overcrowding is a common reason people give for dropping their membership).

In 2007, another report commissioned by IHRSA, *Fitness American Style III,* was released. In this report, consumers were asked to compare health/fitness clubs to other businesses in the community (Figure 5-1). Among the most interesting insights from this study were the following:

- The club industry is perceived favorably to other retail operators, including Starbucks, when it comes to the industry's commitment to providing its customers with good service.
- The club industry is seen more favorably than other businesses when it comes to being seen as being engaged in their local community and being environmentally conscious.

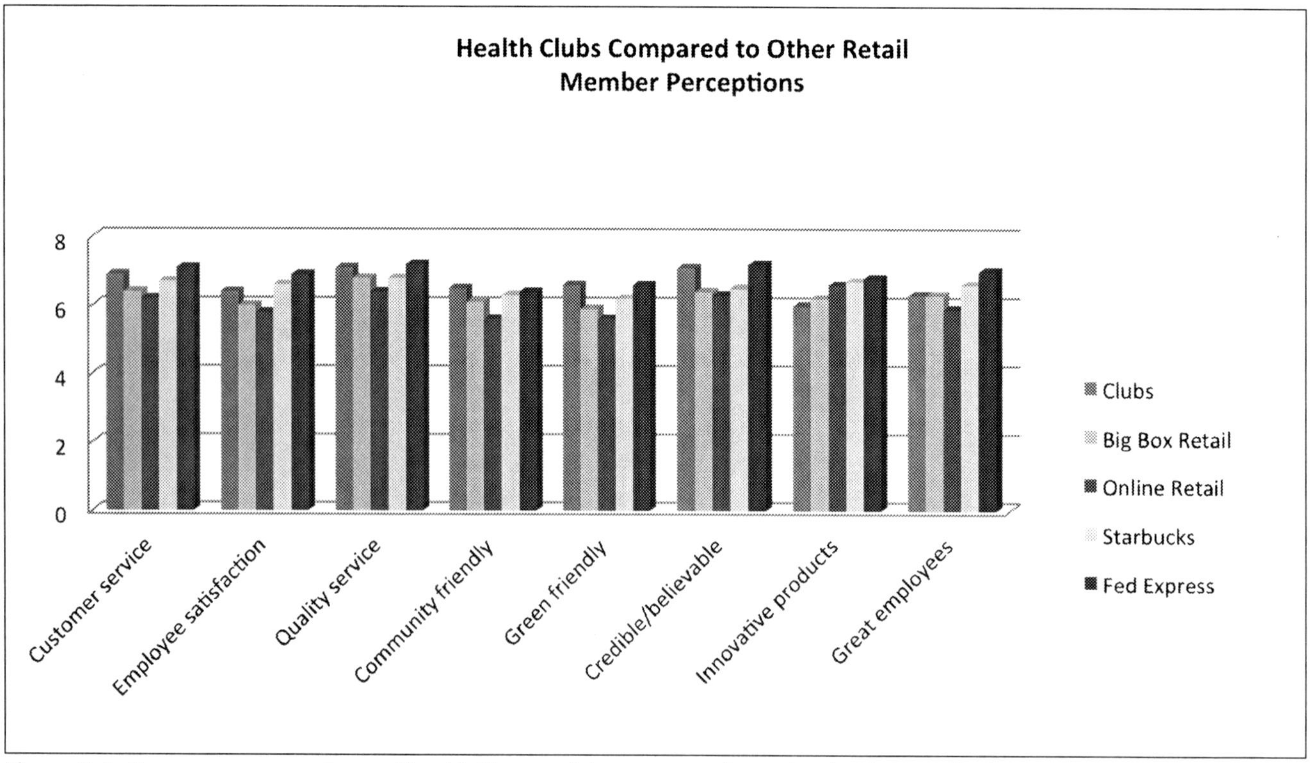

Figure 5-1. Consumer perceptions of health/fitness clubs compared to other businesses in the community

- The product and service that clubs offer are perceived as having better value than those offered by other businesses, with the exception of the services offered by Federal Express and Johnson & Johnson.
- Clubs are seen as being less innovative in their product and service offerings than other industries (not a real surprise).

While consumers, in general, express positive perceptions about health/fitness clubs, both from a general perspective and when compared to other businesses, consumers also have some lingering negative perceptions about clubs. It is interesting to note that these negative perceptions closely align with the reasons members give for resigning their membership (refer to Chapter 6). Another important insight is that while positive perceptions are important influencers of consumer behavior, negative perceptions, even if less prevalent than the positive perceptions, tend to have a stronger influence on behavior.

Why Consumers Join a Health/Fitness Club

Consumers join health/fitness clubs for a variety of reasons. According to *Fitness American Style III,* prepared for IHRSA in 2007, the top three reasons that new members have for joining their club were as follows:

- Get in shape (64% of respondents)
- Convenience of a place to workout (54% of respondents)
- Stay in shape (49% of respondents)

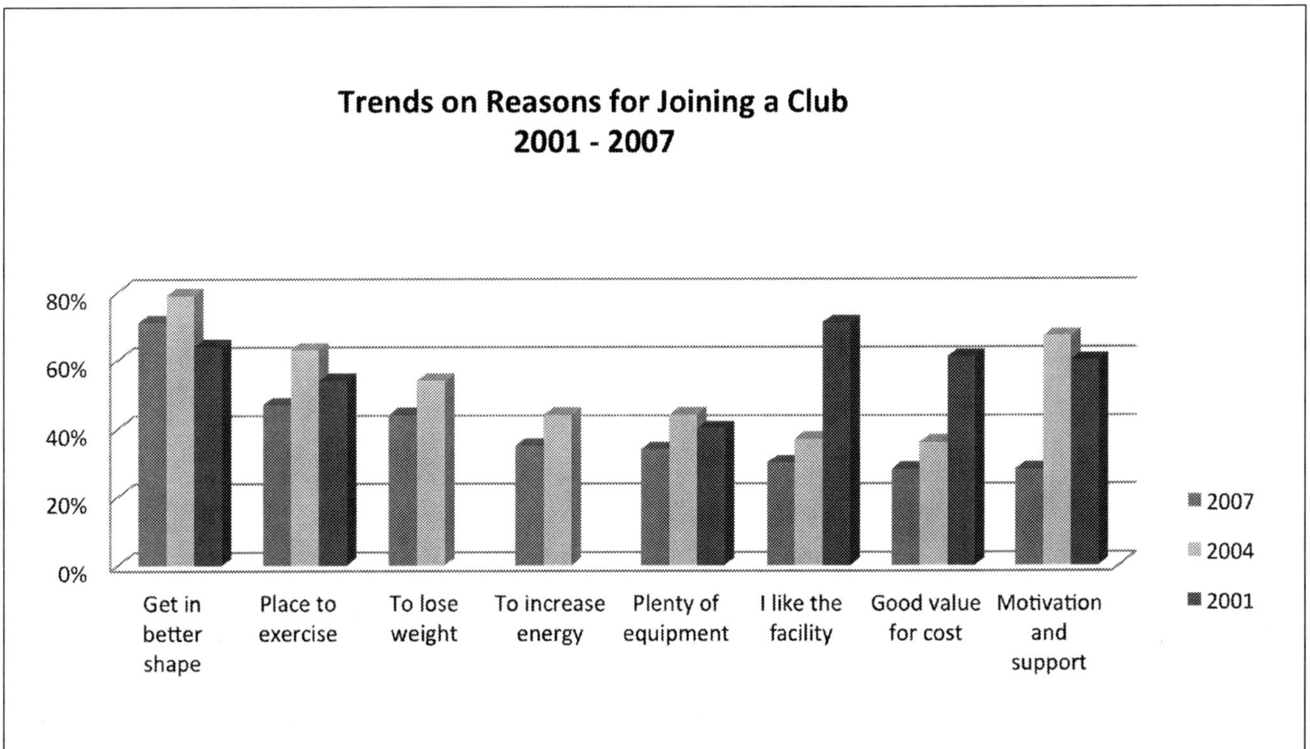

Figure 5-2. The trends concerning the reasons that consumers give for joining a health/fitness club

A subsequent examination of reports from 2001, 2004, and 2007 indicate that the leading reasons for joining a health club, as well as the level of importance behind a specific reason, had changed somewhat. Figure 5-2 graphically illustrates the trends from 2001, 2004 and 2007, as they relate to reasons consumers give for joining a health/fitness club. Among the insights that can be derived from these trends are the following:

- While getting in better shape remains the top reason members join a club, the percentage of consumers who indicate this factor was the top priority dropped from nearly 80% of respondents in 2004 to 64% in 2007.
- While needing a place to exercise was the third most frequently given reason for joining a club in 2007 (49%), it received a significantly lower response rate then in either 2004 or 2001, when nearly 60% of respondents indicated this factor was their rationale for joining a club.
- In 2001 and 2004, close to 60% of respondents indicated that they joined a club to provide them with motivation to exercise, but in 2007, only 20% of respondents indicated this factor as their reason.
- In 2001, consumers indicated that their number one reason for joining a club was because they liked the facility (70%), followed closely by their perception that the club was a great value (60%), and finally, the fact that the club was a place to get in better shape. In 2007, liking the facility or indicating it was a good value had less importance.

It appears that over the course of the first seven years of the 21st century, consumers moved from an "extrinsic goods" perspective (placing their reason for joining in terms of the look or the cost of a facility) to more of an intrinsic reasoning, related to their personal goals.

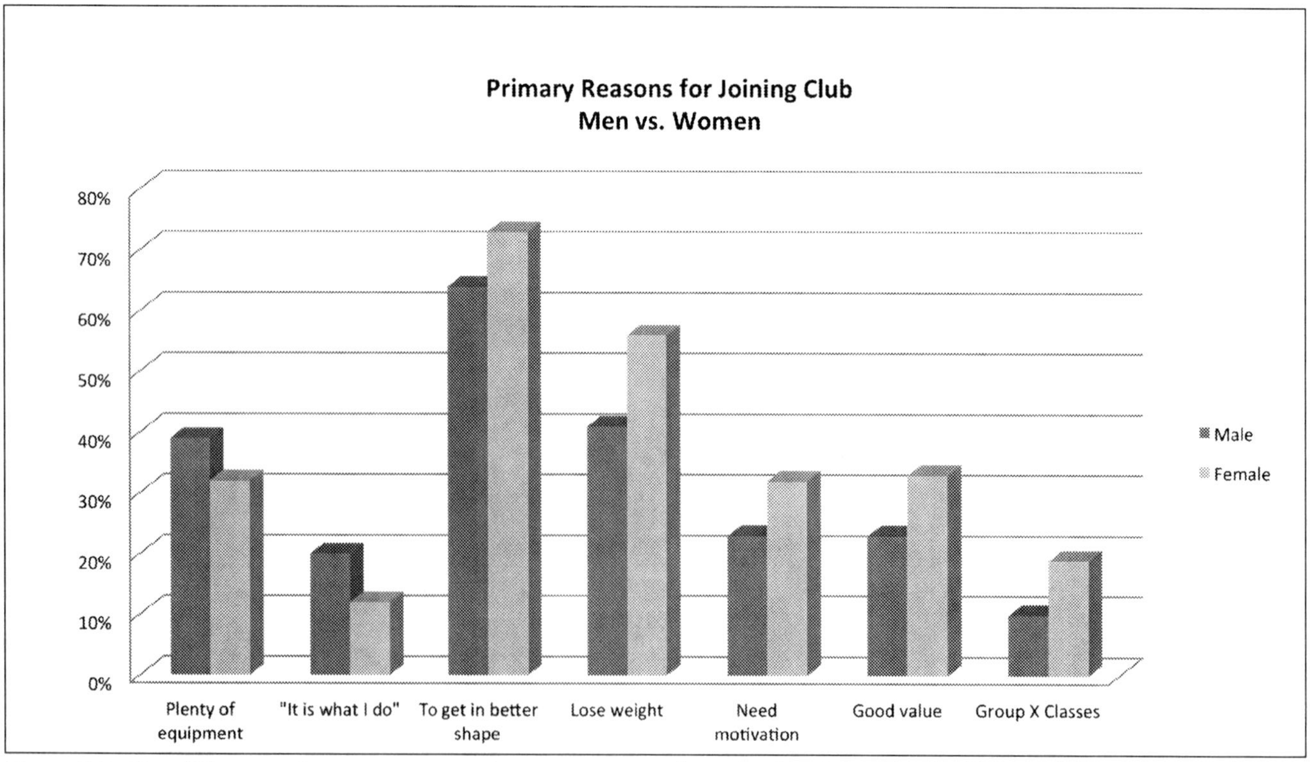

Figure 5-3. The differences between men and women concerning why they join a health/fitness club

In *Fitness American Style III,* the researchers looked at the differences between why men and women join a health/fitness club. The differences are considerable and are reflected in Figure 5-3. The most salient points derived from this comparison of gender reasons for joining a health/fitness club were:

- Men place the heaviest weight for joining a club on having a place to exercise. Sixty percent of men cited this factor as a reason for joining, while 50% of women indicate it is a determined for their joining.
- Women place a far greater emphasis for joining a club on a motivating environment, an educated and friendly staff, and friends who are members. For each of the aforementioned reasons, women indicate that it is important by a margin of more than 50% than men.

Approximately two years after *Fitness American Style III* was released by IHRSA, a new report was issued as part of the publication, *2009 Profiles of Success.* In this updated report, members indicated what their leading reasons (Figure 5-4) for joining a club were based on:

- Improve overall well-being (70% of respondents)
- Access to a variety of equipment (49% of respondents)
- Opportunity to work out and not socialize (46% of respondents)
- Access to group-exercise classes (24%) and fitness programs (20%)
- Having friends and family as members (18%)
- Access to the social aspects of the club (16%)

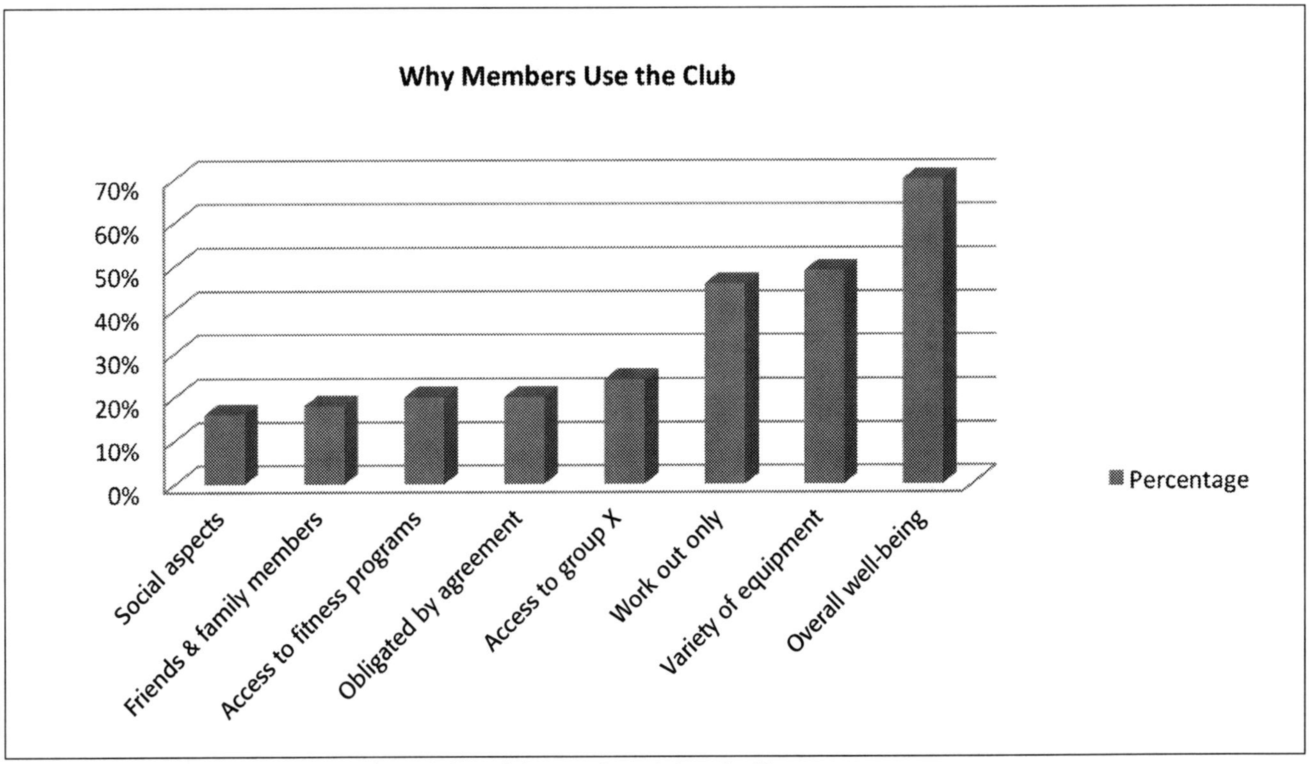

Figure 5-4. The primary reasons why existing club members join a facility

When the responses were segregated by gender (Figure 5-5), several important differences arose, including the following:

- Women are far more likely to list looking better (70% for women and 55% for men) and to feel better about self (70% of women to 63% of men).
- Men were far more likely to indicate building muscle (43% of men and 34% of women), maintaining bodyweight (39% of men and 32% of women), and addressing a specific medical concern (29% of men and 23% of women).

The authors of the 2009 report also looked at generational differences regarding why members join and use a club. The generations they studied included the Eisenhower generation (those born before 1945); the baby boomers (those individuals who were born between 1946 and 1964); generation X (those individuals who were born between 1964 and 1981); and finally generation Y or the millennial generation (individuals born after 1981). A summary of the key findings of this report is shown in Figure 5-6. The most interesting insights from this research are:

- Using a club to improve a person's self-image and sense of self is much more important to those individuals of generation Y (77%), than it is to any of the other generations (63% to 65%).
- Those individuals in generation Y also indicate that "looking better" is a significant factor for their joining and using the club, a response that was significantly higher than the other generations indicated (41% to 69%). It is interesting to note that baby boomers were not far behind generation Y in this regard.

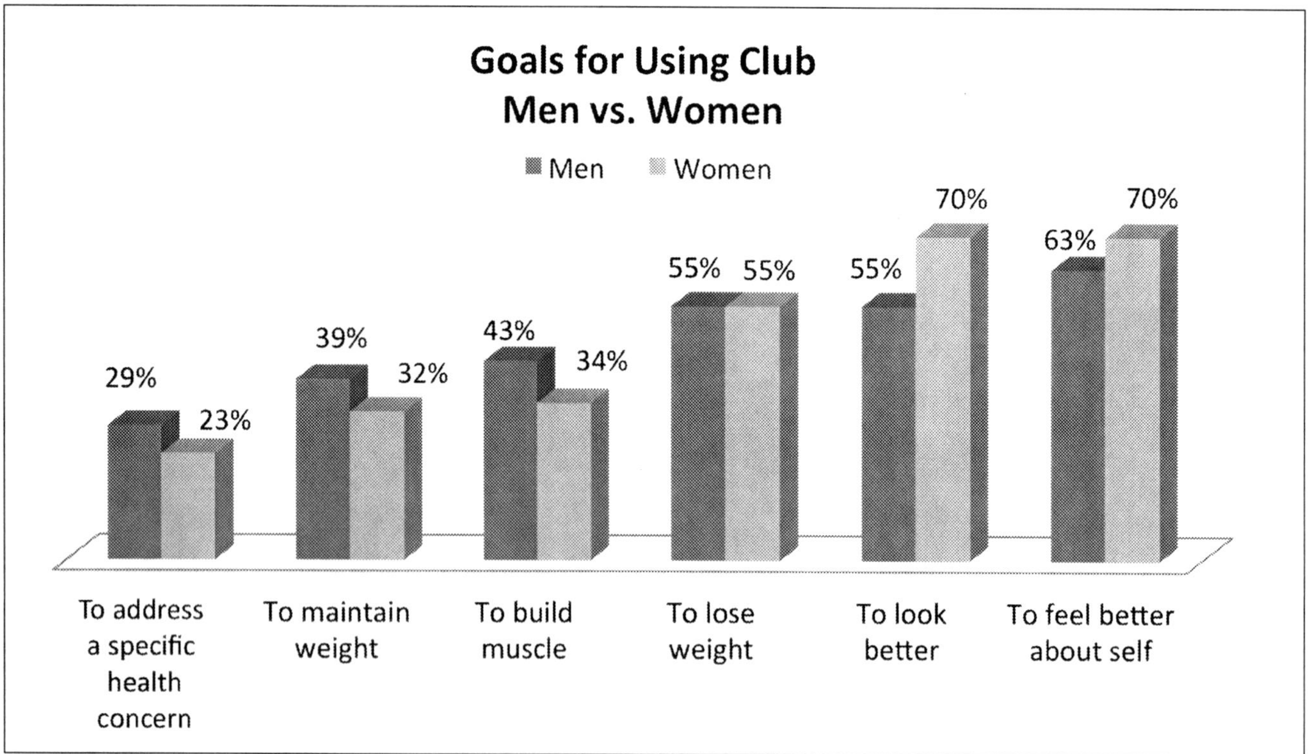

Figure 5-5. Gender differences between the goals of men and women for using a club

- Baby boomers list losing weight (70%) and looking better (69%) as their leading rationales for joining and using a club.
- Generation X, similar to generation Y, consider self-image and looking better as their top reasons for joining a club. Only the percentage of generation X that expressed this reason was 12% lower than the percentage of generation Y who expressed this rationale.

Another interesting question the researchers asked involved ascertaining to what consumers perceived to be the barriers to joining a club. Perceived barriers are important to understanding joining behavior, as was discussed in previous chapters. Unfortunately, perceived barriers can often overwhelm good intentions. As a result, they can impact the influence of rational reasons for joining and even remaining a member of a club. Figure 5-7 provides a graphic representation of these barriers. The leading perceived barriers according to the research were as follows:

- The club is too expensive, or I cannot afford it (61%).
- I exercise elsewhere (30%).
- I feel out of place (18%).
- The club is not convenient (16%).
- The club is too crowded, and I don't know anyone at the club (12% apiece).

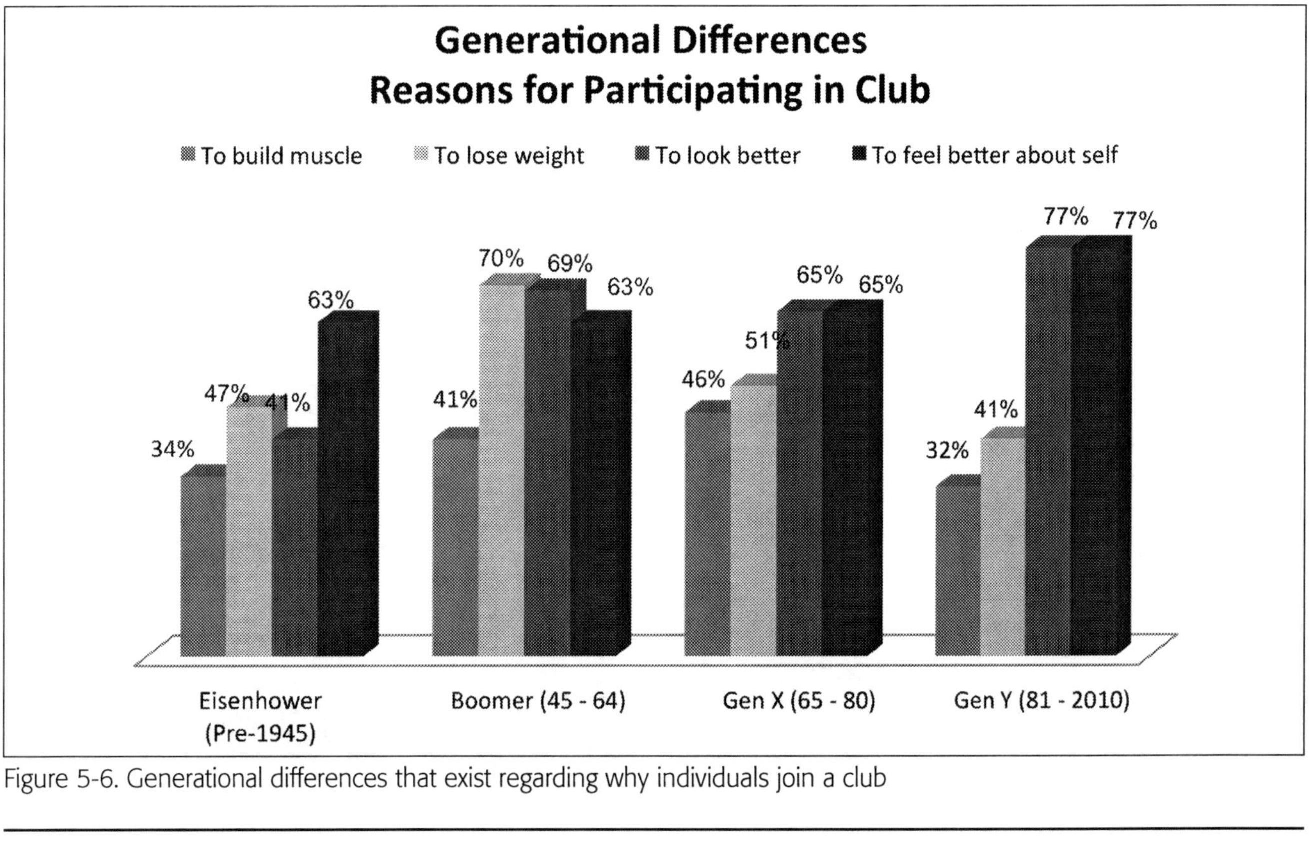

Figure 5-6. Generational differences that exist regarding why individuals join a club

Research presented in a report entitled, *Why People Don't Join,* prepared by IHRSA in 2006, listed the following top reasons given for not joining a club:

- A lack of time
- The membership costs too much.
- The club was intimidating.
- A lack of a social support network

It is interesting to not that the reasons for not joining a club in 2006 are not too dissimilar from the barriers that consumers expressed in 2009.

Reflections and Insights on the Data

As was indicated previously in this chapter, understanding why people join or don't join a club is important to creating a club environment that is conducive to retaining members. As a result, several essential insights can be gleaned from the information presented in this chapter, including the following:

- The general public has a reasonably favorable impression of the health/fitness club industry. The public's perception of the value of the industry's product offering, its business focus on customer service, its involvement in the community, its industries environmental consciousness is better than most big-box retailers and other service organizations.
- Consumers definitely see value in the investment of joining a club, but that investment is highly correlated with usage. The perceived value of a health/fitness club membership drops precipitously if the member does not use it.

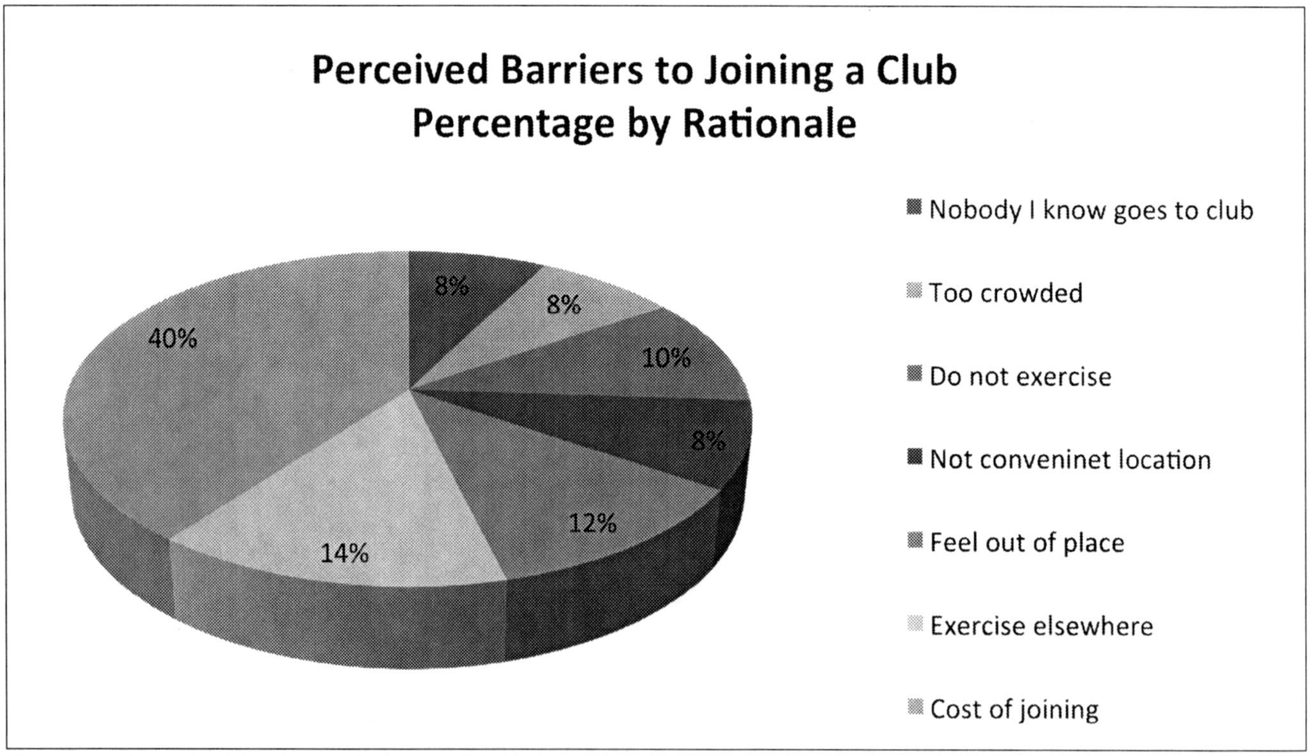

Figure 5-7. Perceived barriers to joining a club

- Consumers also believe that health/fitness clubs offer a "fun" environment, a perception that is different than the opinions expressed about exercise itself.
- Consumers still retain some negative perceptions about health/fitness clubs. In particular, consumers view clubs as being overcrowded (a strong influencer of member retention), a place for young and fit people, and a pick-up place. What is most interesting to note is that some of these perceptions have been around for decades, and yet our industry has not been able to shake them off. The perception of overcrowding may be the most damaging, especially since club members and former club members have a stronger perception of this factor than non-members.

If people join a club for a specific reason, that reason becomes the foundation for their expectations.

- Regardless of an individual's gender, the primary reasons for joining a club are related to getting in shape, staying in shape, or enhancing self image. Granted, women look more closely at feeling better and looking better, while men are more inclined to focus in on availability and gaining muscle. Each of these variables impacting the decision to join a club also plays a role in why members remain a member, a topic that will be addressed in the next chapter.
- Women place much greater emphasis on the quality of the club's staff, whether friends or family are members of the facility, and if there is a socially engaging environment. While not detailed as a leading reason, women believe that the cleanliness of a facility is also very important.
- Men desiring to join a club are assessing the facility more than the anticipated experience. Men seek out a variety of equipment, convenience and a competitive environment. Men also seem to be more inclined to look at a club for health reasons, counter to what they express when asked about exercise.
- Generation Y seems to be far more concerned with the club's ability to assist them in looking better and feeling better about themselves, which is much different than the reasons expressed by the other primary generation—the baby boomers. For baby boomers, it's about losing weight and looking better.

Club operators should consider the aforementioned insights, not just with regard to why individuals choose to join a health/fitness club, but as a window into the minds and emotions of members once they have joined. It should be kept in mind that if people join a club for a specific reason, that reason becomes the foundation for their expectations. If they are unable to achieve those expectations, they are more than likely to terminate their membership.

6

Retention: What Drives Members to Engage or Resign?

Chapter 5 explored the perceptions of consumers concerning health/fitness clubs, as well as the attitudes and beliefs that impact their decision to join a facility. This chapter takes the next step in the retention journey, which is to look into the general reasons and rationales behind why members remain members, as well as the reasons they give for ending their membership experience.

The intentions of people immediately after joining a club do not shift much from the reasons that drove them to become a member in the first place.

The Reasons Members Express About Remaining a Member

General Reasons Members Provide for Using Their Club

The reasons members give to researchers regarding why they are health/fitness club members do not vary significantly from the rationale that they provide for joining a club. The intentions of people immediately after joining a club do not shift much from the reasons that drove them to become a member in the first place.

In IHRSA's 2009 industry survey of the U.S. health and fitness clubs, *Profiles of Success,* consumers indicated a host of reasons for utilizing their membership. The leading reason, shared by more than 60% of members, was to enhance their overall level of well-being (Figure 5.4), followed closely by the opportunity to choose from a large variety of equipment on which to train. While health enhancement and access to equipment and programs were important elements behind using the club, these members also identified the social aspects of being a member as important (15% of respondents) and having family and friends as members (16% of respondents).

In this same study, members shared with researchers the goals that they expected to achieve as a result of being a club member. For women, looking better and feeling better about themselves were the two leading reasons driving participation, while for men, these two goals were also a high priority, as well as the desire to build muscle. Finally, when the researchers looked at responses, based on generation (refer to Chapter 4 for a description of demographic generations), they found that three of the four generational groups identified feeling better and looking better as their top priorities. The only generation whose profile was dramatically different were baby boomers (individuals born between 1946 and 1964). Baby boomers saw weight loss as their top priority, followed closely by looking better (Figure 5.6). It is interesting to note that the generation that is aging and experiencing health problems would not have "feeling better" as a top priority.

Other Elements of the Club Experience That Influence a Decision of an Individual to Remain a Member

In a study of 24,000 members of U.K. health/fitness clubs in the earlier part of the 21st century that was conducted by Paul Bedford, Ph.D., the importance of customer interaction to a member's decision whether to remain a member was explored. His research, which involved over 24,000 individual interviews, identified several of the key elements that impact an individual's decision to remain a member, all of which go beyond the reasons detailed in IHRSA's studies. His research uncovered several interesting factors, including the following:

- Members want to be recognized. Members indicated that they wanted to be approached by members of the club's staff. Members indicated it was important to be welcomed to the club with a hello and smile, and just as important to be recognized for making an effort to get to the club.
- Members want to know that staff is available to assist them if needed. The individuals in these interviews made it clear that they valued receiving coaching and guidance, especially when the staff was proactive in approaching them. The members also indicated that staff should not interrupt them when they are actively exercising, and that staff should be sensitive to reading a member's cues about when they wanted to be approached.
- Members want to be confident in how they use the club. Individuals interviewed in this study indicated that it is important that they have confidence in how to navigate the club. Members do not want to be seen by other members as being a "rookie' or someone who looks out-of-place in the club setting. Fitting-in is a critical determinant of a member's experience. If members sense that they look out of place, they will be far more likely to resign their membership. One example given in the interviews conducted by Bedford involved the use of an exercise card. Members reported that they felt embarrassed to have only one exercise card, when other members had either several stapled together or even had a diary for recording their exercise practices.

Members do not want to be seen by other members as being a "rookie' or someone who looks out-of-place in the club setting.

- Members want to have competence in how they use the club. Those individuals interviewed indicated that it was important for them to understand the relevance of exercise to their specific needs. These individuals believe that it is important for them to see the connection between what their goals are and the exercises and programs in which they are engaged.

Reasons Members Give for Terminating Their Membership

In IHRSA's publication entitled, *Why People Quit,* researchers identified six key drivers that lead to members resigning from their club (Figure 6-1). Three basic reasons were expressed by members: they could not afford the club (23%), followed closely by overcrowding (20%) and not having enough time to use the club (19%).

If the aforementioned reasons that members express for leaving a club are compared to the rationale provided for joining a facility, with the drivers of member satisfaction, as well as with responses related to consumer perceptions of the club experience, two responses stand out. The first is overcrowding, which existing members indicated is a barrier to overall satisfaction with the club experience. This factor was also listed as a leading negative perception by consumers. It would appear that the perceptions of consumers are valid. Even worse, it seems that the industry has been unable to overcome an important negative influencer of member satisfaction and membership retention. When the rationale for resigning is separated into intrinsic reasons, intentions driven by the individual's perceptions of their own experience, operational factors, or causes that reflect club management's approach to the members, several valuable insights can be identified.

When looking at the intrinsic reasons members give for resigning their membership (Figure 6-2) the top three reasons involve the level of club usage, the lack of motivation, and not having an exercise partner.

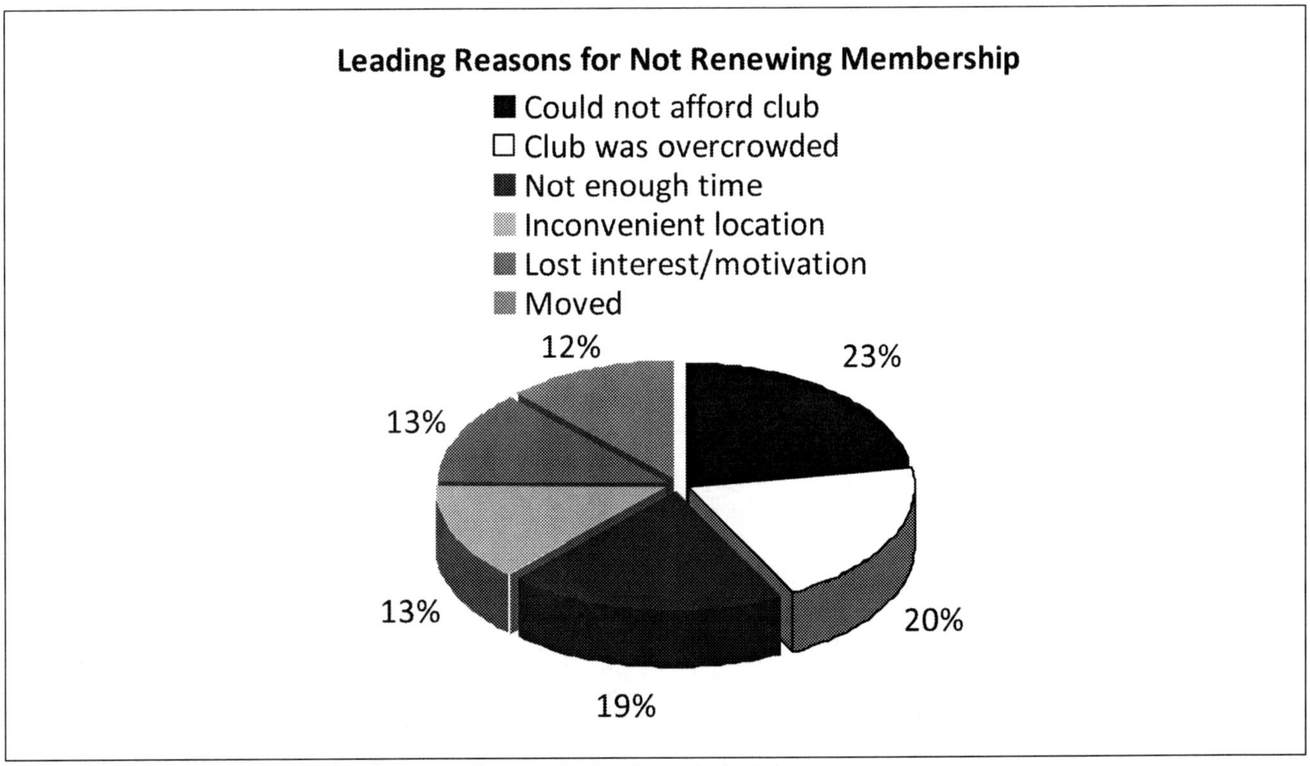

Figure 6-1. Six key drivers that lead to members resigning from their club

It is obvious that individuals who don't use the club frequently enough see less value in the membership, and therefore identify it as a reason for leaving. This rationale has been proven correct in numerous studies and is detailed in Chapter 7 that addresses the relationship between member participation and membership retention.

It can be argued that the other two intrinsic reasons that consumers provide for resigning from their club are even more important—lost motivation and a lack of an exercise partner. Each of these factors is a key driver of member usage, which indicates that members expect clubs to provide them with an environment that is motivating and supportive.

The aforementioned reasons also indicate that clubs may have a responsibility to help members connect with other members, at least if retention is important to their business model. When members share their reasons for joining a club, neither motivation nor having an exercise partner is identified on top of the list, although for women having friends and family as members is seen as important by women. It is essential to understand the discrepancy between the reasons influencing joining behavior and those factors impacting a member's reasons to resign. It seems that the expectations of individuals change once that they join a club, or, they don't realize how important certain factors are until they actually join a facility.

When the research looked at the extrinsic reasons (Figure 6-3) that people provided for choosing to resign, or was detailed earlier, the reasons influenced by the approach of management concerning its customer and business model,

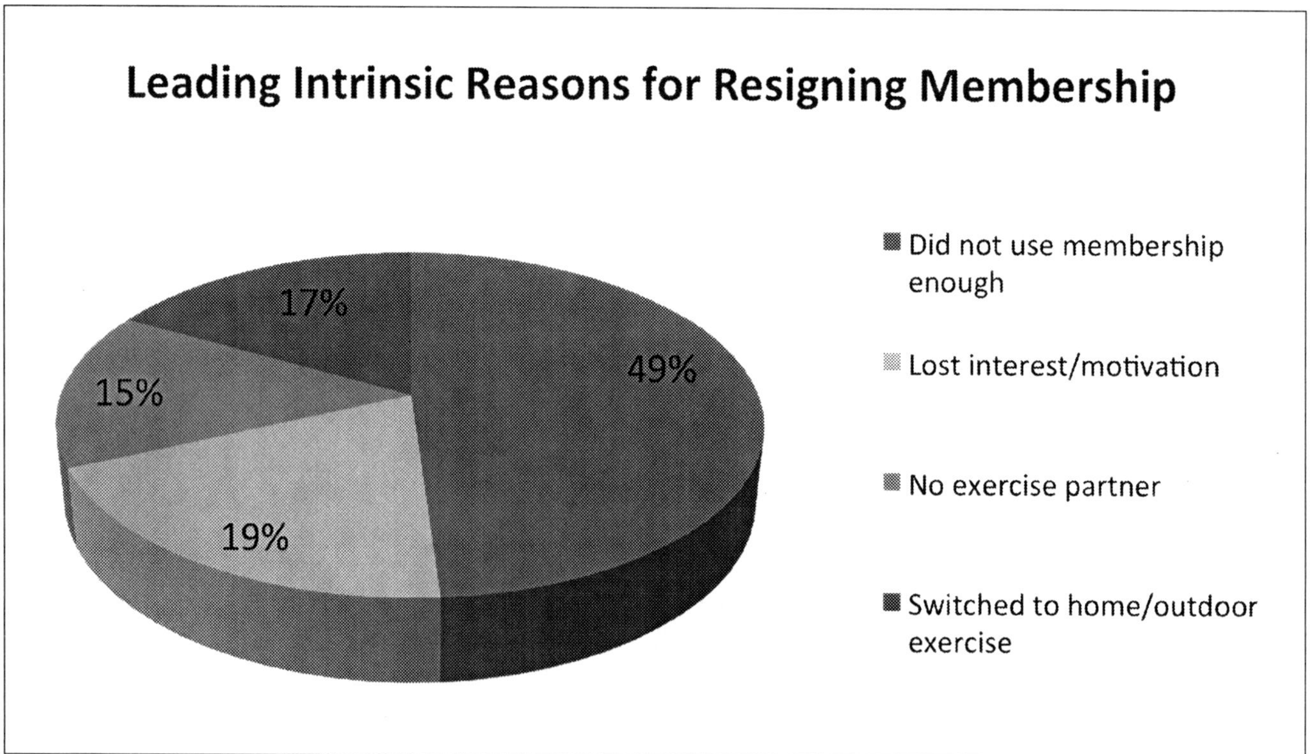

Figure 6-2. The intrinsic reasons that members give for resigning their club membership

several alarming issues arise. One is the fact that overcrowding of the club is the leading reason given (41%) by members for resigning. As was discussed previously in this chapter, as well as in earlier chapters, consumers have a negative perception of clubs concerning this factor. Concurrently, existing members indicate the lack of overcrowding is a key driver of satisfaction. While the issue of overcrowding can be easily managed, the industry's "lust" for overselling memberships (i.e., selling more memberships than a club can actually accommodate), is, in large part, to blame for this leading driver of membership terminations. An example of the overcrowding phenomena can be seen in some of the low-cost, high-volume clubs, such as Planet Fitness in the U.S. and Mcfit in Germany, where as many as 7,500 memberships are sold for a club that encompasses 15,000 to 20,000 square feet of space.

What is possibly a more interesting reason for leaving than overcrowding, are three factors that are directly linked to management:

- *Dissatisfied with staff.* This factor suggests that the members are either dissatisfied with the qualifications of staff, the level of staffing, or the manner in which staff treats members.
- *Lack of attention from staff.* This factor is a simple measure to interpret. Members feel that the club staff does not focus their efforts on providing members with assistance and guidance. This issue tends to be exasperated by the industry's current love affair with paid personal training, which has resulted in many clubs forgoing any type of service to members who are unwilling to pay additional fees for guidance. In research conducted in the United Kingdom by Dr. Paul Bedford, in which he interviewed over 24,000

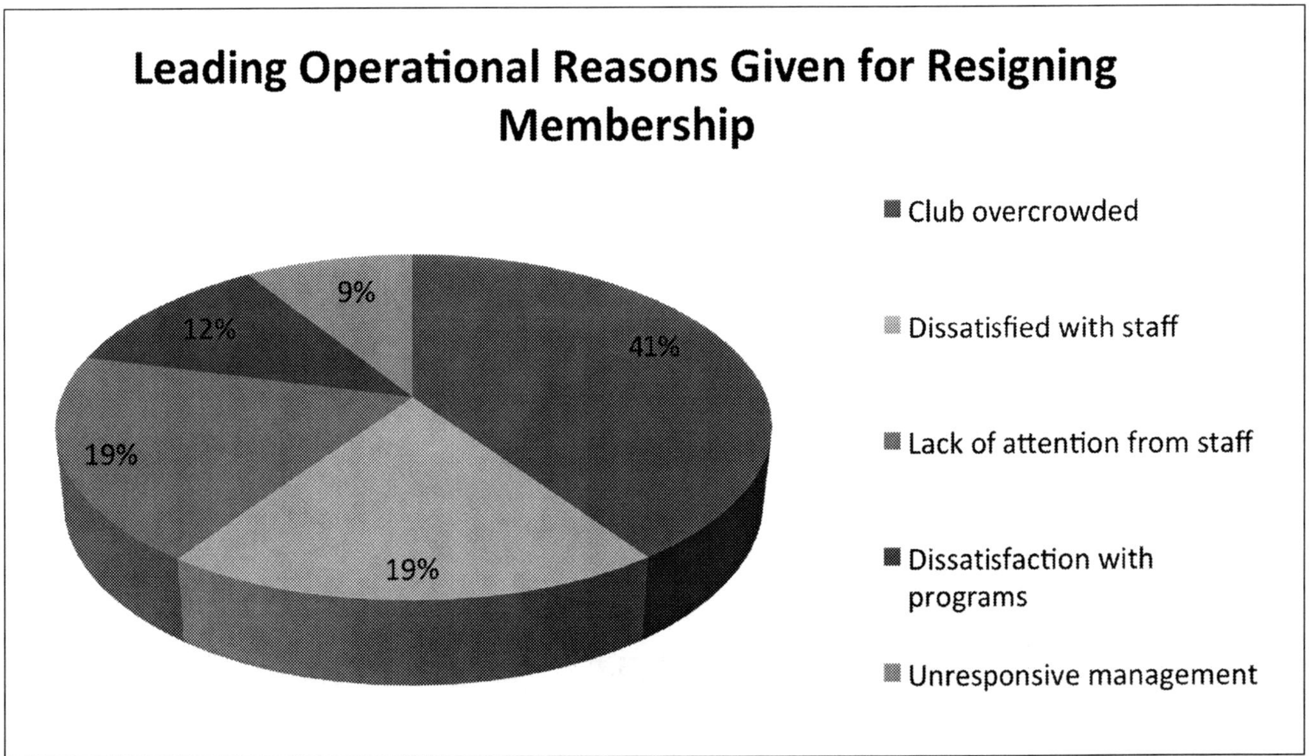

Figure 6-3. The extrinsic reasons that members give for resigning their club membership

club members, the issue of attention from club staff also arose. It seems that in many cases, members had not been approached by staff since they joined their club, which, in numerous instances had been over one year.

- *Unresponsive management.* This factor refers to the inability of management to resolve member issues in a timely and satisfactory manner. It is connected to the communication and transparency between management and the members.

In another study commissioned by IHRSA in the early part of the 21st century, members were asked why they resigned, and how these factors would impact their decision to rejoin, they indicated reasons (Figure 6-4) that were very similar to the aforementioned intrinsic and operational measures, including the following:

- No exercise partner
- Lost interest
- Did not fit in
- Favorite staff left

These responses, like the others detailed in this chapter, indicate that individuals expect clubs to provide staff, programs, and a social environment that motivates them to continue their membership.

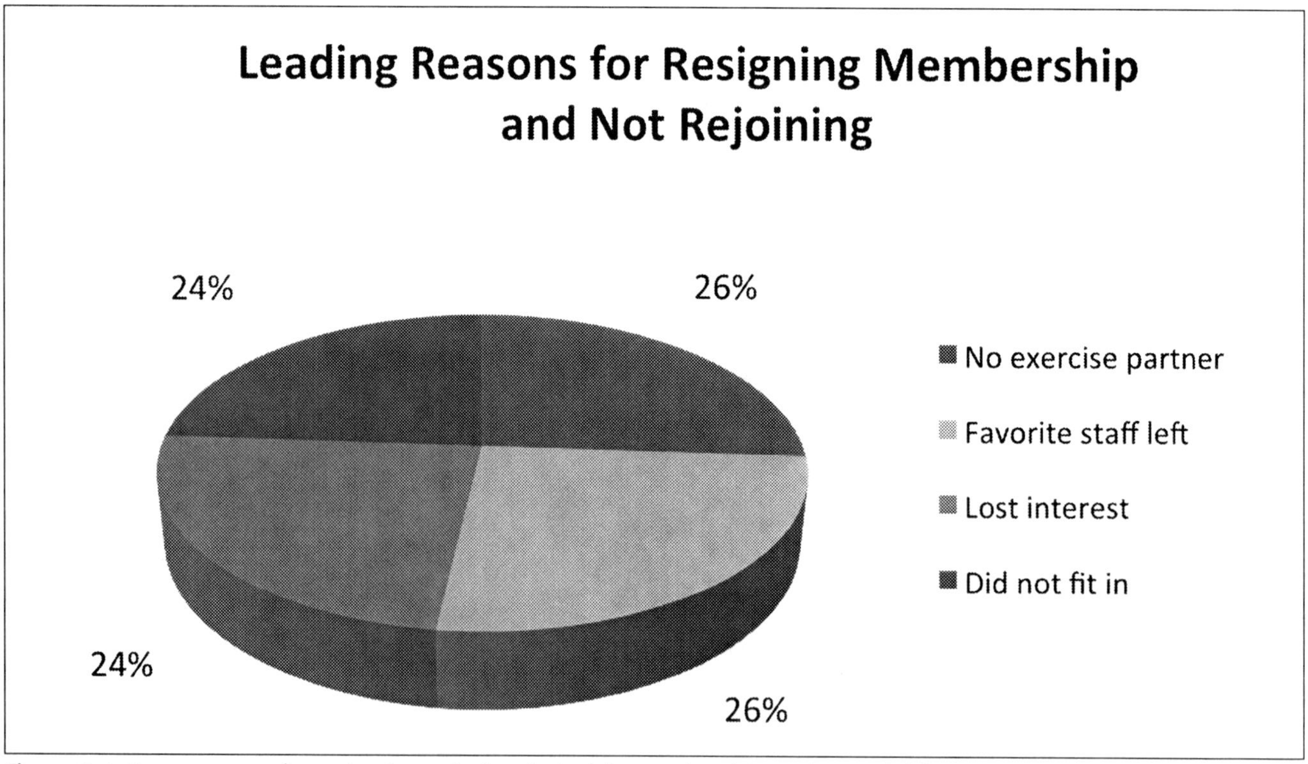

Figure 6-4. Reasons members give for resigning their club membership and not rejoining

Reflections and Insights

- Membership satisfaction is important to membership retention. The higher members rate their level of satisfaction, the more likely they are to use the club, and as a result, the more likely they are to remain a member.
- Several variables influence member satisfaction, including how crowded the club is, the quality and attentiveness of the staff, the social ambiance of the club, and the ability of members to achieve their expressed goals.
- When individuals report their reasons for leaving the club, the leading influencers are very similar to those factors that are important to achieving a high level of member satisfaction. These influencers encompass a number of factors, including the quality and attentiveness of staff, the responsiveness of management, an environment that promotes social interaction and connection (exercise partner), an environment in which the member feels comfortable (fits in), and an environment that is motivating (satisfactory programs, staff involvement, social support network, etc.).
- The reasons that individuals give for joining a club are different than the factors that drive their level of satisfaction with the club experience, as well as ultimately their decision to remain a member. This disconnect may partially be the result of how the industry sells itself and how it services its customers. What it does mean is, that understanding why people purchase a membership will only partially impact on the effort to helping clubs keep individuals as members once they join. To retain members, clubs need to focus more effort on identifying each member's intrinsic needs and beliefs, and then find a balance between what creates a short-term sale, and what sells for the long-term.
- Since understanding a member's needs, goals and aspirations is critical, clubs should apply more effort in this aspect. Uncovering an individual's needs early in the member experience can contribute to the effort to identify viable actions that can help involve that member in the club life.
- Members want to be recognized by club staff. This recognition goes beyond just receiving a hello or smile. It also involves staff being proactive in approaching members. As such, club staff needs to be sensitive to the nonverbal cues that members express so they can respond accordingly in providing coaching, support, and guidance.
- Members want to "fit-in" with the crowd. This desire to fit-in extends beyond just their physical appearance. It also by involves being perceived as having confidence and competency in how they navigate the club. Clubs should make sure that every new member understands the policies of the club, knows how to obtain assistance when needed, understands how to use various areas and amenities of the facility (sauna, pool, equipment, towels, vending stations, etc.), and knows which classes are appropriate for their particular skill level, etc.

To retain members, clubs need to focus more effort on identifying each member's intrinsic needs and beliefs, and then find a balance between what creates a short-term sale, and what sells for the long-term.

7

Behaviors and Demographics That Drive Member Retention

The average U.S. health/fitness club member visits their club 102 times a year or an estimated twice a week.

Chapter 6 explored the reasons that drive individuals to either retain or terminate their club membership. This chapter looks into several additional behavioral and demographic variables that have been found to influence membership retention.

Understanding How Members Use Their Club and Its Impact on Retention

Studies of membership retention over the past two decades have shown that one of the most influential variables on membership retention involves how frequently members visit their club, both at the commencement of their membership and throughout the tenure of their membership. As a result, understanding the patterns of member usage, both from a frequency perspective and from the aspect of what activities in which they actually participate, can present opportunities for impacting those behaviors and ultimately influencing member retention.

How Often Do Members Use Their Club?

As discussed in Chapter 1, the average U.S. health/fitness club member visits their club 102 times a year or an estimated twice a week. In other countries, the average usage level tends to be lower, with the typical club member using their club 50 to 60 times a year. In an unpublished study conducted in 2007, the investigation compared participation rates between IHRSA clubs, 24 select clubs in Russia, a select group of 25 premium clubs from across the U.S., and two publically held health/fitness club companies in the U.S.

In 2007, the average member usage among IHRSA clubs, according to IHRSA reports, was 92 visits annually. In the Russian clubs, members averaged 51 visits a year, while among the group of 25 premium-club operators, members visited their clubs 115 times a year (Figure 7-1). For comparative purposes, one of Northern Europe's most successful club operators had an average annual use per member of approximately 40 visits. One of the two public club companies in the U.S. reported an average of slightly over 100 member visits per year. In the Russian clubs, which averaged 51 visits annually per member, the range of annual visits was relatively consistent across the 24 clubs. In contrast, in the group of 25 premium U.S. clubs, member usage ranged from 65 to 195 visits annually.

The industry has often placed members into two groups: core members (i.e., individuals who use the club a minimum of 100 times annually) and casual members (individuals who frequent the club less than 100 times a year). Within the casual-member category, a sub-group of members exists that can be defined as infrequent users, or those individuals who use their club less than six times a year. Based on industry statistics, the following factors are known about these primary member usage groups:

- An estimated 42 percent of U.S. club members can be classified as core members (i.e., individuals who use the club approximately two times each week). The percentage of core members in U.S. clubs has fluctuated over the past 20 years between 33 percent and 42 percent, while over the past decade, it has remained relatively stable between 40 percent and 42 percent (Figure 7-2).
- The percentage of members who participate less than 100 times annually, casual members, has ranged from a peak of 67 percent back in 1990 to a low of 58 percent in 2009.

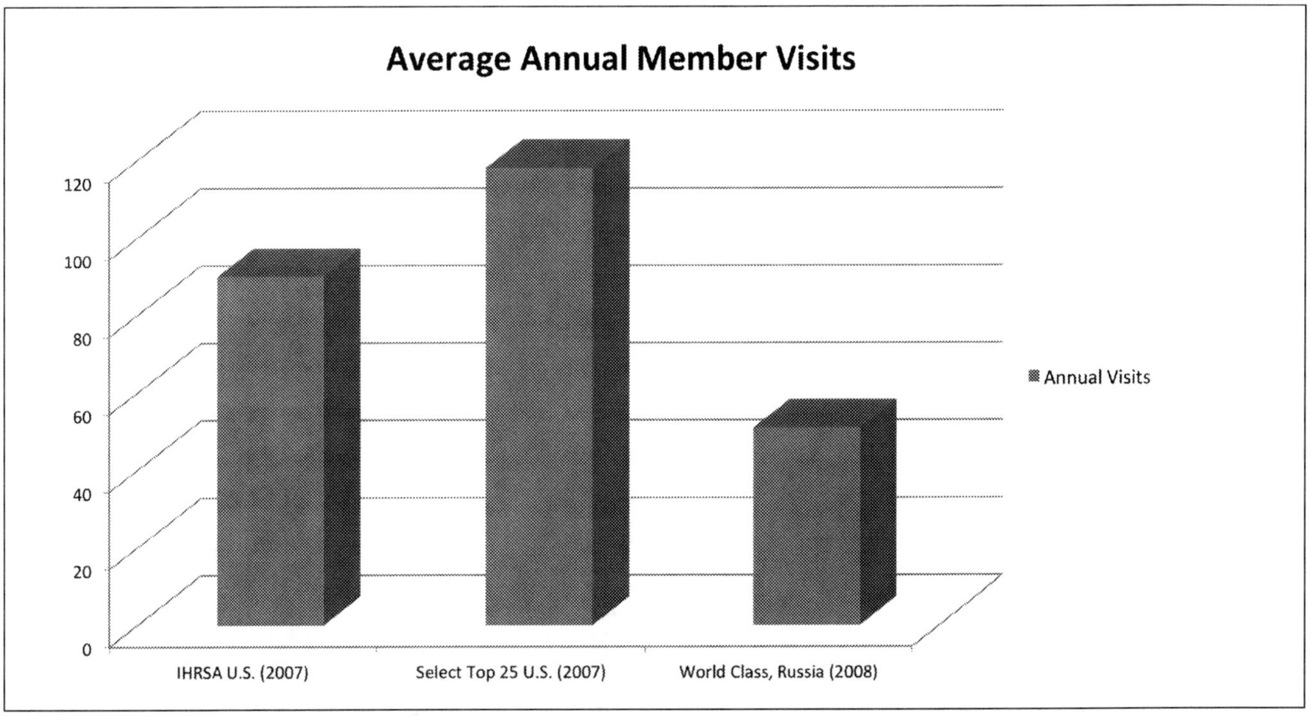

Figure 7-1. Average member visits to their club annually

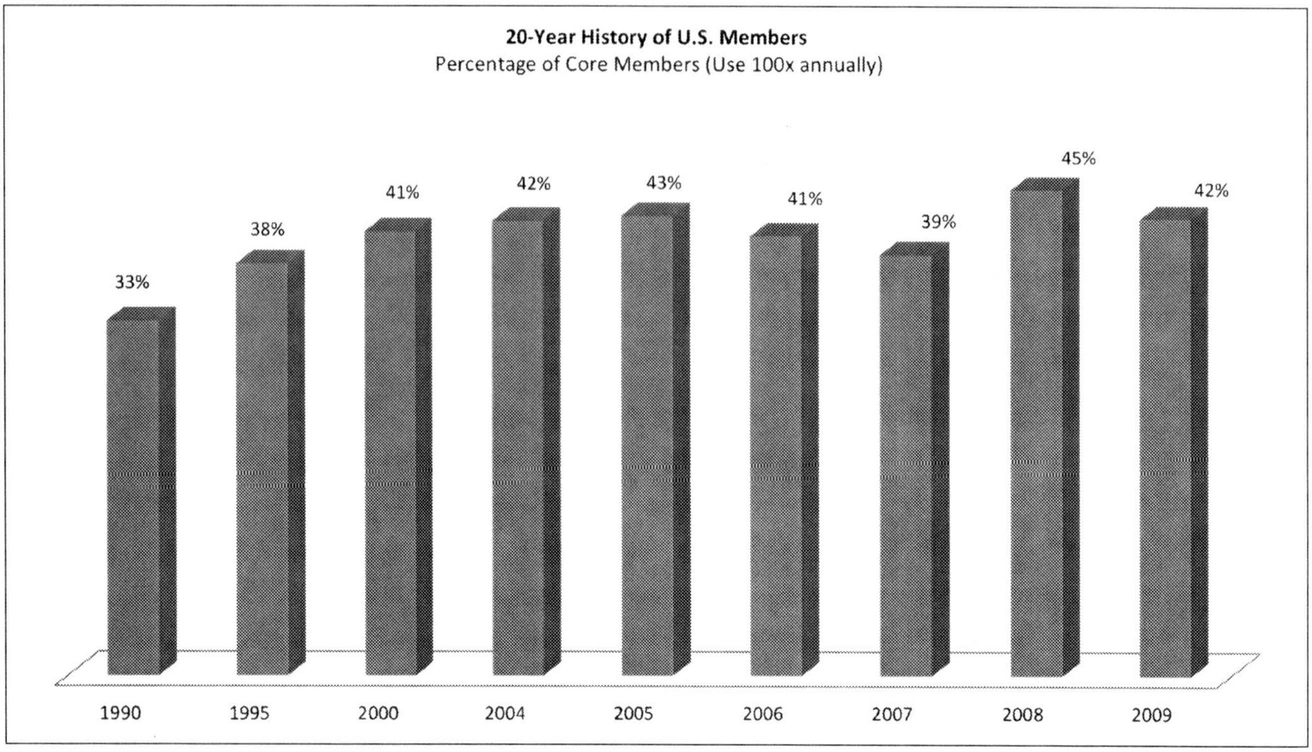

Figure 7-2. A twenty-year overview of the number of U.S. club members who are core members

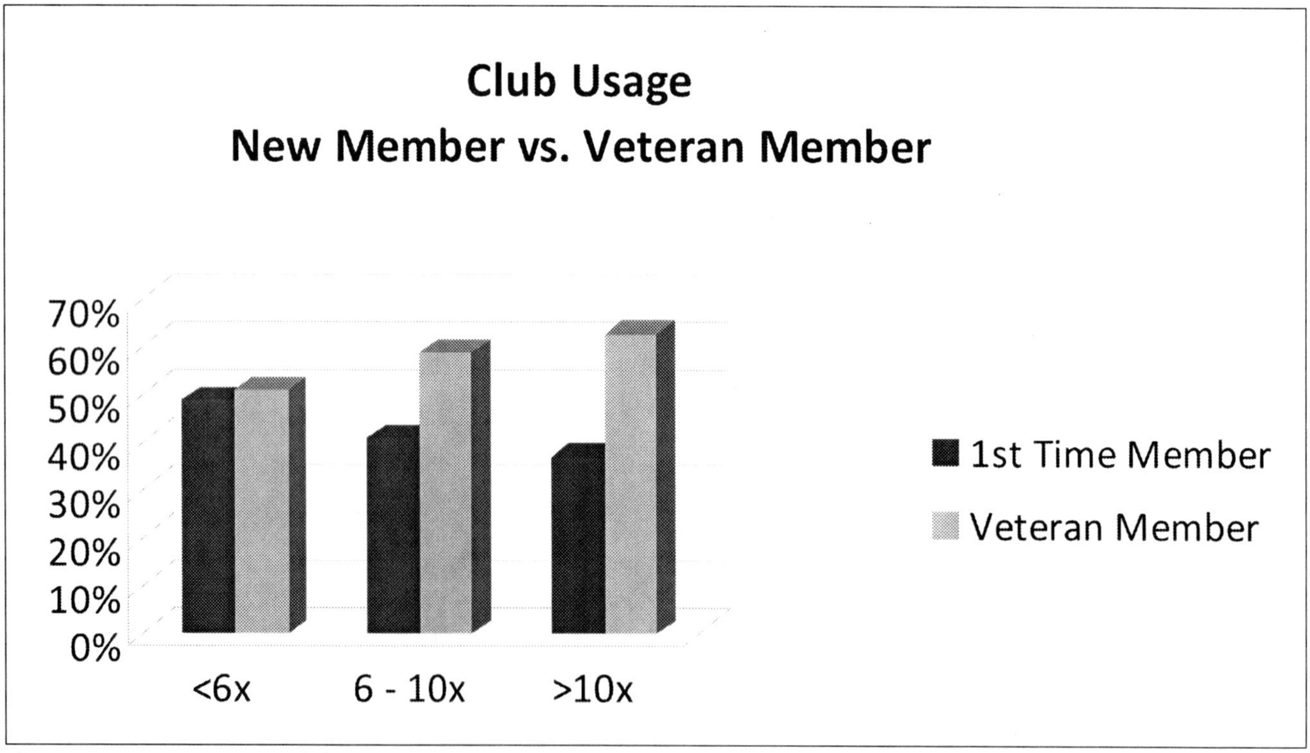

Figure 7-3. A comparison of club usage between new members and veteran members

- The percentage of members who could be classified as infrequent users, or those individuals who visit their club less than six times annually, has ranged from a peak of 26 percent in 1990 to an estimated 15 percent in 2009. Over the past three years (2006 to 2009), the percentage of infrequent users has remained relatively stable at 14 to 15 percent of the membership base.

One study found that member usage for veteran members (i.e., those individuals who have previously been members of a club) is significantly more frequent than for first time members. Figure 7-3 provides a visual comparison of usage levels between new members and veteran members. The most dramatic differences seem to be in the percentage of these two member groups who use the club 6 to 10 times a month and more than 10 times a month, compared to veteran members who use it 15 percent and 30 percent more often, respectively.

Among the 24 Russian clubs the author studied in the investigation, the usage patterns of members were separated into four distinct groupings based on their average visits per month (less than once a month, one to four times a month, five to eight times a month, and more than eight times a month). Over the course of a year the percentage of members who fell into each of these activity categories were as follows:

- Approximately 30 to 45 percent of club members used their club less than once a month, which is nearly two to three times higher than the level reported for the members of U.S. clubs.
- Approximately 30 percent of the club members visited their club between one and four times a month.
- Approximately 20 percent of the club members visited their club between five and eight times a month.
- Approximately 15 percent of the club members visited their club more than eight times a month, nearly one third the percentage witnessed in U.S. clubs.
- On average, 50 percent to 60 percent of these club members used their club once a week or less.

One study found that member usage for veteran members (i.e., those individuals who have previously been members of a club) is significantly more frequent than for first time members.

In a 2001 Fitness Industry Association of England (FIA) report on retention entitled, *Winning the Retention Battle,* researchers studied the retention levels of members by their level of club usage (less than four visits per month, 4 to 7 visits per month, 7 to 11 visits per month, and more than12 visits per month). The researchers then tracked these groups over the course of their first year of membership. Several interesting facts were derived from this study (Figure 7-4), including the following:

- The percentage of members who frequented the club less than four times a month was 29 percent in the first month, a figure that had increased to 44 percent by the sixth month.
- The percentage of members who used their club between four and seven times a month remained relatively consistent during the first six months, ranging from 30 to 28 percent.

- The percentage of members who frequented their club 8 to 11 times a month dropped from 21 percent in the first month to 15 percent in the sixth month.
- The percentage of members who used their club more than 12 times a month went from 21 percent in the first month to 13 percent by the sixth month.
- The average member used the club six times a month, which would equate to approximately 72 times annually.

It is interesting to note that the numbers from the U.K. study, especially those individuals using the club less than four times a month, are not too dissimilar from the member usage levels witnessed in Russia. Concurrently, the percentage of members in the U.K. who are frequent users is also not significantly different from the percentage of frequent users in Russia. In both instances, the usage patterns are lower than those reported in U.S. clubs (Figure 7-5).

Among the common variables that "pop-out' from the attendance data are the following:

- An estimated 15 percent and 40 percent of club members actually use their club at least twice a week, a level of usage that exercise authorities would consider the bare minimum for achieving any noteworthy physiological benefit.
- Approximately 30 to 50 percent of members frequent their club less than once a week.

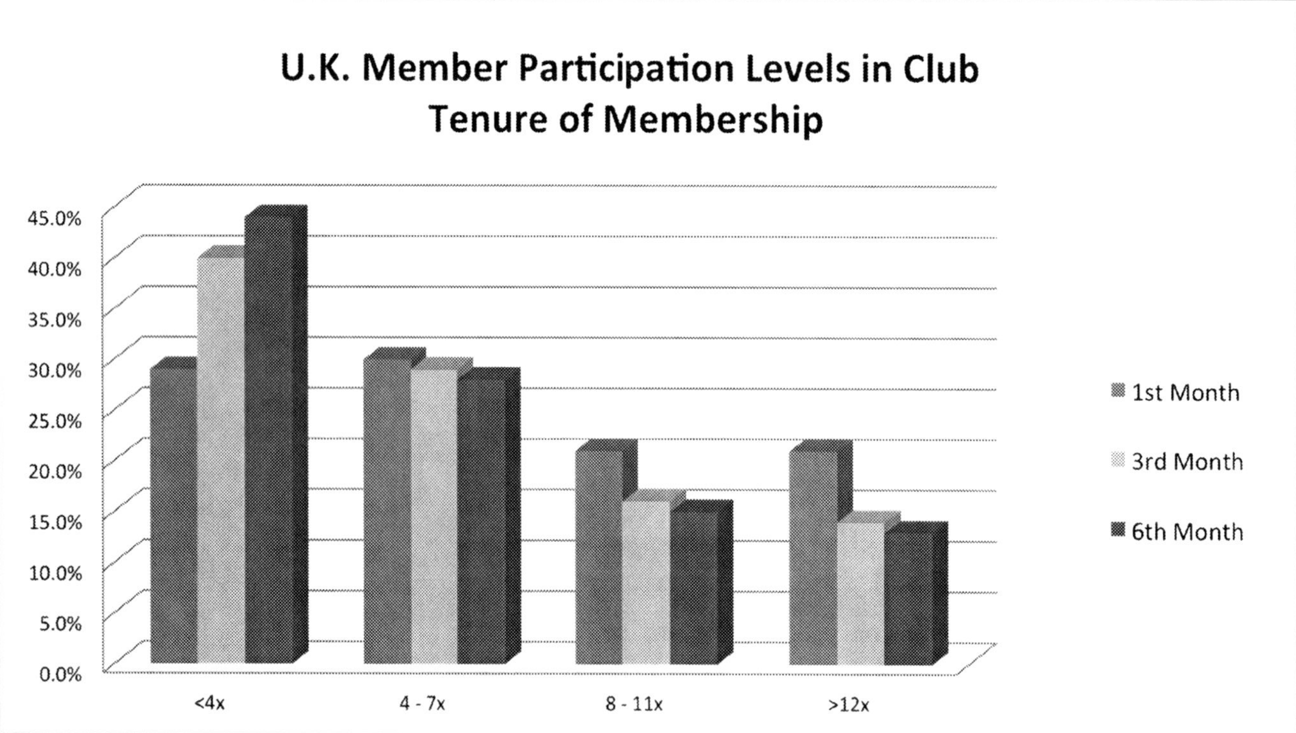

Figure 7-4. A comparison of member participation in U.K. health/fitness club with regard to the length of their membership

- Approximately 50 percent of members use their club between once and twice a week, not enough to experience real fitness benefits, but potentially enough to influence membership retention.
- Member usage tends to wane with each successive month of membership. This drop in usage eventually contributes to the decreasing level of membership retention over time.
- The health/fitness club industry has not done a very good job engaging members. Other than core users, who tend to be "exercise enthusiasts," the industry has not done what is needed to insure that members are actively using their club to the point that would allow them to derive any particular physiological or fitness benefit.

What Do Members Do When They Visit Their Club?

In IHRSA's *2010 Health Club Consumer Report,* researchers looked at how members actually use their club (i.e., in what activities do they actually participate). The report separated activities into four primary categories—cardiovascular machines, resistance machines and free weights, group exercise (step, high impact, low impact, etc.), and soft exercise (Pilates, yoga, stretching, tai chi, etc.) Based on the data in this report, the usage of treadmills and resistance machines ranked at the top, with approximately 45 percent of members indicating they use these machines to pursue their fitness goals. Among the key statistics that can be gleaned from this report are the following:

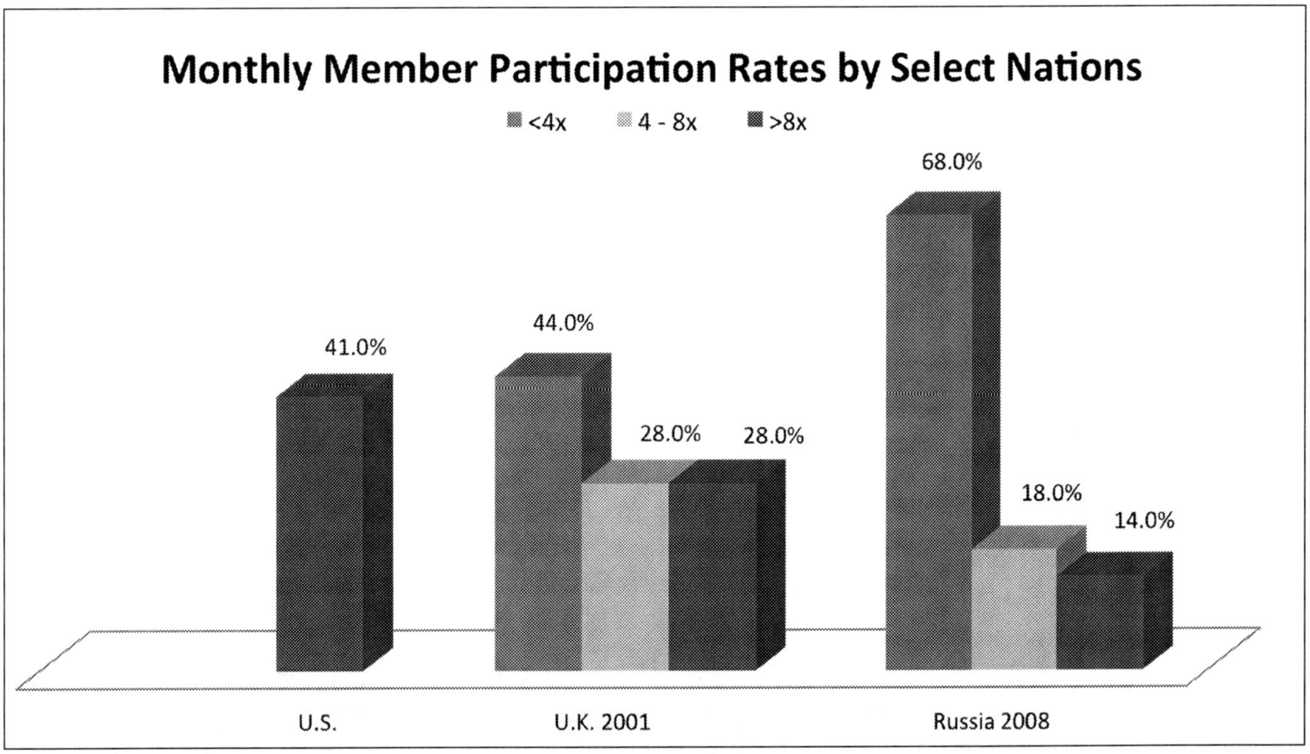

Figure 7-5. Monthly member participation rates by select nations

- Among the five most popular activities pursued at clubs are using the treadmill (45 percent), using resistance machines (45 percent), lifting free weights (37 percent), using elliptical trainers (30 percent), and participating in group exercise (20 percent).
- Among women, the most popular activities were group exercise (approximately 64 percent of respondents indicated that they participated), soft exercise (61 percent), cardiovascular machines (47 percent), and resistance-training exercises (44 percent).
- Among men, the most popular activities were training on cardiovascular equipment (58 percent), working out on resistance equipment (52 percent), performing soft exercise (39 percent), and engaging in group exercise (36 percent).
- Among individuals in generation Y (the millennial generation), the two most popular activities were training on cardiovascular equipment and using resistance equipment, while among baby boomers, soft exercise, and cardiovascular exercise ranked the highest.
- The most popular group classes were low-impact, with nearly a 20 percent level of involvement, and classes that involved a variety of movements (e.g., Zumba).
- The most popular form of soft exercise was stretching, with 24 percent involvement. The second most popular soft exercise was yoga with nearly 16 percent participation.

The five most popular activities pursued at clubs are using the treadmill (45 percent), using resistance machines (45 percent), lifting free weights (37 percent), using elliptical trainers (30 percent), and participating in group exercise (20 percent).

Data collected as part of member-satisfaction research with Russia's leading operator of health/fitness clubs, showed that approximately 80 percent of members used cardiovascular and resistance machines, while 67 percent participated in group-exercise classes. When evaluated from a gender perspective, 92 percent of men indicated that they used the resistance and cardiovascular equipment, while 75 percent of women reported that they utilize the cardiovascular and resistance equipment. Approximately 83 percent of women indicated they participate in group exercise, while only 33 percent of men indicated that they participate in this form of activity. These reported figures from Russia are similar to those presented in IHRSA's *2010 Health Club Consumer Report,* especially with regard to the percentage of women and men who participate in group exercise, as well as those individuals who utilize the equipment in the fitness center (referred to as a gym in Europe).

In the aforementioned study, which looked at retention and usage among a group of 24 Russian clubs and 25 premium clubs in the U.S., data was collected regarding what percentage of the daily usage of clubs could be attributed to group-exercise participation. In the 25 premium U.S. clubs, the average group-exercise participation levels represented 26 percent of the overall daily attendance, with a range of 16 to 50 percent. In the Russian clubs, group-exercise participation ranged from 25 percent to approximately 50 percent, with an average of slightly over 30 percent.

In a study reported by Les Mills International in 2011 that looked at group-exercise participation among Les Mills-licensed clubs, it was found that approximately 33 percent of all club attendance could be attributed to group exercise, with the top club in this study attributing 57 percent of its daily attendance to group exercise. This study indicated that the industry norm for the percentage of daily visits attributable to group exercise was 10 to 20 percent, with levels of 30 percent or greater being considered high. Based on the aforementioned data, it would seem that between 20 and 40 percent of club members who visit their club participate in group exercise.

Specific data on what members actually use when they visit the club is not nearly as comprehensive as the data on daily and annual usage or group-exercise usage. As a result, it is difficult to reach any concrete conclusions regarding what members pursue when they visit. Understanding what members actually do when they visit the club is an essential element of the usage equation, and as will be discussed subsequently, an important driver of membership retention.

Demographic Variables That Influence Member Participation

In the research commissioned by IHRSA, the data shows that education, household income, and education level influence how active members are in their club.

In Figure 7-6, it can be seen that the higher the attained education level, the more likely the member is to use the club. Figure 7-7 indicates that as the average household income of a member increases club usage rises. Furthermore, Figure 7-8 shows that members between the ages of 35 and 65 tend to represent the most active member populations (this particular piece of data parallels what the FIA researchers found in their studies of U.K. members).

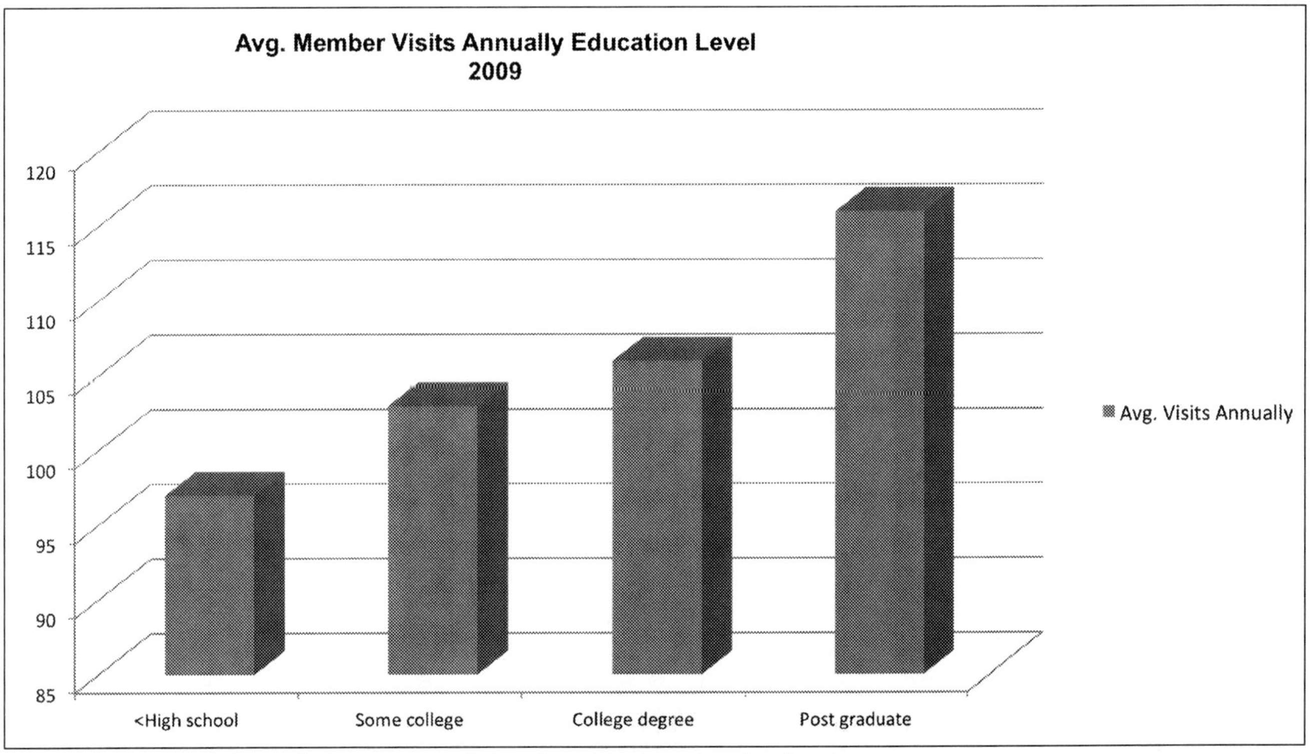

Figure 7-6. A comparison of average annual member visits by education level

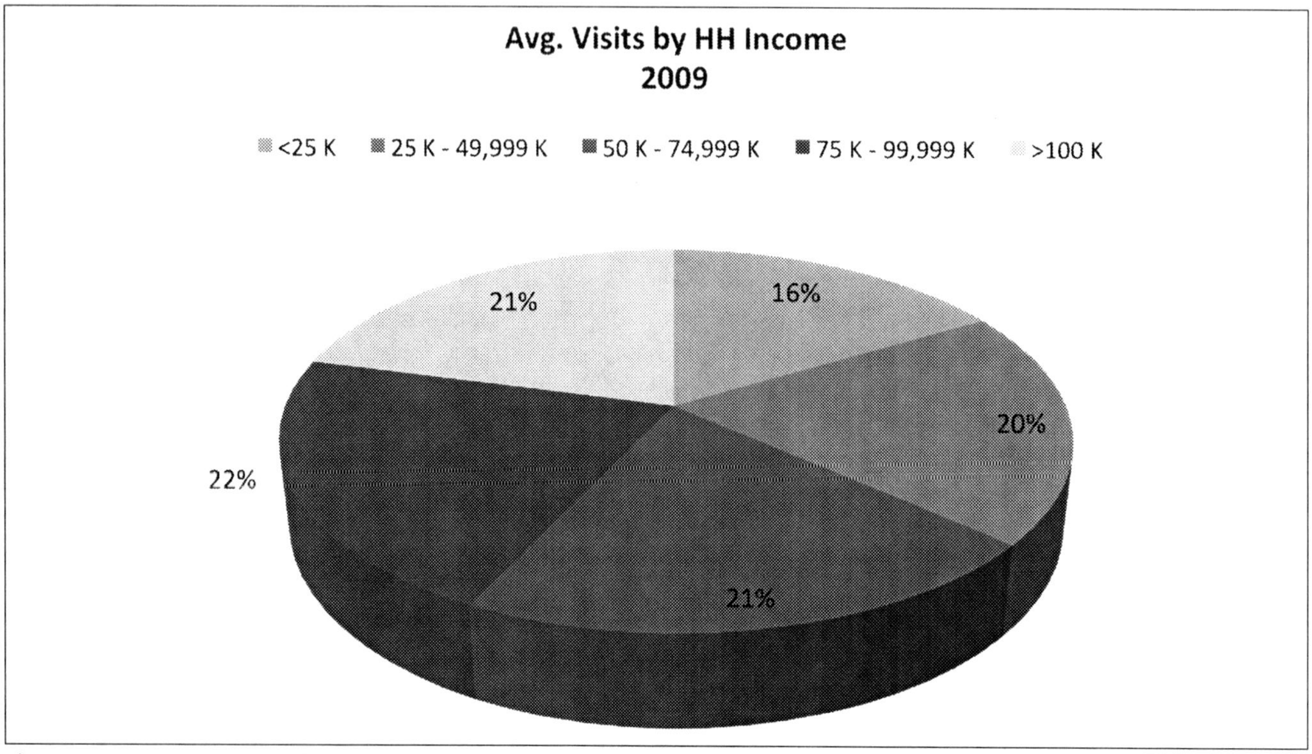

Figure 7-7. A comparison of average club visits by household income (2009)

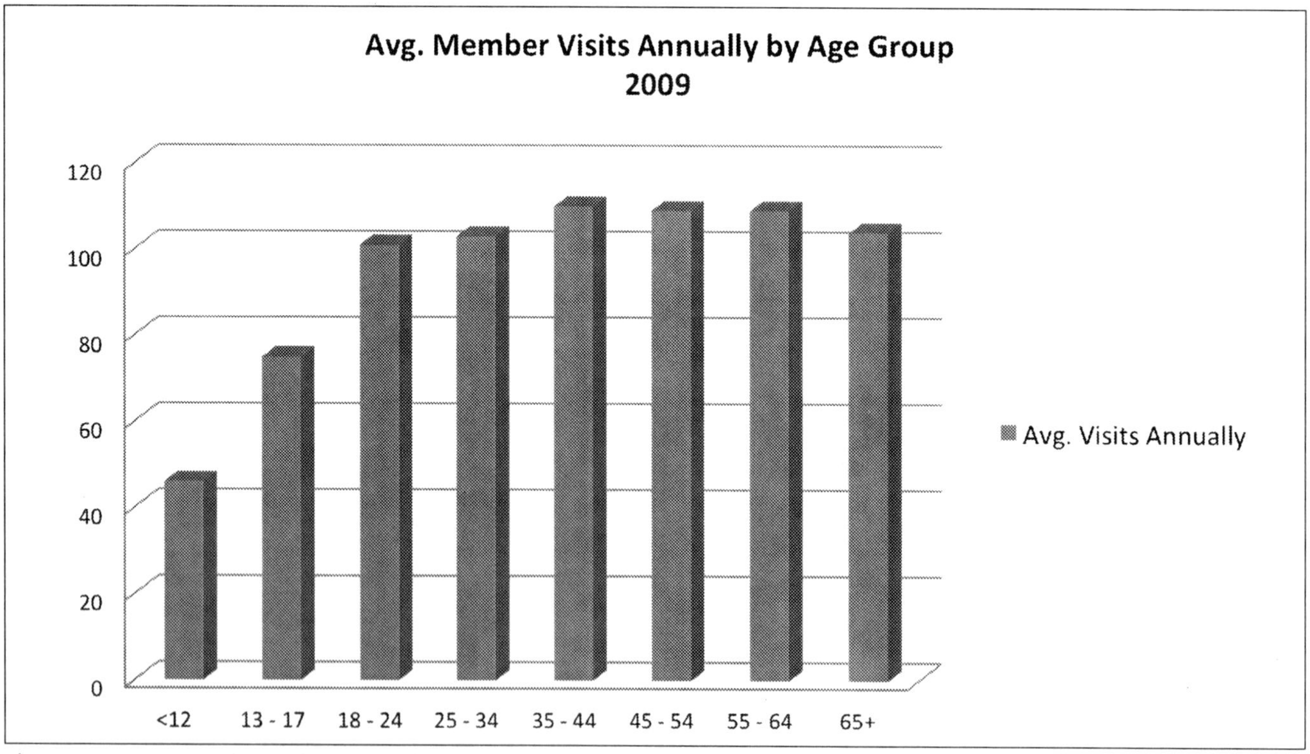

Figure 7-8. A comparison of average club visits by age group (2009)

The Impact of Member Usage on Member Retention

In the 2001 FIA report entitled, *Winning the Member Retention Battle,* researchers showed a high correlation between member usage and member retention. The report found that after one year, members who used the club less than once a week had a retention level of 59 percent, while those individuals who used it more than three times a week had a retention rate of 80 percent. Figure 7-9 illustrates the impact of these varying levels of member usage on the overall retention rate after one month, three months, six months, nine months, and one year. Figure 7-10 shows the retention rates for the four defined categories of usage for U.K. members after one month and again after 12 months.

This data clearly indicates, at least during the first year of a membership, that a dose-related relationship exists between member usage and member retention, with member retention levels improving as average weekly usage increases. In the *2008 National Retention Report* commissioned by the Fitness Industry Association of England, researchers again were able to show that a strong correlation exists between the frequency of club visits and member retention levels.

Using data collected in 2009 on 24 clubs in Russia, the relationship between the average percentage of members who used the club daily and the annual retention rate (Figure 7-11) was studied, as well as the relationship between annual retention rate and four distinct levels of usage (Figure 7-12). The data, while not statistically valid, found the following relationships between retention and participation levels:

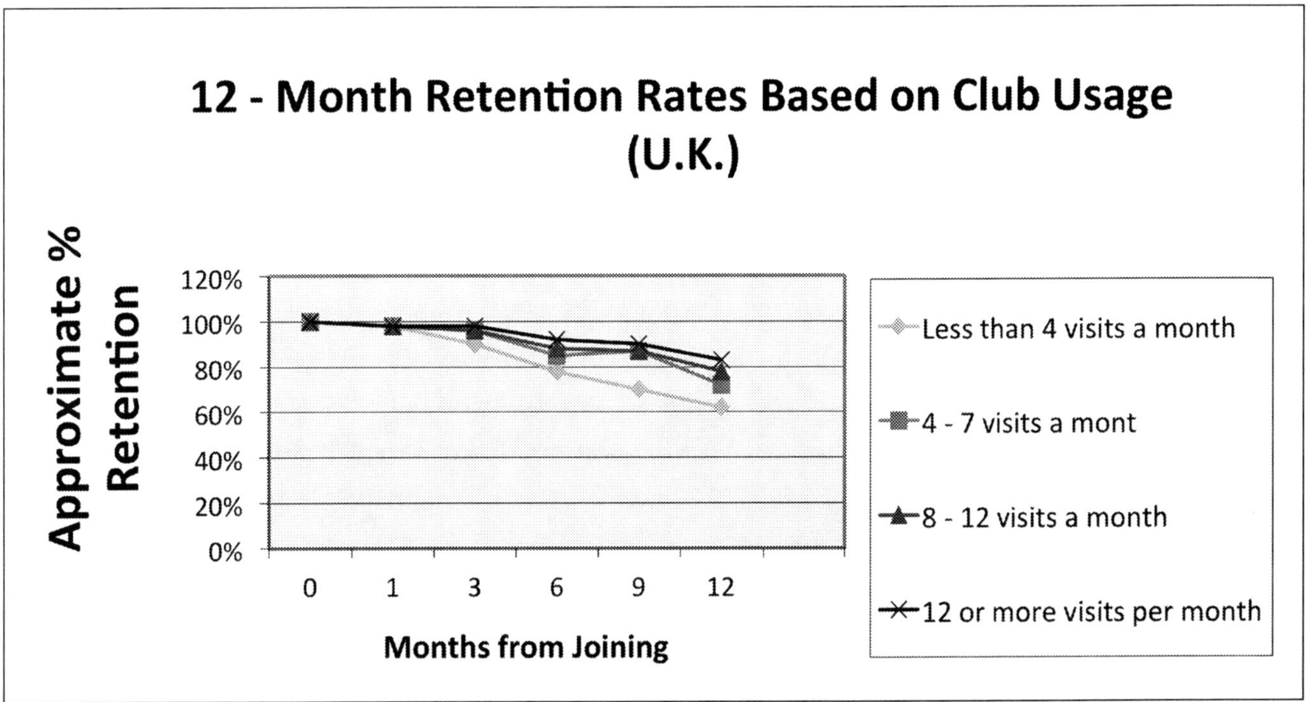

Figure 7-9. Twelve-month retention rates, based on club usage (U.K.)

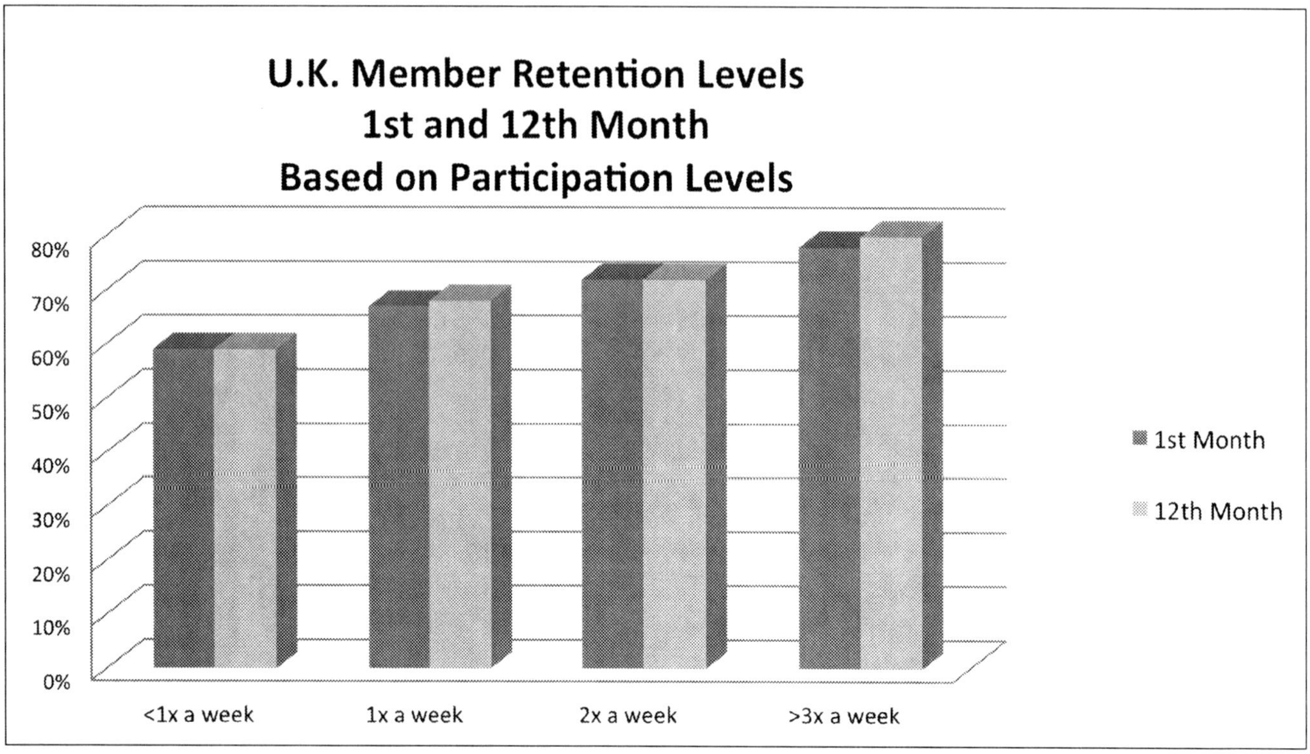

Figure 7-10. U.K. member retention levels during the first and twelfth months, based on participation levels

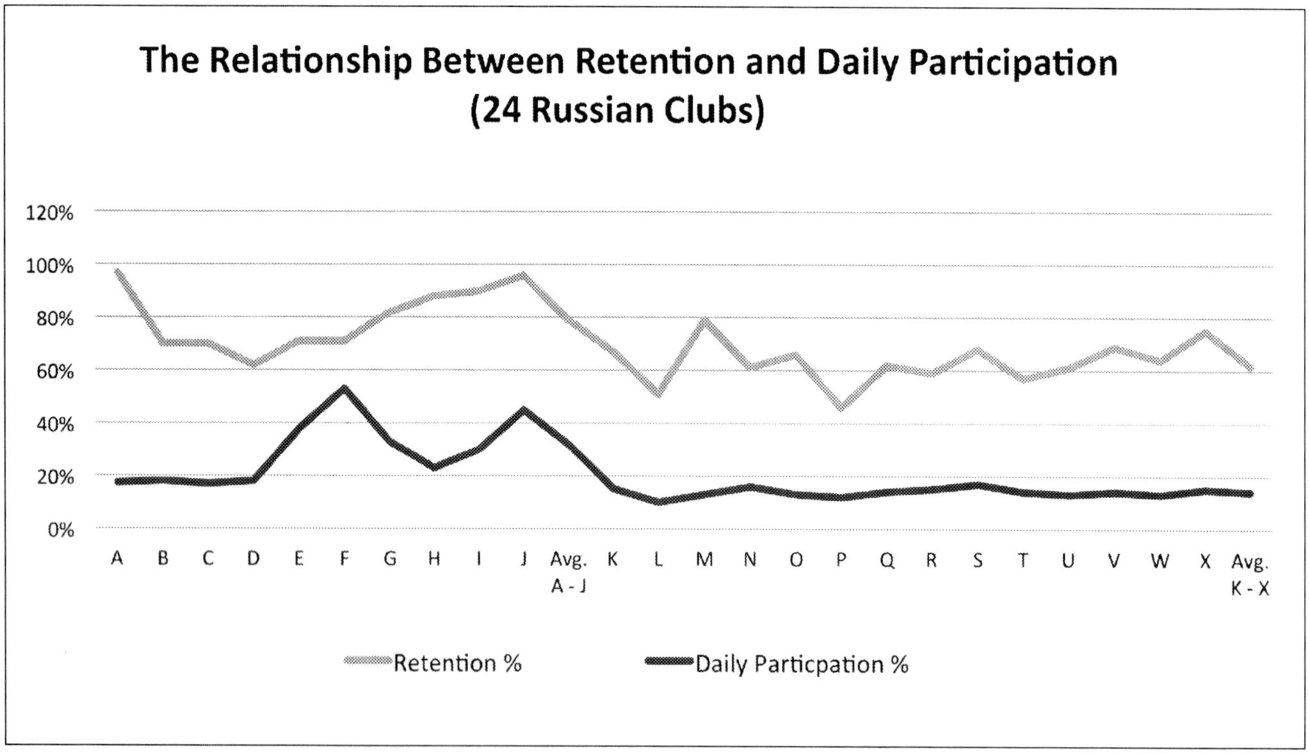

Figure 7-11. A comparison of the relationship between member retention levels and daily participation

- The clubs with the highest annual retention rate had the highest level of member usage (i.e., the percentage of total members using the facility on a daily basis).
- A stronger relationship existed between the member retention percentage and the percentage of members who used their club at least five to eight times a month or more than eight times a month than existed between the member-retention percentage and levels of usage that were less than four times per month.
- In Russia, approximately 15 percent of members visit their club on a daily basis, with 8 to 10 percent of members visiting during any one peak time period. In Europe, a similar percentage of members visit their club on a daily basis, while in the U.S. daily attendance approaches 20 to 30 percent of the member base.

Membership Pricing, Contract Length, and Its Impact on Retention

Membership Pricing and Retention

One variable that is believed to influence membership retention is pricing, a factor that includes initiation fees (e.g., also known as enrollment fees, induction fees, joining fees, etc.) and dues.

In the 2001 retention study commissioned by the FIA, researchers identified the following relationship between membership pricing and membership retention:

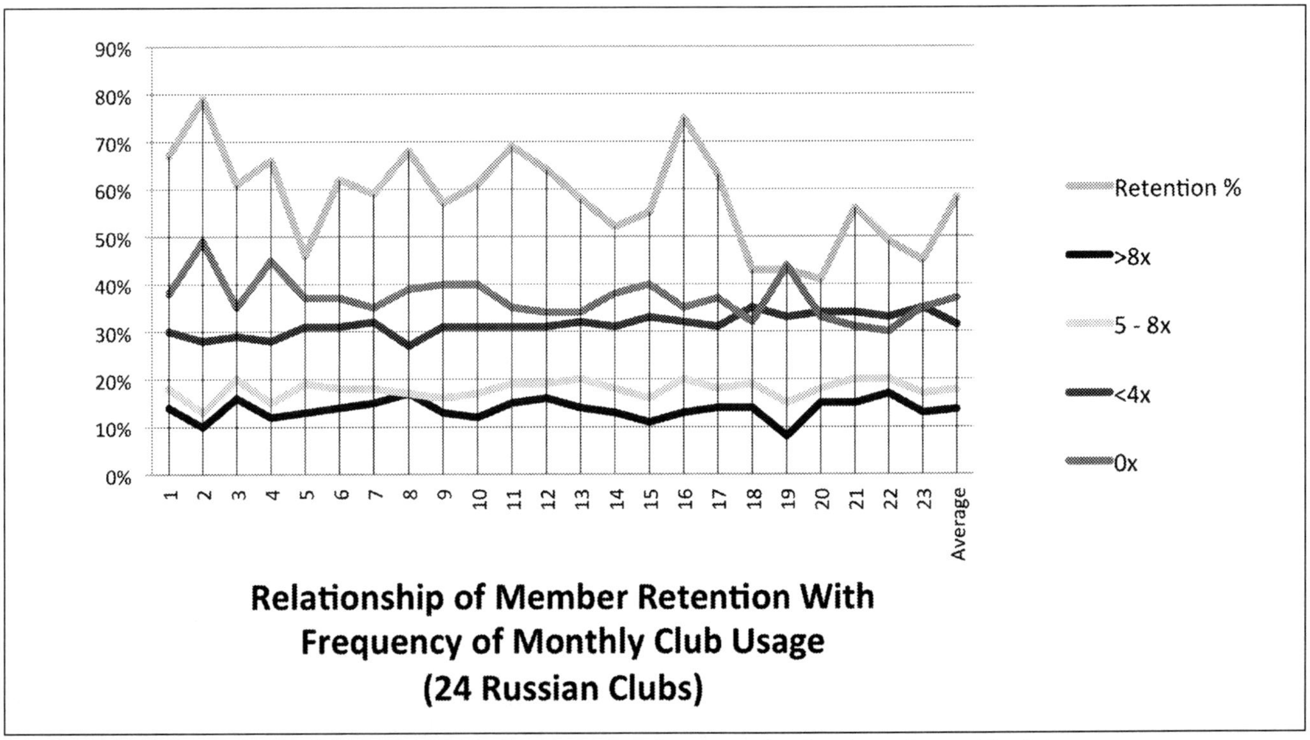

Figure 7-12. A comparison of the relationship between member retention levels and monthly club usage

- The 12-month retention rate for members who paid a joining fee was 21 percent higher than for those individuals who did not pay a joining fee. Those members who paid a joining fee had a retention rate of 68 percent after one year, compared to 47.4 percent for those individuals who did not pay a joining fee. Figure 7-13 provides a visual depiction of the relationship of joining fee to retention over the first 80 weeks of membership.
- Paying a joining fee increased member retention levels at the 80-week mark by approximately 20 percent.
- Individuals who paid an annual membership fee (often referred to as paid-in-full charge) had a retention rate compared to those members who paid monthly for 48 weeks that was 16.4 percent higher (78.7 percent to 62.3 percent). Even after 64 weeks, the retention rate of those members with an annual membership remained approximately seven percent higher (60.3 percent vs. 53.2 percent). Figure 7-14 provides a visual representation of the differences in retention rates over 12 months between those individuals on an annual membership and those members on a month-to-month membership.
- Members who pay for their memberships on a monthly basis are 56 percent more likely to resign by the 68th week, compared to those individuals who initially paid for their membership in full.

In the most recent FIA-commissioned research on retention, the *2008 National Retention Report,* the lead researchers in the study found that enrollment-fee pricing (joining fees) still had a high correlation with retention.

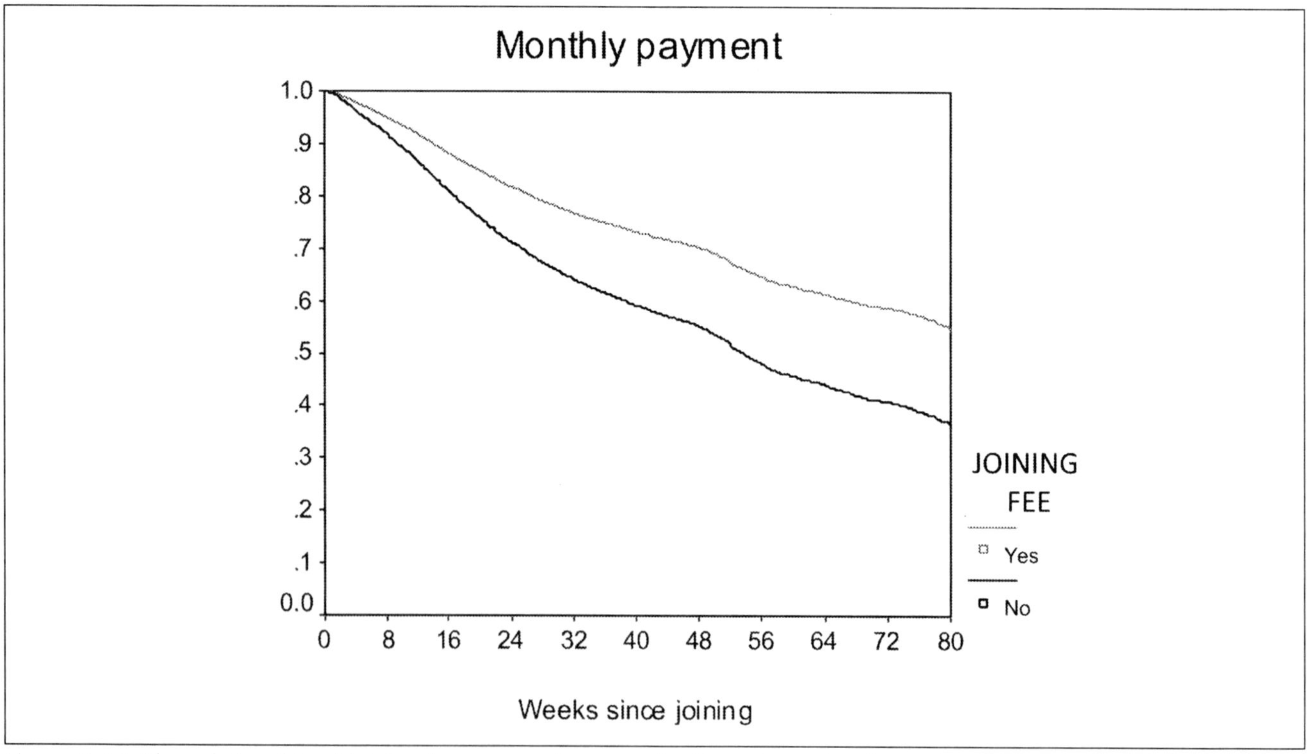

Figure 7-13. The relationship of joining fee to retention over the first 80 weeks of membership

As such, retention levels were shown to decline with lower joining fees. It is interesting to note that the researchers did not find a significant relationship between actual monthly-dues pricing and retention. In their research, they discovered that clubs that charged monthly dues of over 50 pounds actually had lower retention levels at 12 months than clubs who charged less, based on a month-to-month membership.

In the previously discussed informal retention and usage study of 24 Russian clubs and 25 U.S. clubs conducted in 2007, the relationship between dues pricing and retention levels was explored. The data showed a casual relationship, though not a statistically significant relationship, between dues pricing and retention. Retention levels were higher in those clubs who had the highest card price. Among the key factors identified in this investigation were the following:

- The three highest priced U.S. clubs, with average annual card prices ($4,440, $4,000, and $3,100) had the highest retention levels (97 percent, 96 percent, and 90 percent respectively).
- The U.S. clubs with the three lowest average annual card prices ($600, $725, and $920) had the lowest retention levels (62 percent, 70 percent, and 71 percent respectively).
- The Russian clubs that had the highest average annual card price had the highest levels of retention, even if they did not have the highest level of member visits.

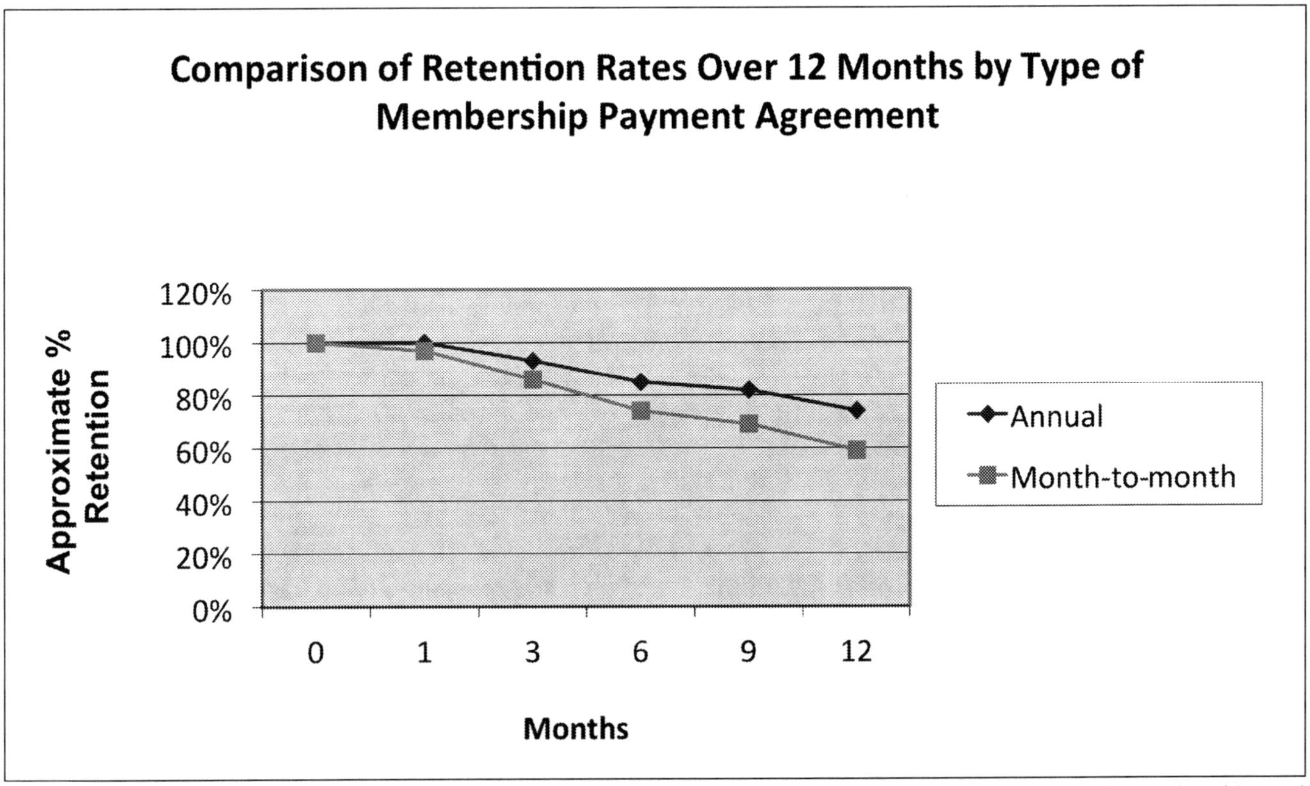

Figure 7-14. The differences in retention rates over 12 months between those individuals on an annual membership and those members on a month-to-month membership

As shown in the data from FIA, as well as the previously discussed Russian study, membership retention levels are influenced by both the pricing of the membership and the method of payment, with membership retention being higher when the card price is higher, the club has a joining fee, and when memberships are paid in full, versus monthly.

When the price point is relatively very low (under 20 dollars, 20 Euros, or 20 pounds), and the fees are pulled from either a credit card or bank account, the member is less likely to scrutinize the cost-value relationship.

A Pricing and Retention Blip

One of the more interesting pricing and retention relationships seems to exist in the high-volume, low-priced clubs or budget clubs (i.e., clubs that typically charge less than 20 Euros, 20 pounds, or $20 a month). Anecdotal data shows that these low-priced clubs actually have retention rates that are equal to or possibly higher than the IHRSA-reported industry averages (i.e., several budget clubs report retention rates of around 70 percent). This relationship would seem to fly directly in the face of other industry studies that suggest that higher prices lead to higher retention levels.

One plausible explanation for the aforementioned discrepancy is that when the price point is relatively very low (under 20 dollars, 20 Euros, or 20 pounds), and the fees are pulled from either a credit card or bank account, the member is less likely to scrutinize the cost-value relationship. This circumstance is similar to what the authors describe as the Bally principle, which was discussed previously. This postulate ascribes to the perception that if the price is low enough, members will tend to retain their membership in order to not give up a good deal, and because the fee tends to fly under their expense-management radar.

Membership Contracts and Retention

In the *2008 National Retention Report*, released by the FIA of England, a strong relationship was seen between contract length and member-retention rates. The information included in this report showed that members who sign a 12-month contract have significantly higher retention levels at 12 months than members who have signed contracts of shorter duration (e.g., month-by-month, three-month, or six-month). It is interesting to note that once the 12-month contract ends, retention levels drop precipitously. For example, at 11 months, the retention rate for those on a 12-month contract is 75 percent, while by the 13th month, the rate drops to 40 percent. Members who are on monthly plans with no contract are nearly 2.5 times more likely to terminate their membership during the first year compared to those individuals who had signed a 12-month contract. In fact, members who signed a 24-month contract were 70 percent less likely to cancel their membership than individuals on a month-by-month plan with time restraints. This report also showed that members paying less than 20 pounds a month, compared to those individuals with a 24-month contract cancelled at a rate of 32.7 per 1,000 and 65.4 per 1,000, respectively.

Other Demographic Factors Influencing Membership Retention

In the 2001 FIA study, *Winning the Member Retention Battle,* researchers looked at several other demographic factors that might influences membership retention, including age and membership tenure.

Member Age and Retention

- Members who are over the age of 45 have a higher retention rate than those individuals in other age groups. At year one, the member-retention rate for those individuals over the age of 45 was 71 percent, compared to 68 percent for members 35 to 44 years old, 60 percent for members 25 to 34 years old, and 50 percent for those members under the age of 24.
- In the most recent FIA national retention report, released in 2008, members over the age of 45 were 52 percent less likely to terminate their membership than those individuals between the ages of 16 and 24. In this study, the data indicated that retention tends to show a significant improvement in months 3 through 12, once individuals reach the age of 35, with retention rates being significantly higher for those individuals over the age of 35 and 45 (Figure 7-15).
- The average length of a membership for those members over age 35 was 80 weeks, while for those individuals under the age of 35, it was only 61 weeks—a difference of nearly 25 percent.
- Those individuals over age 55 are 46 percent less likely to resign at 68 weeks than those members under the age of 24. Even adults between 45

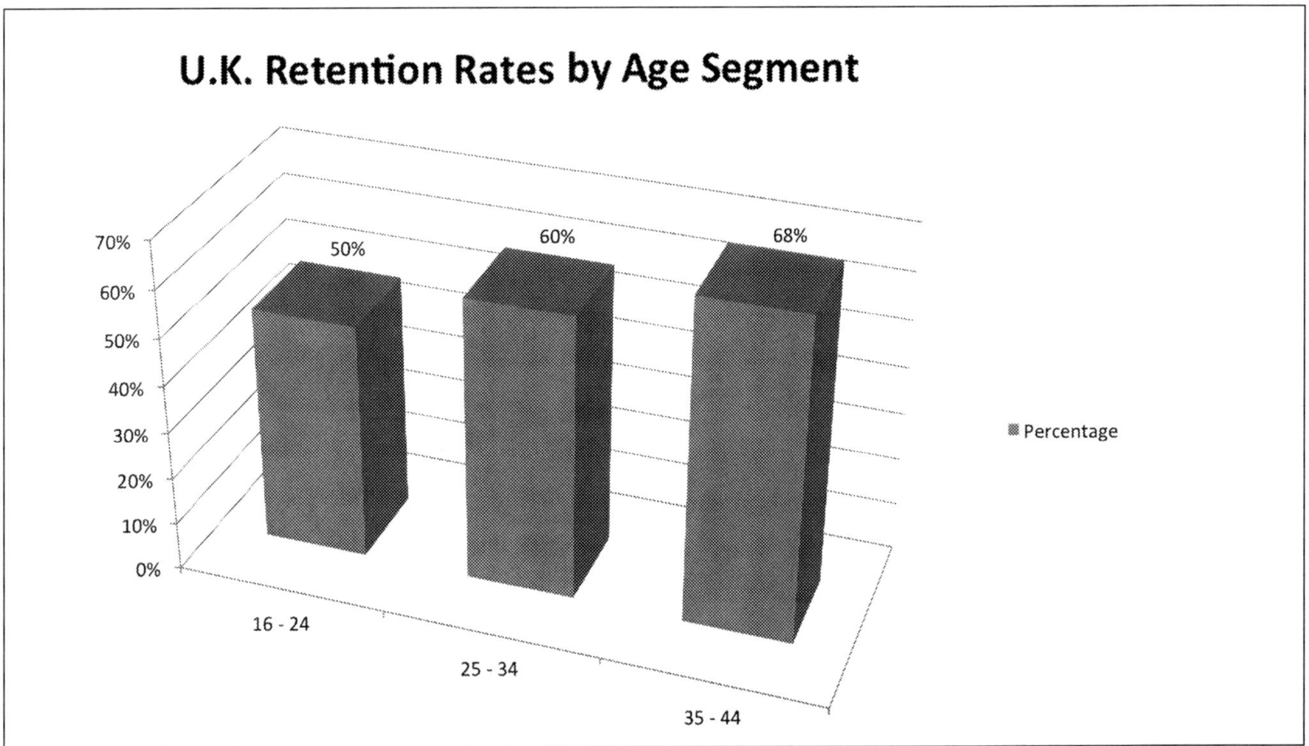

Figure 7-15. Retention rates in U.K. clubs by age segment

and 54 and 35 and 44 are 45 percent and 38 percent, respectively, are less likely to resign than those under the age of 24.

- Members who are part of a family membership are 31 percent less likely to cancel their membership than a single member at the 68-week period of membership.

Retention and Tenure of Membership (Figure 7-16)

- Member-retention levels decline with each successive week of membership during the first year. The data shows a significant change between 12 and16 weeks, an indication that this time period is critical in the retention equation.

Reflections on the Data—What Might It Mean?

This chapter focused primarily on those factors, both demographically and operationally, that influence retention levels in the health/fitness club industry. Several key understandings can be taken away from this chapter by club operators, including the following:

- Membership-dues pricing does not significantly influence membership-retention levels. Rather, such levels are more dependent upon the combination between pricing and the actual experience the club offers. All factors considered, it seems that very low monthly pricing, such as is reflected in budget clubs, may actually provide some benefit for retention. Furthermore, clubs that have very high monthly pricing that simultaneously

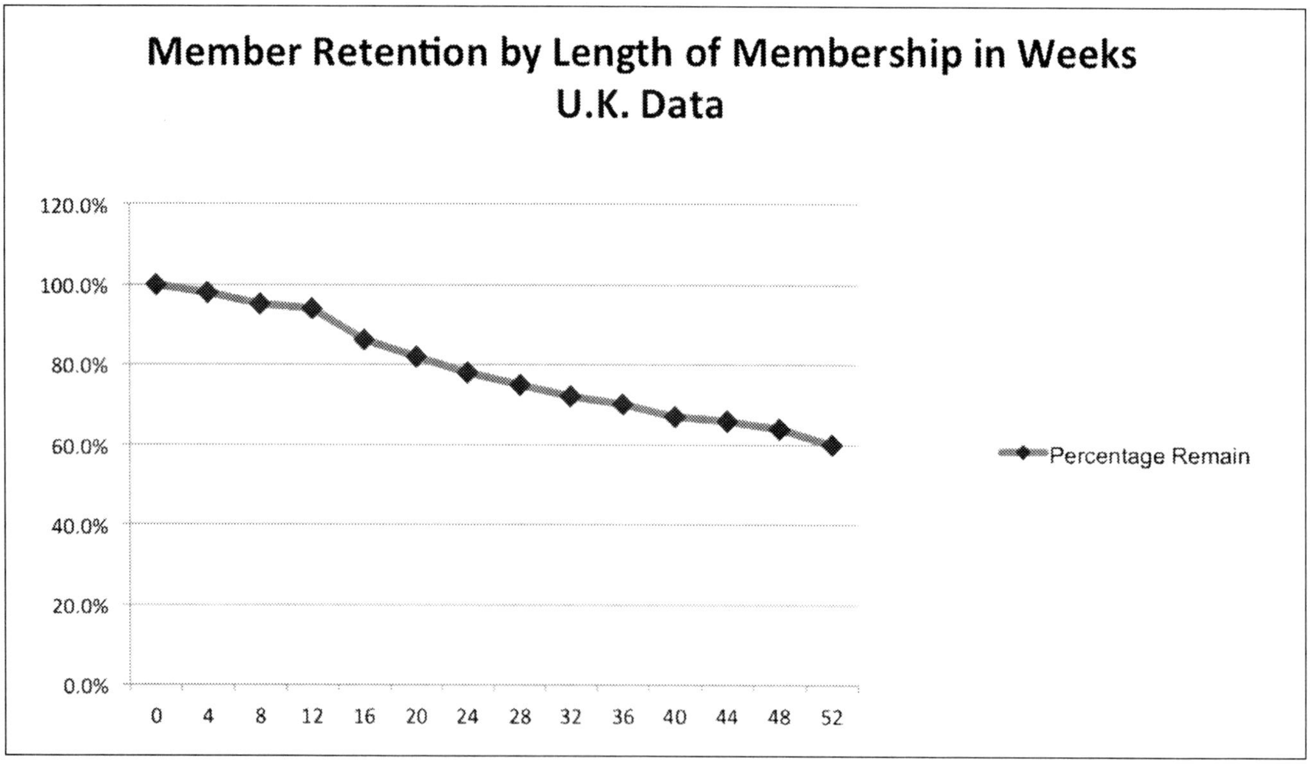

Figure 7-16. Member retention rates by the length of membership in weeks in U.K. clubs

deliver a luxury experience also reap some retention benefits. As such, it appears that dues structures, accompanied by a member experience that falls between budget and luxury, are not highly impacted by a slight variance in dues pricing. The take-away is that operating in either the budget segment or the luxury/premium market provides the greatest opportunity to enhance the value proposition of membership through, in part, the dues pricing.

- Lowering enrollment fees (joining fees) or not charging enrollment fees will generate lower retention levels, while instituting enrollment fees will increase membership retention. Enrollment or joining fees can be seen as a barrier to departure. The underlying premise is that consumers will be less inclined to walk away from their initial investment, especially if they perceive that an opportunity exists to get a return on that investment (i.e., achieve desired results). With no upfront investment, the consumer or member has no additional incentive or barrier to keep them from walking away from their membership if they are not using the club. This conclusion apparently seems to indicate that the industry practice of lowering fees to generate sales can have a rebound effect that can negatively impact the ability of clubs to retain their members once they have made the sale.
- Offering annual memberships or requiring members to sign membership contracts can have a positive influence on membership retention. It would seem that by paying up-front for an annual membership, individuals are making a stronger commitment to their investment. As a result, they are more likely to expend more effort in getting a return. Furthermore, by requiring individuals to sign a contract that commits them to monthly payments for a period of 12 to 24 months provides some protection against attrition. The downside of this practice, of course, is an extended sales cycle.
- Member participation is a critical variable in retention. Members who use their club at least eight times a month, and even those who use it five to eight times a month, have significantly higher retention levels than those individuals who use it less frequently. The explanation for this factor may be two-fold. First, members who use the facility more frequently perceive greater value (i.e., a lower price point per visit). Second, those individuals who use the club more frequently are more likely to achieve their fitness goals, as well as establish relationships with the staff and other members. The secret is getting members at all stages of their membership into the club.
- Membership activity and membership retention levels drop with each month of membership. Between the third- and fourth-month mark, a drastic drop off in activity occurs, which then continues through the first year of membership. As a result, clubs need to especially focus on getting members actively engaged in the club during the first 90 days of membership, and then keeping them engaged. The key seems to be getting members into the club more than four times during each of the first three to four months if the facility really wants to make a dent in their retention levels.
- The participation practices of men and women are considerably different. Women prefer to engage in more social group activities, whereas men

Members who use their club at least eight times a month, and even those who use it five to eight times a month, have significantly higher retention levels than those individuals who use it less frequently.

prefer to work out on equipment. As a result, clubs need to pay close attention to how it balances the diverse activity requirements of each of the genders, if they want to promote higher usage and therefore higher member retention in the club.

Individuals who receive a multiple-phase induction over their first four weeks of membership are more likely to remain members than those people who only receive a one-time induction to the club.

- Individuals who receive a multiple-phase induction over their first four weeks of membership are more likely to remain members than those people who only receive a one-time induction to the club. The key variable seems to be providing more interaction and coaching from staff, which allows members to gain greater confidence in their ability to exercise and navigate the club.

8

Driving Member Retention Through Member Loyalty and Satisfaction

According the *Service Profit Chain,* a principle first introduced in the early 1990s out of Harvard, member loyalty is considered the second-to-last link in the service-profit chain, following customer satisfaction and proceeding profitability. What the proponents of this model proposed was that highly profitable businesses must have loyal customers, which result from a series of other actions taken by the business. Since the model was initially released, research has shown that businesses that do the best job retaining customers do so because of their ability to cultivate customer loyalty (e.g., Apple, Starbucks, etc.).

This chapter expands on the principle of member loyalty and satisfaction (satisfaction is the first step in moving toward member loyalty). In addition, information is presented in this chapter that demonstrates the impact of member loyalty on membership retention and profitability.

Understanding Member Loyalty and Satisfaction

Defining Member Satisfaction and Member Loyalty

Member satisfaction is defined as the collective feeling or sense of fulfillment that members have about their experience with a club. When members are satisfied with their experience, it reflects the fact that the club has objectively met their needs and allowed the members to achieve the initial expectations that they had when they joined the facility.

Member loyalty is considered the second-to-last link in the service-profit chain, following customer satisfaction and proceeding profitability.

Satisfaction is a non-emotional response. It does not create an undying or fanatical desire to continue to use a product or service, or in the case of a club, to remain a member. What it does refer to is the fact that the club has temporarily met each member's expectations and that unless a better service or experience arises in the market, each member will continue to utilize their current club.

The potential downside of this factor, from a business perspective, is threefold. First, once a member is satisfied, their expectations change, resulting in a higher level of performance having to be delivered by the club to drive the satisfaction of the member going forward. Second, member satisfaction only allows a club to retain the member until such time as either a perceived better experience is offered by the club or another club in the market brings forth an experience that a particular member may perceive to be better. Finally, it should be kept in mind that member satisfaction is not member loyalty. Because it does not fully engage the emotions and passions of the member, it does not create the bond that can retain members for life or can drive them to spend more at the club.

Member loyalty occurs when a business captures the heart and soul of the customer.

Member loyalty occurs when a business captures the heart and soul of the customer. The following quote from Lord Burleigh does an excellent job of putting member loyalty in perspective, *"Capture their hearts and you have their hands and purses."* What Lord Burleigh was saying is that loyal members are those members whose heart and soul are one with the club, when members become the apostles and disciples of a facility, or as Ken Blanchard coined in his book, *Raving Fans.* "Raving members" are individuals who have the highest level of retention and who spend the most money in their club.

The Value Equation Underlying Member Satisfaction and Loyalty

How does a club first achieve member satisfaction, and then move beyond it to establish member loyalty? It begins with understanding the underlying elements of how a customer, or in the case of the club business, a member, perceives value and how that value creates either satisfaction or emotional passion and loyalty. In fact, a member's perception of value can be calculated using the following formula:

$$\text{Value} = \frac{\text{Facility Quality} + \text{Product Quality} + \text{Service Quality} + \text{Emotional Quality}}{\text{Price} + \text{Time}}$$

Numerator:

- Facility quality is defined by the overall quality of a facility and includes several elements, such as cleanliness, amount of equipment, accessibility of equipment, condition of the facility, etc.
- Product quality is defined as the overall quality of a club's products offerings, based on the expectations that the members have. It includes an array of elements, such as class schedule, special events, training programs, etc.
- Service quality is defined as the level of service a club provides, based on the expectations of the members, and includes a number of elements, such as smiles, greeting members by name, fast and courteous attention, service recovery, etc.

- Emotional quality is defined as the level of emotional attachment that is created for the member by the club experience and depends on a variety of elements, such as relationships with staff, relationships with other members, a sense of pride in the club, etc.

Denominator:

- Price reflects the actual cash price that individuals pay to use their club and is comprised of enrollment fees, dues, and on occasion, fees for extra services. It may also involve whether the payment is made monthly or annually.
- Time reflects the time that an individual must allocate to gain benefit from being a member of the club, which involves elements, such as visits per week, time spent each visit, and any time allocations involved in getting to and from the club.

Member satisfaction occurs when the numerator is higher than the denominator. On the other hand, loyalty can only occur when the emotional quality in the numerator is incredibly high. For example, Apple has created an incredible level of customer loyalty, because all of the elements in the numerator in its perception-of-value equation are powerful, particularly the emotional quality. A recent article that appeared in the January 2011 edition of *Advertising Age*, written by Doug Levy and Bob Garfield, indicated that if you Google "I love Apple," you will get 3.27 million hits, more than any other firm, including Starbucks, which received 2.7 million, Zappos with slightly more than 1.1 million hits, and AT&T wireless with only 21,000 hits. Everyone is aware of the fact that Apple products are not inexpensive (typically, they're more expensive than comparable products). The key point to keep in mind is that the numerator contributors, when combined together, are far more valuable and powerful than the costs reflected in the denominator.

The basic takeaway is that for clubs to establish a high value, they must deliver the facility, product, and service, along with emotional engagement, at a level far greater than the actual cost and time required for a member to use the club.

Measuring Member Satisfaction and Loyalty

The standard approach for measuring satisfaction is to survey the membership on a regular basis, asking a series of questions or proposing specific statements to which members can then respond, using a simple five-point Likert scale (a basic scale commonly employed in surveys). The Likert scale (a simple Likert scale is five points, while more advanced scales can be seven or nine points) is a standardized psychometric tool that allows researchers to easily assess respondent answers. The basic five-point scale is as follows:

5 = strongly agree
4 = agree or somewhat agree
3 = not sure, or neither agree or disagree
2 = disagree
1 = strongly disagree

For clubs to establish a high value, they must deliver the facility, product, and service, along with emotional engagement, at a level far greater than the actual cost and time required for a member to use the club.

By using this scale, researchers are able to accurately measure the degree of satisfaction or dissatisfaction that exists around a specific situation, series of situations, or an entire experience.

The most frequently used and quoted metric or indicator of member loyalty is called the *"Net Promoter Score,"* a measure that was introduced in 2003 by a Harvard University professor, Fred Reichheld. The term *Net Promoter Score* is actually a trademarked title of Reichheld, Bain & Company. The purpose of the *Net Promoter Score* is to clearly identify those customers and/or members who are actual promoters of a particular business (loyal members, raving fans, etc.). While Net Promoters are typically determined by using a 10-point scale, the metric can also be applied, using the aforementioned simple five-point Likert scale. A *Net Promoter,* or a loyal member (raving fan), is a member or customer who rates the club as either a 9 or 10 on a 10-point scale or 5 on a five-point scale (Figure 8-1).

The Net Promoter Score is determined by taking the percentage of members who rate a facility as a Net Promoter and then subtracting that number from the percentage of members who rate the club as a detractor. The resulting number is the facility's *Net Promoter Score* (Figure 8-2). A score of zero or better is considered good and a score greater than +50 is considered excellent.

Figure 8-2 depicts two clubs—one, Club A, with a *Net Promoter Score* of -10, and the other, Club B, with a score of +20. The club with the positive score is definitely doing a better job at creating an environment that promotes member loyalty. In reality, many club operators, with a score similar to that of Club A (30 percent of members gave the club a 5 and 30 percent gave the club a 4 on the survey), would tend to think, "Hey, we have 60 percent of the members who are either satisfied or delighted with their experience, so we must be doing a good job." The underlying error in this type of logic is that

Description	10-Point Scale	5-Point Scale
Promoters	9 to 10	5
Passives	7 to 8	4
Detractors	6 and below	3 and below

Figure 8-1. The ten-point and five-point scales for determining the Net Promoter Score of member loyalty

they don't understand that a merely satisfied member has no emotional buy-in, and that with more detractors than promoters, the club is in danger of losing members.

A number of businesses focus on one simple question to determine their overall Net Promoter Score—*"How likely are you to refer a friend or colleague?"* Truth be known, many researchers believe that this single question and the resultant *Net Promoter Score* are not a true indicator of customer loyalty. Rather, it is a score that indicates how likely a member is to refer another member. The pervading rationale of these researchers is based on the premise that a club needs to develop the *Net Promoter Score,* using the responses to a series of questions. As such, in the health/fitness club industry, one leading market researcher has built the Net Promoter Score off of members' responses to the following four questions:

- How likely are you to remain a member over the next 12 months?
- How likely are you to refer someone for membership over the next 12 months?
- How would you rate your overall experience with the club?
- Do you love your club?

In reality, taking the responses to these four questions and calculating the percentage of responses that fall into each of the three response categories (promoter, passive, detractor),totaling them up, and then subtracting detractors from promoters provides a far more accurate portrayal of a club's Net Promoter Score. Figure 8-3 shows the results of a club that used a survey that measured each of the four aforementioned questions in order to determine its overall Net Promoter Score. In this example, the club scored a +45, a tally that is excellent.

With a Net Promoter Score in hand, a club can more easily identify the general level of loyalty that exists within its membership. Even with a Net Promoter Score in hand, businesses should also be aware of how important

Category	**Club A** **Percentage Responders**	**Club B** **Percentage Responders**
Promoters (5)	30%	35%
Passives (4)	30%	50%
Detractors (1 – 3)	40%	15%
Net Promoters	**-10**	**+20**

Figure 8-2. An example of the Net Promoter Score for two different clubs

it is for them to get a reading on other important questions, as well as most importantly, to understand the specific variables that contribute to driving its Net Promoter Score upward

The Russian Fitness Group, an owner and operator of 30 health/fitness clubs in Russia, conducts a survey with its members on a semi-annual basis. As part of its survey process, a Net Promoter Score is calculated for each club, as well as for the respective brands it operates. In addition, important information is obtained pertaining to the actual influencers of its Net Promoter Score.

In October of 2010, 20 out of 21 premium and luxury clubs of the Russian Fitness Group had a positive Net Promoter Score (a number that is considered good), based on the aforementioned four questions. Twelve out of 21 clubs had a Net Promoter Score above 25 (a level that is considered very good), and one club had scores of over 40 (a total that is considered excellent). In fact, the average Net Promoter Score across the company's premium segment was +25, an increase of 14 points from the scores it had achieved one year earlier and four points higher than it had recorded in a survey performed just six months earlier.

Figure 8-4 provides a graphic representation of the overall survey scores for the Group for three time periods over a period of one year. As Figure 8-4 illustrates, the clubs increased their percentage of fully satisfied members during each successive survey period. Correspondingly, the clubs decreased the percentage of members who were less than satisfied, while concurrently maintaining the same level of satisfied members. The underlying basis behind their increased Net Promoter Score is the result of decreasing the percentage of dissenters and increasing the percentage of promoters.

Category	Promoters %	Passives %	Detractors %	Net Promoter Score
Likely to remain 12 months	30%	40%	30%	
Likely to refer a member	30%	50%	20%	
Overall experience	35%	55%	10%	
I love my club	20%	70%	10%	
Total Score	115	215	70	+45

Figure 8-3. Example of the use of survey results to determine a club's Net Promoter Score

Member Satisfaction and Loyalty as They Relate to Driving the Value of Membership

While it is important to be aware of the reasons members have for using a club, studies from other industries show that understanding a customer's level of loyalty or satisfaction is equally important in determining how a business can perform better at retaining its customers. An FIA report from 2001 entitled, *Winning the Retention Battle,* studied member satisfaction and the drivers behind it. When members were asked what the most crucial factors were driving their level of satisfaction with the club experience (scores over one), the following was indicated:

- Overall quality of the staff (rating of 1.16). This response not only reflected the knowledge and expertise of the staff of the facility, it also measured the club's level of attentiveness in serving the members.
- Club management (1.15). This measure refers to the club's management practices regarding servicing the members and management's responsiveness to issues raised by members.
- Level or member compaction (1.08). This score is an indication that one driver of satisfaction relates to whether members feel the existence of personal space or if they feel "caged-in."
- Feel like they fit in (1.02). This result is based on the premise that members believe that their level of satisfaction is drawn, at least in part, from feeling a sense of being perceived to fit in, or not standing out as being different.

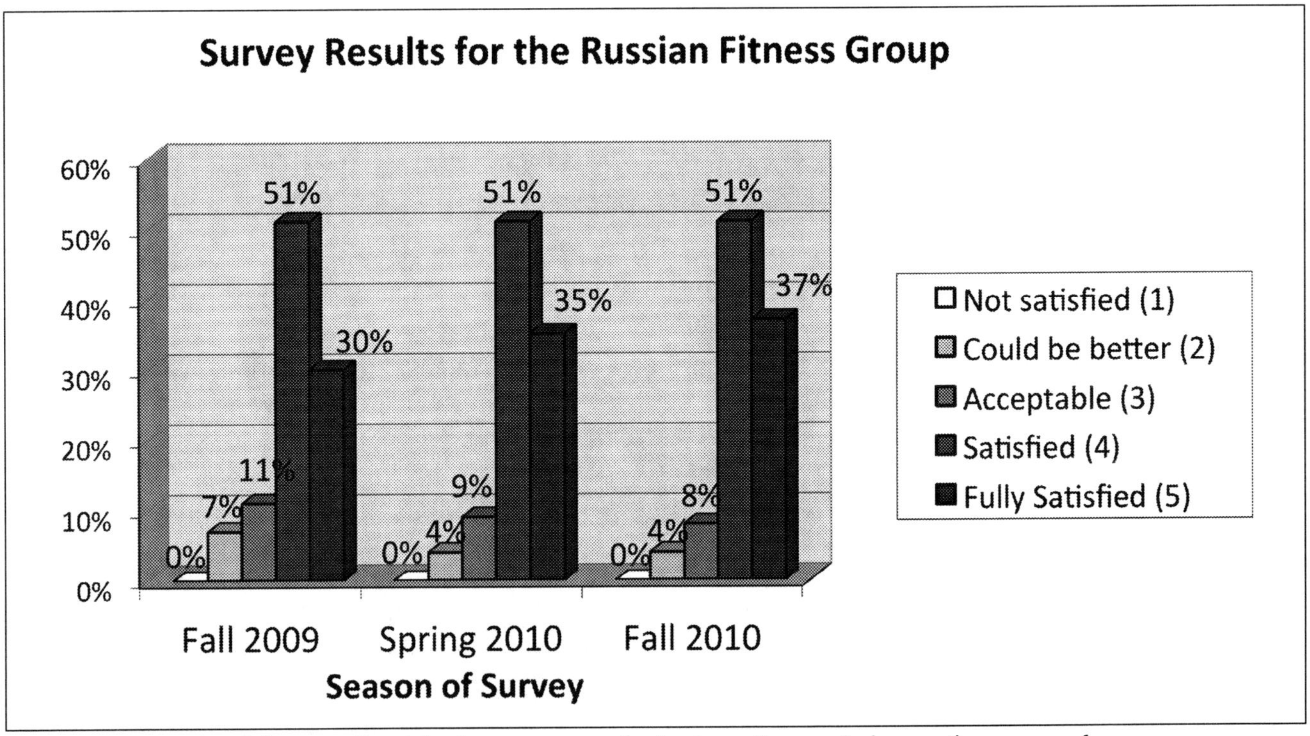

Figure 8-4. Example of the overall satisfaction survey results for three time periods over the course of one year

- Social ambiance (1.02). This reply reflects the fact that a club that affords members a chance to socialize with other members and, in essence, connect with other member is important to their overall club experience. The measure is also an indication that the club needs to provide a social engaging environment.

Members who responded that they were very satisfied with their club experience were significantly more likely to refer someone for membership.

Similar to the aforementioned findings, the researchers also identified the following categories as receiving the highest percentage of agreement, with regard to being rated as excellent or very good (9 or 10 on a 10-point scale) in their contribution to member satisfaction:

- Overall value for the money spent (54 percent) and general club atmosphere (52 percent) received the two highest totals, with regard to having a role in the satisfaction levels of members.
- Fitting in (46 percent), social ambiance (36 percent), and not too crowded (36 percent), were close runner-ups when it came to factors that are important to the level of member satisfaction.

In a 2007 study conducted on behalf of IHRSA, *Fitness American Style III*, the researchers looked at member satisfaction with the club experience. They found that 91 percent of current members were either very satisfied or somewhat satisfied with their club. It should be noted that because current customer research shows that the key response to driving customer loyalty and retention is the *Net Promoter Score*, the responses reflected in this IHRSA-commissioned study may not be the best barometer of member loyalty.

If this IHRSA study is examined more closely, only 42 percent of respondents indicated that they were very satisfied. In this report, 93 percent of members indicated that they would be very likely or somewhat likely to refer a friend as a member. What is not known, however, is the true percentage of promoters and passives that comprise this number, and whether an overall positive Net Promoter Score existed. It is interesting to note that members who indicate that they had an excellent relationship with the staff scored significantly higher on overall satisfaction with their club than those individuals who did not have an excellent relationship with the staff of the club.

In fact, the research by the FIA in 2001 and the research reported in *Fitness American Style III* from 2007 both indicate that members who are very satisfied with their club experience are more frequent users of the facility. In addition, according to data included in these studies, those members who responded that they were very satisfied with their club experience were significantly more likely to refer someone for membership.

Member Loyalty in Russia and Its Value to Membership Retention

Results from market research on member satisfaction in Russia parallel the results seen in the IHRSA and FIA research. Research completed in 2009 and 2010 with the Russian Fitness Group showed a direct correlation between the level of member satisfaction and retention, with those clubs having the highest positive *Net Promoter Scores* having the highest level of retention and member usage. Interestingly, the top 10 drivers of member loyalty, as defined by a high positive *Net Promoter Score* included the following:

- Pride in belonging to the club
- Reputation and image of the club
- Comfortable environment (general club atmosphere)
- Feeling of exclusivity (fitting in)
- Family and friends are or can be involved
- Staff knowledge
- Helpfulness of the staff
- Responsive management in dealing with the concerns of members
- Warm and welcoming environment (social ambiance)
- Availability of equipment (compaction and overcrowding)

The final eight of the aforementioned factors are the drivers or attributes that influence club member loyalty in Russia, which consumers in both the FIA and the IHRSA studies also identified as key influencers of their remaining a member. Nearly every one of these drivers can be attributed to the interaction of employees with members, and members with members. In fact, collectively they had much less to do with the standard reasons that members indicate are important prior to joining.

Member Sacrifice and Its Impact on Member Loyalty

An article that appeared in the July/August 2010 issue of *Harvard Business Review* indicated that one of the leading drivers of customer loyalty relates to the ability of a business to solve customers' problems. In 2010, World Class, a brand operated by the Russian Fitness Group, asked the same question. After doing its first member loyalty study, it found it had a brand loyalty score of 43 percent. Concurrently as part of this investigative effort, it was found that 21 percent of members had experienced a problem, of which 70 percent reported the problem and 55 percent of those who reported the problem indicated the problem had been resolved to their satisfaction. Based on this information, World Class embarked on implementing strategies to address the problem. Twelve months after implementing these strategies, the percentage of members reporting problems had dropped from 21 percent to 17 percent. Furthermore, while the same percentage of members having problems reported them, 59 percent of those individuals reporting a problem indicated that their problems had been resolved. Paralleling this four-percentage point drop in the number of reported problems and a four-percentage point improvement in problem resolution, member loyalty increased by six percentage points from 43 percent to 49 percent. While these results only reflect the results of one company, in this case a Russian firm, they clearly indicate the impact of reducing member concerns on driving loyalty, and more importantly, the need to solve problems in an effort to enhance member loyalty.

One of the leading drivers of customer loyalty relates to the ability of a business to solve customers' problems.

Reflections on the Data—What Might It Mean?

To really have a positive impact on driving member loyalty, and ultimately membership retention, club operators need to obtain a clear understanding of the key drivers or influencers for their facility.

- It is critically important for clubs to understand the nuances involving their level of member loyalty. The desired degree of awareness can be achieved by performing member surveys on a regular basis, preferably with the assistance of a qualified market-research firm.
- The level of member loyalty as defined by the Net Promoter Score is a positive indicator of membership usage and retention. By driving up its Net Promoter Score, a club can positively impact its overall level of membership retention.
- To really have a positive impact on driving member loyalty, and ultimately membership retention, club operators need to obtain a clear understanding of the key drivers or influencers for their facility. Although clubs will differ between each other to a degree, in many cases, they will be similar.
- The influencers of loyalty are more than likely those attributes that solicit or create a positive/memorable emotional response from the members. The strongest influencers tend to be related to relationships that members have with staff, the quality of and level of attention staff provides, the relationships that members have with other members, the social ambiance of the club, the pride that a member has in belonging to the club, and the feeling by members that they fit in. While these influencers powerful, it is essential that clubs address certain core basics (i.e., they must first provide the facility quality, product quality, and service quality that their members expect).
- By reducing the number of member sacrifices and by more effectively solving the issues that arise, a club can have a positive impact on member loyalty.

STRATEGIES FOR ENHANCING MEMBER RETENTION

Section Four

The first section of this book provided an overview of the value of membership retention. The second section provided a detailed overview on the state of membership in the global health/fitness club industry, as well as a look at some of the key demographic characteristics of the industry. The third section offered an in-depth examination of the attitudes, behaviors, and perceptions of consumers and members with regard to why they seek out clubs; how members actually use their club; the drivers of member loyalty; and the reasons why some members ultimately choose to resign their membership. The fourth section of this text focuses on strategies that club operators can employ in an effort to enhance membership retention in their respective clubs.

This section of the book is separated into five chapters, each of which centers in on a different potential influencer of retention. Chapter 9 looks at strategies to improve engagement or induction of a new member into the club environment. Chapter 10 explores what clubs can do to get their members more actively involved in the club life. Chapter 11 hones in on strategies that clubs can implement to establish memorable experiences and deliver great member service. Chapter 12 reviews club design and details how this factor can be addressed to improve membership retention. Finally, Chapter 13 presents summaries of actual case studies from U.K. clubs that implemented strategies that are designed to have a positive influence the level of membership retention of their businesses. In addition, Chapters 9, 10, and 11 will feature the following:

- Stories from clubs around the world. These stories are intended to provide insight concerning how various global operators address the retention issue. In some instances, the stories are general, while in others, they address topics that are quite specific.
- Insights into the club stories. As such, the story of each club is broken down, and a unique perspective is offered concerning why these clubs are successful with retention, and why their approaches are effective.
- A series of interesting strategies that have been obtained from club operators around the globe, with specific guidelines concerning how to implement these strategies
- Stories of specific situations that point out strategies or specific elements of a strategy
- Reflections and insights that summarize each chapter's key points

It could be argued that, all factors considered, of all the sections in the book, this section may prove to be the most helpful to operators as they strive to improve the level of membership retention in their clubs.

9

Engaging the New Member: Getting Members Off to the Right Start

When individuals first join a club, they are usually excited—as people tend to be whenever they've made a substantial investment. On the other hand, new members may also feel a little overwhelmed by the many offerings of their club, as well as feel alone, if they don't know anyone else in the facility. New members may also feel slightly or completely bewildered because they have no short- or long-term exercise-related goals, and don't know how to begin. It is important to note that all of these factors can quickly dim the so-called "new buyer" excitement and cause new members to lose interest and motivation when it comes to exercise.

As discussed in previous chapters, new buyer excitement can quickly wear off. In fact by day 90, member participation begins to dramatically drop off, at which point, membership resignations begin to climb.

Research conducted by the FIA indicates that the manner in which new members are inducted into a club can have a significant influence not only on their future level of participation, but also on their future commitment to remain a member. FIA's research clearly shows the importance of getting members actively inducted and involved during both the first 30 days and first 90 days of their membership. One of the real keys, according to this research, was to get members active at last four times a month during those first three months, and if their activity levels exceed eight times a month, all the better. This period is also when members require the greatest level of guidance, education, motivation, and social support.

The manner in which new members are inducted into a club can have a significant influence not only on their future level of participation, but also on their future commitment to remain a member.

In a report published in January 2009 in *Health Club Management* and that appeared online in Cybertek, the lead author and researcher, Paul Bedford, Ph.D., summarized his doctoral research that addressed new member inductions and member retention. Bedford's efforts compared the retention levels of a control group and an experimental group through survival analysis. The control group of members received a single 60-minute induction, while the experimental group was given 120 minutes of induction over a four-week period. The experimental group's 120 minutes were separated in an initial 60-minute orientation followed by three additional sessions held over three weeks that encompassed 30 minutes, 20 minutes, and 10 minutes duration respectively.

Six months into their membership, the experimental group members had a retention level of 90 percent compared to a retention level of 70 percent in the control group. After 13 months, the retention level of the experimental group was 70 percent, while the retention level for the control group was only 40 percent. The attrition rate of the experimental group was 24 per 1,000 members, compared to 77 per 1,000 members for the control group.

Figures 9-1 and 9-2 provide a graphic representation of the results of Dr. Bedford's research. On average, an individual in the experimental group remained a member for seven months longer than a person in the control group. In this regard, Bedford concluded that providing a multiple-phase induction process that involved instruction and behavior coaching had a significant impact on improving retention.

Based on the research published in England, as well as data collected in the U.S., it is evident that how club management engages a new member immediately after that person joins the facility can have a significant and

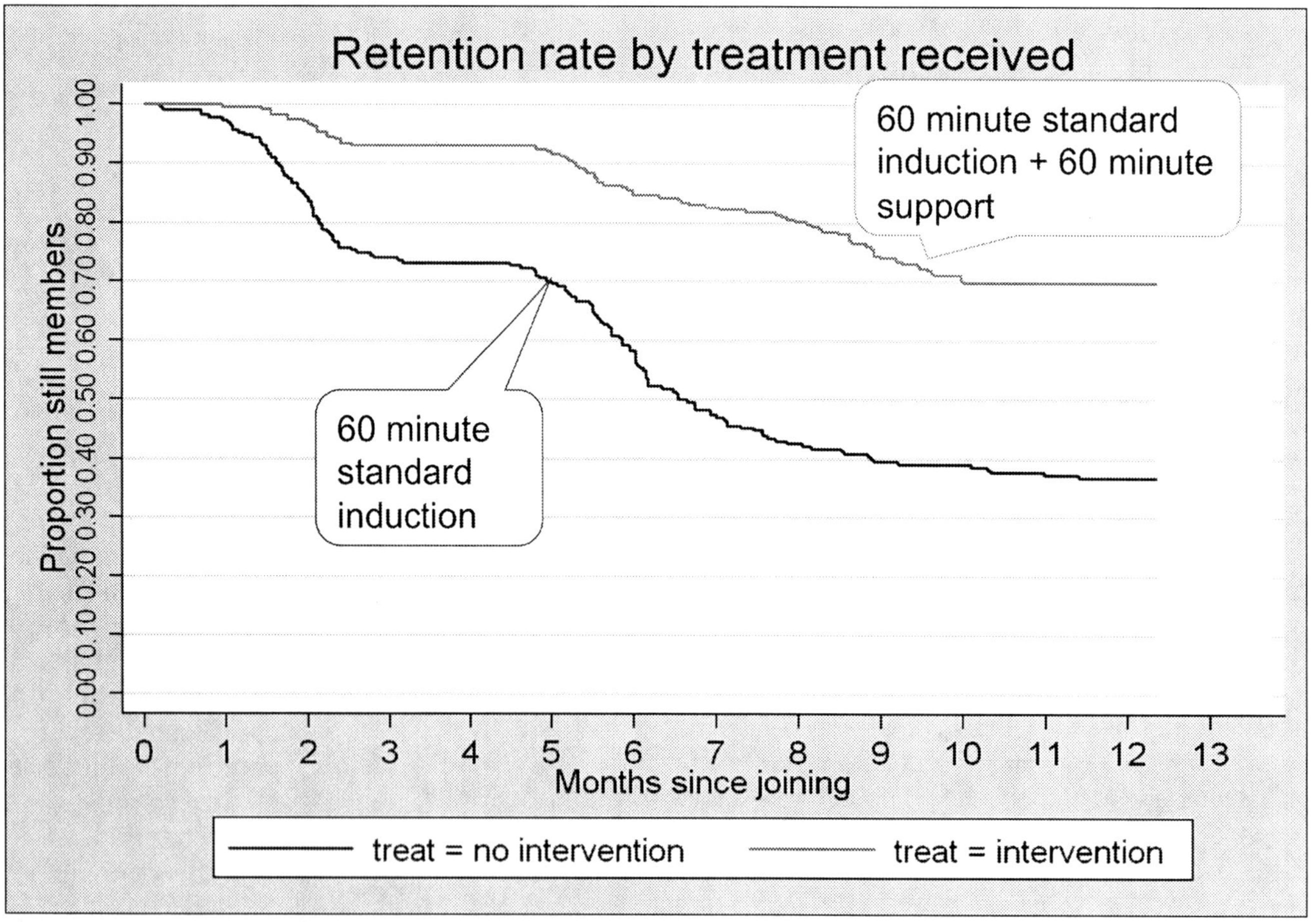

Figure 9-1. A comparison of the retention rate between two different types of member induction programs

noteworthy impact on overall membership retention. Accordingly, club operators need to introduce systems and practices that will make it far easier for new members to pursue and achieve their initial goals, as well as begin to "fit in" to the club's culture.

This chapter features club stories from a number of actual clubs, as well as several valuable strategies that club operators from around the globe have found beneficial in helping them engage and introduce new members into the club life. Hopefully, the information, ideas, and insights that can be derived from these stories and strategies can provide a pathway to better understanding and appreciating the importance of getting new members off to the right start at the club.

Attrition Rate	
Intervention group 60 minutes + 60 minutes support	24.3 per 1000 per month
Control group 60 minute standard induction	77.6 per 1000 per month

Figure 9-2. A comparison of the attrition rate between two types of member induction programs

Real Stories of New Member Engagement

It Begins at the Sale
body + soul (www.bodyandsoul.ag)
Munich, Germany
Owner: Dr. Ralf Kriegel
Average individual monthly dues: 57 Euros ($81)
Average annual retention: 80% across clubs and 90% at top club

From the perspective of the club lifespan of a typical member, retention begins with the initial customer acquisition. At member acquisition, the first unique selling proposition of body + soul can be identified. The club benefits from a 70 percent member referral rate and 80 percent retention rate (it should be noted that the top club in Munich, with dues of over 80 Euros a month, has a retention level approaching 90 percent). This high level of both member retention and member referral is an effective form of new member acquisition, and is representative of a high level of member satisfaction.

Stephen Tharrett

Exterior, body + soul

Stephen Tharrett

Mind-body studio entry, body + soul, Munich, Germany

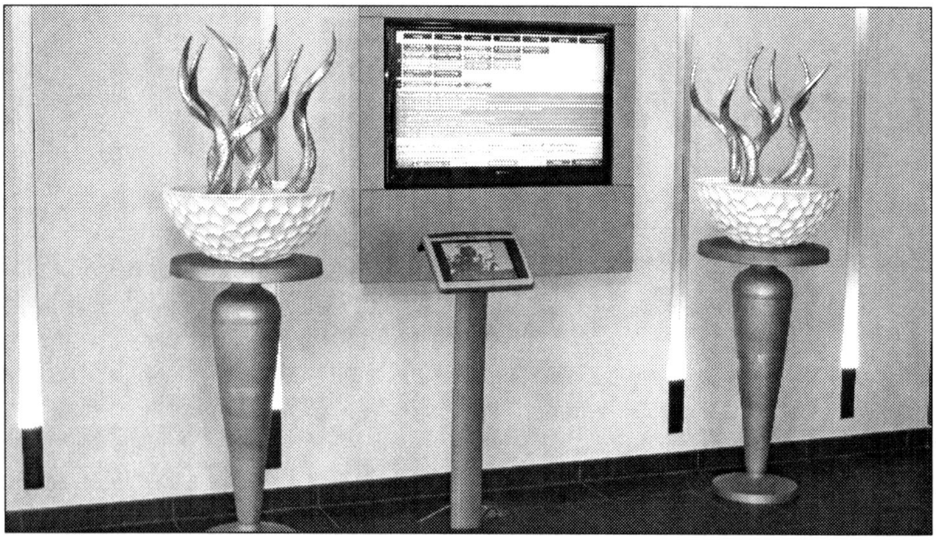
Stephen Tharrett

Group exercise studio entry area, body + soul, Munich, Germany

At body + soul, new members, who are referred by current members, are exposed to the first step in the process of driving member loyalty—the positive first impression that they receive prior to joining. This positive impression comes from the referring member vis-à-vis the expected service body + soul calls "fitness." This factor, engrained in the initial phase of the club/member relationship, is the foundation for long-term member satisfaction.

Another important factor in the context of member loyalty is the club's membership agreement. body + soul's goal is to "WOW" its fitness clientele on a daily basis. This factor is also the underlying reason for the club's unique membership structure, one that is based on keeping its members through emotional, rather than contractual, means.

Memberships at body + soul consist of a basic period that then transfers automatically to a monthly cancelling phase. Furthermore, an option exists to freeze the membership for a set period. The current fluctuation rate among all seven of the body + soul clubs is less than 20 percent, which is evidence that few members actually take advantage of this freezing option.

Another factor of note is the fact that sales team members are not referred to as "salespersons." Instead, they are referred to as consultants and product representatives. This approach emphasizes body + soul's desire to implement so-called "soft selling." Potential customers are presented with an authentic offer, without sensing sales pressure.

In conjunction with the exceptional features that exist in its facilities, body + soul's strategy for new member acquisition, as well as the identification of staff as part of the total enterprise, allows the clubs to achieve a closing ratio of 80 to 95 percent. This approach to selling allows the initial journey of its members to be grounded in authenticity, sincerity, and trust—all of which are foundations for a secure relationship in the future, as well as enhanced member retention.

Customer satisfaction is monitored from the outset of a new member's enrollment or induction through "Welcome-Calls." These member calls are not performed centrally. Instead, they are organized and conducted by the staff of each respective club. Why? The member relationship is a personal one, a factor that is particularly true in the initial phase of an individual's membership.

When the desired relationship exists, the staff in the clubs can sense and "feel" the member. When the member establishes a trusting relationship with the club's staff, and when the staff identifies themselves as part of the organization's culture, members perceive a strong sense of loyalty. As such, a sense of partnership exists between the members and the employees of the club.

When the member establishes a trusting relationship with the club's staff, and when the staff identifies themselves as part of the organization's culture, members perceive a strong sense of loyalty.

At body + soul, the role of the trainer and the consultant take on the function of "entertainer," an individual whose task and functions intertwine. This inadvertent redundancy leads to significant member contact, lessens miscommunication and lost information, and establishes the entire team as having their "ear to the customer." Furthermore, the club's fitness offerings include exceptional and unique group-fitness programs that mirror the organization's culture.

While the group X program is always at the forefront of current industry and popular culture trends, it is balanced by a level of professionalism that ensures that those "trendy" programs without a solid foundation are not incorporated. In this instance, a special emphasis is placed on the appeal of the senses. The partnership is always focused on members' needs and desires. It is of course not always possible to fulfill every wish of each individual member. On the other hand, the goal of body + soul is to find a common denominator. As such, "magic moments" are celebrated at regular intervals, and in some cases, spontaneously. These "magic moments" may be small presents given to members or special events that are offered, generally without an additional charge. body + soul has an enduring passion and commitment to bring joy and a rewarding experience to the membership each and every day and hour.

The staff at body + soul practices an all-inclusive principle of member service.

The staff at body + soul practices an all-inclusive principle of member service. For example, a trainer and a customer service representative are available at a "flat rate." Both individuals are always on tap to answer questions for the members concerning the body + soul product. By virtue of this emotionally motivated member contact with staff, it is possible to express individual invitations to friends and acquaintances of our members.

Finally, through the very intensive member contact handled by staff in each of the individual clubs, body + soul empowers its staff to accommodate members who may be experiencing problems continuing their membership at body + soul.

All of the aforementioned are organized in coordination with the individual clubs and the central administration of body + soul. The administrative staff treats the situations of each member individually and offers alternatives to the members who are having problems, such as the transferring a membership or freezing the membership for a period of time, or even releasing the member from the contractual obligation.

Collectively, these steps, in the aggregate, are the basis for the body + soul credo: "The whole is more than the sum of its parts." As such, the approach of the organization leads to a successful retention strategy, which ultimately plays an important role in the overall success of the company. The success experienced by body + soul is reflected in a few key performance indicators, such as its attrition rate or the referral rate. At the end of the day, the entire team at body + soul understands that fitness is a service and a "people business," and that our true success for the company is best measured by a smiling member.

Reflections and Insights on body + soul's Approach to New Member Engagement

- The company is focused on the new member's integration at the time of the sale. Every effort is made to ensure that even during the sales process, the prospective member understands that the club's objective is to provide them with the proper start. The philosophy of having sales staff as consultants, relying on the "soft sale" approach, and not selling by features and price, and instead by the experience, is an excellent strategy for framing their overall retention philosophy.

- The club indicates that its membership agreement is based more on an emotional contract than a legal one. Essentially, this approach, which is clearly communicated to new members, establishes a framework for members that says, "We are here to WOW you, not tie your hands." The freezing option, while a feature of the membership, provides a subtle undertone that indicates the membership is tailored to each individual.
- The new member welcome calls are quite unique, especially since they involve the club's trainers and frontline employees. These welcoming calls let members know that they are more than just a sale, and that the staff really cares about them as new members. Since the research clearly shows that club members value receiving staff attention and recognition, having staff make personal new member calls is a great start.
- The team at body + soul is focused on creating trusting relationships at every stage of the new members' experience, realizing that this emotional bond is the key to retention. The trainers are referred to as entertainers, and are asked to get to know the members, and to make sure that as part of the education process, they also entertain the members. It is interesting to note that the members can access staff for information, coaching, and general guidance without having to pay for personal training (this factor was an important data point brought forth in research concerning what members seek in their club experience). For a new member with a lot of questions, or an individual who is intimidated by the initial club experience, it is nice to know that professional and courteous expertise is available whenever it is needed.
- The owners make note of their celebration of magic moments, which reinforces to the members the special memories that they receive from a particular experience. These celebrations also reinforce to the employees the value that they create when they are able to generate magic moments for the members.

First and Last Impressions Matter

Body Care Health Club

Albany, Australia

Owner/Manager:	*Amber Cekerevac*
Retention %:	*72%*
Average Daily Usage:	*20% of members on weekdays*
	14% of members averaged over entire week

The team at body + soul is focused on creating trusting relationships at every stage of the new members' experience, realizing that this emotional bond is the key to retention.

Body Care Health Club is located in Albany, Australia, a town of 35,000 in Western Australia. Since the club is located in a small market, it has a limited surplus of potential new members. As a result, retaining existing members is a priority. The club focuses on three fundamental elements of retention: offering an induction or enrollment process that engages new members immediately;

rewarding existing members on both a short-term basis and a long-term basis for their participation and loyalty; and not allowing inactive members to hide in the shadows, or as they say in Australia, "remain sleeping dogs."

Body Care believes strongly that retention efforts take precedence, beginning with the first day of an individual's membership. At Body Care, a program is offered called, "Around the Club in 30 Days." This program involves giving each new member a 30-day new member induction card. During the member's first 30 days, each time a member participates in a club-sponsored activity, the staff signs off on the card. At the end of the 30-day period, based on the documented activity, the member receives a special reward. As such, this program has been found to successfully invite members to become more involved in the club at the beginning of their membership, as well as encourage them to try new activities.

As noted previously, rewarding members for their involvement is a second tenant of Body Care's retention efforts. In this regard, one of Body Care's short-term reward programs involves providing group-fitness cards to those members active in group fitness. Each time the member attends a class, their card is stamped. At the end of each month, every member who has completely filled up their card is entered into a random drawing to select a winner. The member whose name is selected receives a special reward. This program is conducted each month and gives every member a chance to win.

On a long-term basis, Body Care rewards its most loyal members (those individuals who have been with the club for at least two years) by giving them the opportunity after two years to purchase a special VIP membership that provides them with special rates on membership and club services. It has been found that once members earn the VIP status, they don't want to lose it. As a consequence, they want to continue with their membership.

The third, and final, aspect of Body Care's retention plan is the fact that it does not allow "sleeping dogs" to lie silent. As such, when members are identified who have not been in the club for a while, they are contacted and scheduled for a complimentary re-induction, program update, or personal training session. Body Care firmly believes that silence should not be ignored. Rather, silence is viewed as a call for assistance.

Body Care believes strongly that retention efforts take precedence, beginning with the first day of an individual's membership.

Reflections and Insights on Body Care

- Body Care clearly understands the relevance of providing each new member with the proper induction into the club life. As such, it has established a system that encourages involvement during the first 30 days of the new member's experience. Rather than just provide a single induction session or even multiple sessions, Body Care encourages members to experiment with numerous activities and then rewards them for doing so. "Around the Club in 30 Days" also gives members and employees a chance to interact immediately, which helps to establish some initial bonds between the staff and the new member.

- The club's approach to rewarding group-exercise participation every month is also a viable means for promoting involvement, especially in the case of new members who typically are not familiar with the club's offerings. The combination of rewarding participation, while also requiring that the members get staff to sign-off on their program cards, encourages a higher level of member-to-staff interaction. The issuance of rewards on a monthly basis through a raffle of those individuals who have successfully completed the card also creates a sense of fairness and leads to the hope that an individual always has a chance to be rewarded for meeting the activity-level requirements.
- The club's approach to rewarding loyal members encourages these individuals to remain a member longer, thereby enhancing long-term retention, and ultimately future member spend.

First Place Fitness believes in "wowing" its members through great member service and personal recognition.

It Begins With Your Culture and the Initial Engagement

First Place Fitness Club
614 Te Rapa Road
Hamilton, New Zealand

Owner/manager:	*Ryan Johnston*
Retention %:	*61%*
Average daily usage:	*30 visits per member per annum*

First Place Fitness believes in "wowing" its members through great member service and personal recognition. The foundation of its "wow" culture begins by making sure that each member is called by name whenever that individual visits the club, as well as that staff remembers do the little things that are important to each member, such as what did the member do the previous weekend, the names of the member's kids, what the member's favorite hobbies are, etc. Its relentless focus on knowing the little things about its members, and always calling them by name, contributes to helping First Place Fitness wow its members.

First Place
FITNESS CLUB
24 HOUR GYM

Another key aspect of First Place Fitness' retention efforts encompasses the induction or initial engagement of new members. This process involves several steps. The first measure is its "kick start" program, which entails getting each new member connected to a small group of two to five other new members. Kick-start is a social engagement process that is designed to help ensure that new members get connected immediately. In another facet of the process, each new member at First Place Fitness receives a complimentary personal training session. Another step that First Place Fitness undertakes is to actively enroll each new member on its Facebook site as a fan. First Place Fitness uses its Facebook site to post weekly video updates about the club, as well as post recipes, special membership deals, etc. Facebook is viewed as another way to engage its members, even when they are not physically in the club. Finally, all new members are provided with an induction card that rewards them for their efforts during the first three weeks of their membership. For example, if during their first three weeks as a member they engage in the "kick-start" program, they receive a complimentary 30-minute personal training session, as noted previously. Furthermore, if they attend three group-exercise classes, bring a friend to work out, and enroll as a fan on Facebook, then they receive yet another special prize.

As part of its "wow" culture, First Place Fitness believes that it is essential that company personnel remain in contact with members, and especially with its new members. As such, a concerted effort is made to reach out to each member two weeks after they join, six weeks after they join, three months after they join, six months after they join, and finally at the twelve-month mark. These contacts are designed around each member's preference and include text messages, phone calls, emails, and handwritten postcards. It has been found that members respond most favorably to the handwritten postcards.

Recently, First Place Fitness has taken its retention efforts one step further by developing a 12-month activity plan, which features a different member activity each month (e.g., Friday night drinks, fun run, members vs. staff sports day, cooking classes, etc.). The underlying premise of this particular undertaking is that by offering a different activity each month, members will have more reason to visit the club.

As part of this 12-month activity plan, radical fitness classes, a form of group training, have been implemented. First Place Fitness believes that group training is important to increasing retention. While it is somewhat too early to reach absolute conclusions about the plan, First Place Fitness has experienced its best group-exercise numbers since implementing the program, with participation increasing by 50 percent over previous months.

Reflections and Insights on First Place Fitness

- The ownership of First Place Fitness understands that it all begins with the internal culture of the club. In this instance, First Place Fitness has established a culture that promotes personal attention, learning about the needs and interests of their members, exceeding member expectations, and finally, attention to the personal details. Its "wow" culture sets the tone for everything it does.
- The "kick-start" program is exceptional. Ownership understands that the first few days, weeks, and months of an individual's membership are critical and that for members to establish a connection, a need exists to go beyond the physical. Its unique approach to bringing small groups of members together in a social setting is spot-on. Research shows that one of the barriers for new members getting and remaining involved in their club revolves around the relationships that they are able to establish. The kick-start program addresses that issue.
- Ownership sees the induction process as a combination of social and physical engagement. As a result, not only does First Place Fitness provide personal training at the start, encourage group-exercise participation, and establish the "kick-start" social connection, they also reach out to new

As part of its "wow" culture, First Place Fitness believes that it is essential that company personnel remain in contact with members, and especially with its new members.

members by "friending" them on Facebook. What they are doing is making sure the new member is instantly connected to other members, via a small personal group in the club, as well as a larger family on Facebook. The use of Facebook as part of the induction process also ensures that new members receive information about the club, updates on new programs, and testimonials from other members. Previous chapters of the book discussed how important it is for members to have confidence in how they use the club, and how important it is for new members to have a sense of "fitting-in" with other members. The touch of providing a reward for completing the "kick-start" program adds an element of recognition and support to the entire process. In fact, it appears that the club's induction process addresses all of the critical factors that research indicates are important to engaging new members.

- Staying in contact seems to be yet another invaluable aspect of First Place Fitness' approach to induction. Every reasonable effort is made to make sure to remain in regular contact with members via numerous communication pathways. The club's approach to using various media to stay in touch with members and to make sure that the members are engaged is a viable signal to the members that the staff is concerned for them.

Both Body Express and Healthy Inspirations believe that it is critical to communicate to prospective members, as well as members themselves, realistic expectations concerning what they can or cannot achieve as a result of joining the club.

Establishing Realistic Expectations Can Prevent Drop-out

Body Express
Bondi Beach, Sydney, Australia
27 Healthy Inspiration Clubs
Owner & managing director: Jamie Hayes
Australia and New Zealand

Average membership size:	*700 members at Body Express*
	230 members at Healthy Inspirations
Average retention %:	*72%*
Average club usage:	*1.5 visits per week*

Body Express of Sydney and Healthy Inspirations of Australia and New Zealand are both operated under a similar retention philosophy. The approach of these facilities to retention is founded in the belief that attrition is frequently the result of members having unrealistic and unachievable expectations about what exercise can produce. As such, when those expectations are not achieved, frustration and disappointment set in and dropout occurs.

Both Body Express and Healthy Inspirations believe that it is critical to communicate to prospective members, as well as members themselves, realistic expectations concerning what they can or cannot achieve as a result of joining the club. Furthermore, these two companies try to help members manage their expectations in an effort to avoiding having disillusionment occur if those expectations are not achieved. It should be noted that by helping their members understand what realistic expectations are, and then managing those expectations, Body Express and Healthy Inspirations often find themselves in a position where they actually exceed the expectations of their members.

Among the actions that Body Express and Healthy Inspirations take to combat attrition through their philosophy of expectation management are the following:

- Provide each prospective member with a thorough needs analysis as part of the sales process. The goal of analysis is to help each prospect identify their deep emotional reasons for change.
- Assist the efforts of each member to manage their weight-loss expectations (e.g., best weight in the last 10 years and realistic rate of weight loss).
- Provide a first-day introduction of the new member to the staff at the club. This step is undertaken to help establish a foundation for a trusting relationship with the staff.
- Encourage the new member to nominate family and friends to receive educationally based weight-loss support. The underlying premise is that when a member can take the journey alongside someone they know, success is far more likely.
- Make it a habit to have frequent face-to-face, one-on-one diet coaching sessions.
- Offer small-group educational meetings that combine education, entertainment, and social support.
- Make "care" phone calls to any member who does not come in for coaching by Tuesday of the following week.
- Segment each member's weight loss goals into manageable portions, consisting of five pieces—each representing 20 percent of the overall target.
- Provide regular recognition for the achievement of both outcome and process goals through various methods.
- Offer a declining fee structure, in which the member's dues decline as they lose weight.
- Encourage each member to be involved in optional small-group fitness programs or personal training.
- Publish a monthly weight loss e-newsletter.
- Offer four optional six- to eight-week, small-group exercise motivation challenges per year, which provide members with additional social support and incentive toward reaching their expectations.
- Design and implement a comprehensive local Facebook strategy for each franchisee that is designed to help increase member engagement.

The initial step that Body Express and Healthy Inspirations take to help members is to identify realistic goals for their club experience.

While their clubs are not typical in the sense that they are primarily clubs that are aligned with helping members lose weight, the principles that underlie the programs and efforts of Body Express and Healthy Inspirations are equally applicable in any environment in which a member is interested in achieving a personal expectation.

Reflections and Insights on Body Express and Healthy Inspirations

- The initial step that Body Express and Healthy Inspirations take to help members is to identify realistic goals for their club experience. By assisting their members to understand what realistic goals are, they are helping to remove one of the biggest obstacles to success, which is the failure to achieve a specific goal. By helping their members to be aware of what is achievable and realistic and then assisting them in managing those expectations, the club staff creates a framework that will make it easier for the member to experience success.

- Club management makes sure that every interaction is personal, thereby helping to ensure that the members feel the club cares about them. This personal approach is something the research indicates is extremely important.
- The engagement process of both companies involves an introduction of the staff to the members. This simple step represents a huge leap in fostering a positive member and staff relationship, a factor that the research states is critical in the retention equation.
- Management makes sure that recognition and reward are an integral part of the initial induction process. By providing a reward system that is tied to both the process and outcomes, members are more likely to remain engaged for the long run.
- The club also provides a combination of both social engagement and competitive engagement, which demonstrates flexibility in their approach to providing a rewarding environment for different types of personalities.

New Member Engagement Strategies

A number of strategies can be employed to engage new members. In that regard, research and anecdotal evidence suggest that the following eight examples can be very helpful:

- *Explore the past, present, and future of the members.*

  Clubs need to know about their new members, for example, what their interests are. What their past experience with fitness is? What barriers do they face, such as family or work schedules? What their three-month, six-month, or ultimate goals are?

  If clubs want to be serious about starting new members down the right path to success, then they need to know the aspirations and challenges of their new members. One way is to develop a new-member profiling system that will allow them to gather information about their members so that club staff will be able to orient them properly, and remove any potential barriers that the members may face. Among the key information that this initial new member questionnaire might seek out is the following:

  A number of strategies can be employed to engage new members.

  ✓ What past experience do new members have with sports and exercise? If they are active in sports, what sports do they enjoy and if they have exercised in the past, but don't currently, what exercise programs did they enjoy? If they indicated that they exercised in the past, but don't know, inquire about the general reasons that they stopped working out.

  ✓ What are the goals of the new members? The questionnaire will identify their short-term goals, for example over the next 30 days, and then move on to longer-term goals, such as 90 days, 180 days, and possibly even one year. Knowing these goals can help the club staff (e.g., trainers, instructors, etc.) create a realistic plan for each member. Just as importantly, this information can help staff set up intermediate appointments to check on the progress of the members toward achieving their goals. Another benefit of determining an individual's goals is this information can help the staff educate the member about what constitutes realistic expectations so that the member does not form unrealistic expectations that can ultimately end in failure.

Another benefit of determining an individual's goals is this information can help the staff educate the member about what constitutes realistic expectations so that the member does not form unrealistic expectations that can ultimately end in failure.

- ✓ What barriers or challenges do the new members face? Clubs need to know what the time constraints of members are, how they see fitting the club into their schedule, if they have certain time constraints that are important, if certain times of the day or week exist that works best for them, etc. When clubs can identify those particular challenges, they can actually help tailor the experience of the members around them.
- ✓ What is the preferred mode of communication of the new members? Do they want to be called, texted, emailed, etc.? Furthermore, what level of communication would they find acceptable, such as weekly, monthly, or when they have been absent from the club for a certain period of time?
- ✓ What basic demographic profile, such as gender, generation (Boomer, X or Y), exists for each new member?
- ✓ What are the hobbies and interests of the new members? Do they enjoy gardening, hiking, sports, reading, video game playing, etc.? Are a loner (i.e., like to do things on their own) or are they socially oriented (i.e., prefer to do things in a group setting)? This information helps clubs on at least two fronts. As such, it can assist in identifying the profile of the new members so that their program can be tailored accordingly. The information can also help clubs connect new members to other members who have similar interests.

The appendix section of this book includes three forms that clubs could utilize to help them identify what it is members need. Form B provides a template for a basic member profile that could help staff establish a basic profile of the new member. Form C offers an Aspirations & Barriers profile that allows staff to gain information regarding to what a new member aspires and what challenges and barriers that new member may encounter. Form D provides general guidelines for using the Aspirations & Barriers profile.

Recently, Technogym developed what it refers to as an "Aspiration Map," a tool that allows a club to identify the aspiration profile of a new member. Having a new member complete the profile questions enables a club to map out the individual's portrait according to six different profiles–move, shape, balance, fun, sport, and power. While a simplified tool and not as accurate as the Aspirations & Barriers tool included in the appendix section of this book, it can provide club operators with a distinct advantage in knowing more about their new members and designing the best possible orientation to the club for them.

- *Make a behavioral and emotional contract that holds the new member and club accountable for early success.*

  One of the keys to successful behavior change is establishing behavioral accountability. Many behavioral scientists recommend creating what is called a behavioral contract, an agreement in which the individual signs a contract that indicates what behaviors and outcomes to which the person agrees. Concurrently, the organization's representative countersigns the agreement, indicating what behaviors and outcomes to which the organization will agree. All factors considered, when a contract is signed, in which the parties agree to certain goals and actions, it increases the likelihood that both parties will take accountability for their actions. The result is usually a higher likelihood of success in changing the behavior. Form A in the appendix section of this book contains a sample behavioral contract.

  Establishing behavioral contracts has been a strategy that has been employed in fitness programs over the last few decades. The question arises concerning why not take it to another level and create a behavioral contract with each new member, as well as establish a dual level of accountability? As such, a new member behavioral agreement might include the following aspects:

  ✓ Identify specific outcome goals for the first 90-days (this period seems to be crucial for new member engagement). For example, how much weight loss, how many beats per minutes should the resting heart rate be lower, etc.? The agreement could also have as an outcome goal the total number of visits in a given period.

  ✓ Identify specific behaviors or actions (process goals) by which the new member and club will abide. For the member, this factor could involve visiting the club three times a week, participate in one personal training session each week, take a fitness assessment, participate in two group-exercise classes, etc. For the club, their actions could include providing a certain number of orientation or training sessions during the first month, introducing the member to at least five other members, calling the member at the end of each month to check-up, etc.

  ✓ Create a reward for the new member, based on the person's achievement of both process goals and outcome goals. As such, rewards need to be tied to both types of goals. These rewards can be as simple as a 10 percent off coupon on a club service to an extra month's free membership.

  ✓ Have both the member and the staff sign the agreement. The new member should get a copy, while the club should keep a copy, of the agreement.

  ✓ Provide a means to monitor the terms of the agreement.

  ✓ Recognize the members when they achieve the terms of the agreement.

One of the keys to successful behavior change is establishing behavioral accountability.

Form A in the appendix section of this book provides an example of a behavioral contract.

Research from the FIA has shown that one of the keys to driving retention is for members to use the club at least four times in the first month.

- *Stage a play of several acts for the new member club orientation.*

  Research from the FIA has shown that one of the keys to driving retention is for members to use the club at least four times in the first month. Research also indicates that a four-part induction process, consisting of weekly sessions during the first four weeks of membership, is far more effective at driving participation and retention than a single induction session. Accordingly, one possible approach to helping new members create a connection at the start of their membership is to offer a club-orientation process that involves at least four sessions during the initial four weeks of membership. The orientation process can be undertaken on an individualized basis or group basis, much of which depends on the club's policies and the profile of the member. In this regard, the following suggestions could be incorporated into the process:

  ✓ Create a four-stage individualized orientation program that involves a series of scheduled appointments over the first four weeks of the person's membership. Ideally, the program should consist of one session each week. These sessions do not all need to be of the same duration. In reality, they could successively get shorter each week. For example, the first session could be 60 minutes, the second 30 minutes, and the final two could last 15 minutes each.

  ✓ Establish a series of group-orientation classes, each with a different focus. A club might create a new member-orientation package that encompasses four separate group sessions, each with a slightly different focus (e.g., exercise prescription and training, nutrition, group exercise, racquetball session, massage, etc.). It could be very helpful to offer these classes at several times during the week so that new members could register for class times that were convenient for them. Even better, the club could register the new members when they join the facility. Given the current technology, clubs could even create a special page on their website or develop a new member Android or iPhone application just for new members where they could register for the orientation classes.

  ✓ Individualize the orientation process. Whether clubs offer individual-orientation sessions or group-orientation sessions, they need to make sure that the schedule of these sessions allows sufficient flexibility so that the process can be customized to the needs and interests of each new member.

  ✓ Offer a virtual new-member orientation. If the club doesn't have the staff resources to provide either individual or group orientations, for example, a club could develop a virtual, four-part orientation series that could go on its website, burned to a CD, emailed to new members, or be provided in an application for the Smart phone of new members. If the new member is both tech-savvy (millennial generation) and time pressured, this option can be an excellent solution.

  ✓ Think about incorporating a social element into the orientation. As reflected in one of the club stories discussed previously in this chapter, providing a forum for social connection can be an important element of the induction process.

At ClubCorp, the orientation or induction process was entitled "Right Start." In this program, the company developed different systems to accommodate the diverse array of interests and goals of the members. For those members whose primary interest was fitness, the program was called Fit Quest, an undertaking that involved an entire sequence of actions, including pre-activity screening, fitness assessment, multiple orientation sessions, new-member profile, and special events. If tennis was the primary interest of the member, the plan was to employ the Tennis Quick Start program, a venture that involved a combination of social activities, player ratings, and league activities.

- *Offer cookies and ice cream.*

  When growing up, the mothers of many children would offer their offspring either ice cream or cookies when their kids had done something good, or had completed a task without having to be pushed. While clubs don't want to offer their members cookies and ice cream (frankly, it's a situation that is not befitting the health/fitness club industry), a page can be taken from this particular act of generosity. For example, facilities could provide their members with special incentives or rewards for a job well done, especially during an individual's first 90 days of membership (Body Care and First Place Fitness, both discussed previously in this chapter, provide such reward programs). As such, in order to encourage members to use the club during the first 90 days of joining the facility, clubs should consider offering targeted rewards, for example:

  ✓ Establish specific parameters for the rewards and tie them to new member usage and success. For example, a reward could be given to new members for visiting the club at least four times, another for between four times and eight times, and another level for more than eight visits during the first month. Similar levels could also be established for participation in the first 90 days.

  ✓ Award points for trying different club activities during the first 90 days (an effort that rewards behavior that extends beyond just visiting). For example, a new member could be given a certain number of points for using only one activity, but more points if that individual took a yoga class and used weights, or even more points if that person participated in three club activities (e.g., engage in yoga, eat a meal, take a massage). The goal is to create not only usage, but program crossover, an effort that can help establish a greater bond between the club and member.

  ✓ Be creative in establishing the award to be given out. For example, the rewards could take a variety of formats, such as club-based coupons and certificates, discounts on services, a complimentary locker rental for a month, guest passes that the member could give to friends, coupons for community-based services, etc. Some urban market clubs have attempted to make the awards even more relevant to their circumstances, giving out rewards, such as a mass transit passes for a month, a parking spot for a week, tickets to a theatre, etc.

In order to encourage members to use the club during the first 90 days of joining the facility, clubs should consider offering targeted rewards.

- *Create a welcoming committee that meets and greets.*

  Member retention is all about relationships. As the research highlighted in this book establishes, social ambiance, fitting in, and establishing relationships are all important factors in retention, especially for the new member. As such, a logical option, in this regard, would be to create a committee of loyal members who contact new members and invite them to club activities.

Member retention is all about relationships.

  At ClubCorp, the company utilizes welcome committees composed of loyal members. For example, if a new member were a tennis player, a member of the tennis committee at ClubCorp would call and invite the individual to participate in a league or to join them for a game with other members. Frankly, it is amazing how effective this step can be in introducing new members to the various offerings of the club, and more importantly, immediately connecting them to other members. ClubCorp has found that this program creates an immediate sense of belonging for the new member. Among the steps that can facilitate this approach are the following:

  ✓ Create an informal committee or ambassador group, comprised of loyal club members. Ideally, a group of 12 to 20 individuals works best. The sole role of the committee is to serve as ambassadors and greeters for new members.

  ✓ Provide committee members with a list of all the new members at the end of every week. This list should include a very brief description of the core interests of each new member. If the committee is well organized, the members of the committee could assume responsibility for a particular area of interest. As such, committee members could personally become the ambassador for new members with a particular interest. For example, if two members on the committee are yoga enthusiasts, they could call any new members who express an interest in yoga or mind-body.

  ✓ Employ a variety of communication tools, for example, phone, text, email, or even written correspondence. The goal of this initial contact should include welcoming new members to the club, letting them know what resources are available to them, inviting them to a special event or activity, and letting them know that if they have questions, a possible point of contact.

  ✓ Have the welcoming committee, along with the club staff, serve as hosts for new-member events, such as new-member welcome parties, special new-member classes, etc.

- *Establish a calendar of events just for new members.*

  Research suggests that new members are often bewildered and intimidated when they first become a club member. One approach to assisting new members in overcoming these initial hurdles to involvement in the club is to schedule a series of special classes, seminars, and parties each month. The underlying premise is to introduce new members to what the club has to offer, including initiating relationships with the staff and members.

Among the steps that can help facilitate this approach are the following:

✓ Have new-member welcome parties each month and personally invite new members to attend. Even if information about the party is noted on new member and existing club calendars, nothing is more effective than a personal invitation to make it special.

✓ Designate certain group-exercise classes for new members. While these activities don't have to be limited to the new members, they should be classes taught by one of the club's most outgoing instructors and tailored to first-time users. At Virgin Active in the U.K and body + soul in Munich, Germany, the classes that are best suited for new members are noted on the group-exercise calendars of these facilities.

✓ Establish special small-group personal training sessions at various times during the week and designate these classes for new members.

✓ If the club offers racquet sports (e.g., racquetball, squash, or tennis), consider having new-member mixer events or league activities just for new members.

✓ Create a special new-member event calendar that appears on the club's website and Facebook page.

- *Send the new member a welcome letter from the leader.*

  Nothing is like extending the "personal touch" when establishing the foundation for a new relationship. In fact, a number of clubs have a system in place in which the general manager of the facility contacts each new member. In some instances, the manager of the facility actually phones new members and welcomes them personally, typically inviting them to a special event for new members. In other clubs, instead of a phone call, the general manger sends a letter, either by email or hard copy. As such, a call, email, or letter from the general manager can make new members feel highly valued. At some clubs, as part of the manager's welcome, the effort involves extending a special gift to the new member, such as a coupon that can be used toward a club service, a free T-shirt, or some other relatively not-too-costly item.

- *Think buddies and mentors.*

  Research points out that members value a trusting relationship with staff, including knowing that the staff will be attentive to their needs and that the staff is qualified to assist them. Research also shows that members often indicated that their primary reasons for leaving the club involved staff-related issues. As such, one approach that clubs can take to proactively deal with these issues is to establish an early bond between the club staff and new members. In this regard, one viable strategy would be to have employees act as ambassadors or mentors for new members. For example, when a member first joins, the club would assign a staff ambassador to each of the new members. The roles of these ambassadors could include the following steps:

  ✓ Contact the new member immediately after the individual has joined the club and introduce themselves. Under ideal circumstances, the club would make sure that the ambassador was introduced to the new member at the time that the new member had their first appointment.

Nothing is like extending the "personal touch" when establishing the foundation for a new relationship.

It is very important that new members are aware of the fact that a staff person is there to assist them if needed.

- ✓ Serve as a resource for new members by making sure that they receive an orientation and are introduced to the various activities offered by the club. Introduce new members to existing members, especially those individuals with similar interests or workout times.
- ✓ Coach new members during their first 90 days of membership. This factor might include regular monthly appointments to monitor the progress of the new member or regular email exchanges to see how things are going.
- ✓ Participate in a club activity with the new member (e.g., yoga, tennis, Pilates, etc.) so that the individual feels less intimidated.
- ✓ Check behind the scenes to see how frequently the member visits each of the first three months and then contact the new member if the attendance of the new member drops off.

While the buddies-and-mentors type of system can be very informal, it is very important that new members are aware of the fact that a staff person is there to assist them if needed.

10

Getting Members Involved in the Club Life

Industry-driven research shows that member participation, or member usage as it is often referred to, is highly correlated to membership retention, with retention levels increasing when member participation in the club goes up. The available data indicates that the minimal dose of monthly activity for connecting members to the club life is at least four times. In fact, in order to have a significant impact on retention and loyalty, members need to use their club at least eight times each month.

Gender differences and generational differences have also been found in how people use clubs and the results that they expect to obtain. In fact, if clubs want to drive participation, they need to understand these individual nuances of motivation and participation, and then find ways to leverage them in getting members involved and using the club. As discussed previously, member involvement is closely tied to member satisfaction—particularly to the Net Promoters Score that is an indicator of member loyalty. When member loyalty rises, participation levels of the members tend to increase. In turn, retention improves. This chapter shares, discusses, and dissects stories from actual clubs, as well as details several valuable strategies that club operators from around the globe have found beneficial in helping them get and keep members involved in club life.

Gender differences and generational differences have also been found in how people use clubs and the results that they expect to obtain.

Real Stories About Member Involvement in the Club Life

A Home Away From Home
Oase Health & Sports Club
Bochum, Germany

General Manager:	*Vincent C. Bradley (28 years at the helm)*
Retention in 2010:	*83%*
Average dues:	*68 euros for an individual and 200 euros for a family*

Oase Health & Sports Club, Bochum, Germany

Relaxation area, Oase Health & Sports Club, Bochum, Germany

Oase Health & Sports Club, Bochum, Germany

Badminton courts, Oase Health & Sports Club, Bochum, Germany

After more than three decades of operations, the success of the Oase Health & Sports Club can be attributed to a number of reasons. One factor why the club has been so successful in reaching and keeping its members happy lies in the club's philosophy and policy of being the "second home" or "home away from home" for its members. That policy, and more importantly the club's promise to its members, is to establish a club environment that reminds them of being at home.

Oase's ultimate goal is that when members think of not being at home, they think of coming to Oase. Being part of city and community life for so long, Oase has established a reputation as the place to go in the community for individuals who are seeking either to lead an active lifestyle or to socialize with nice people in a great environment.

With the average age among members of 47 years, it is not unusual to have three generations of the same family in Oase at the same time. For example, a grandfather discusses the world with his friends in the Oase café, his daughter works out with friends in the facility's group-exercise studio, and her baby boy is being cared for in the Crèche. Engaging in an active life is an ageless pastime that knows no generational boundaries, a principle that serves all members of Oase well.

Engaging in an active life is an ageless pastime that knows no generational boundaries, a principle that serves all members of Oase well.

Oase undertakes a number of steps to reinforce the home-away-from-home environment. For example, its willingness to reinvest, rejuvenate, and upgrade the facilities to a standard that members expect at home (or higher) helps make its members feel comfortable from the start. In addition, a high level of quality and professionalism is expected from staff, with the result that its members are treated to the highest level of professionalism every time they visit the club. Oase also prides itself on a high level of staff-member communication. In fact, the resulting interaction among members and staff is an important element of the club's success. The consequence of this focus on staff professionalism and staff-member interactions is a club in which the relationships between members and staff and between members and other members are exceptionally strong.

Oase also operates a school program and a corporate health program that reach out into diverse areas of the community, some of which are unexpected. Its aim is to support both programs with its know-how so that their pupils and staff can be encouraged to lead a healthier life.

Oase also is actively involved in the community. For example, it has a seat on the Health Development Forum of the Chamber of Commerce. In addition, it has received an award as German Club of the Year. It is also renowned for its adherence to high educational quality standards in the health/fitness club industry on a European level. As such, collectively, its members take great pride in its actions.

Oase also makes a concerted effort to understand, care for, and value the lives of its members, their families, and their friends. Its unrelenting passion and commitment to its members build a bond of trust and confidence between Oase, its members, and the community. As a club, it takes great pride in being the "second home" for its members.

Reflections and Insights About Oase's Approach to Creating a Home Away From Home

The philosophy of a "second home" is the essence of all great clubs.

- The philosophy of a "second home" is the essence of all great clubs. As far back as the mid-1800s, clubs, such as Triatt's in Paris, Desbonnet's in Lille, France, and Turnvereins in Germany, understood this "home away from home" philosophy. At the present time, in many of today's country clubs, as well as in a number of the more established member-owned athletic clubs (e.g., New York Athletic Club, Olympic Club, Los Angeles Athletic Club, Multinomah Athletic Club, etc.), the entire facility revolves around creating a "home away from home." In London, England, the Harbour Club is an example of a commercial club that is built around the "home away from home" philosophy.
- Oase carries out its "home away from home" concept by offering facilities, programs, and services that encourage members to feel comfortable when they are at the club. This factor involves providing non-intimidating environments for socializing and participation, as well as offering numerous socially oriented activities, such as badminton and group classes.
- Oase goes one step further by establishing a generational friendly environment so that every generation of the family has something to engage in at the club. The key to success in this regard is providing multiple environments so that the particular interests of each generation can be addressed. It is interesting to note that Oase expands on this concept by making sure that the club's environment and offerings create a cross-pollination of generations, a factor that is typically only seen in a nuclear family.
- Oase is fully aware of the link between staff and members in creating a home-like environment. The club's culture encourages staff not only to know members by name, but also to know intimate details about the members and their families, such as names of their children, their interests, their hobbies, etc. Oase's focus on creating closeness extends across the membership, with the result that members begin to feel as comfortable in the club as they do at home.
- Oase gets involved in the local community by hosting and sponsoring activities about which the local community has a passion. In particular, Oase's "adopt a school" program allows it to have a positive influence on families in the community.
- Oase has built its culture around valuing the life of each member. This core value and mission fosters the home-like environment they provide.

Oase's "second-home" philosophy mirrors that of ClubCorp's founder, Robert Dedman, who frequently shared with the company's 23,000 employees that its clubs were the third most important place for members, coming only after home and office. To ensure that every employee understood the importance of this mission, Robert wrote a poem that was eventually placed in each and every ClubCorps club. Robert's poem, entitled A Club, went as follows:

A Club

"A club is a haven of refuge and accord in a world torn by strife and discord.

A club is a place where kindred spirits gather to have fun and make friends.

A club is a place of courtesy, good breeding, and good manners.

A club is a place expressly for camaraderie, merriment, good will, and good cheer. It humbles the mighty, draws out the timid, and casts out the soreheads.

A club is one of the noblest inventions of mankind."

This poem epitomizes what a club is—a place where people can socialize with friends and never feel intimidated. It could well be argued the underlying premise of this poem is behind every action that Oase takes. In later years, Robert's philosophy was adapted into ClubCorp's existing mission statement, which is "to build relationships and enrich lives."

Where Everyone Knows Your Name
Cambridge Group of Clubs
Cambridge Club, Toronto Athletic Club, Montreal Athletic Club and Adelaide Club
Montreal and Toronto, Canada
President: Clive Caldwell

The Cambridge Group of Clubs is a network of four clubs that are based in Montreal and Toronto, Canada. The network includes one of Canada's most prestigious clubs, the Montreal Club Sportif MAA, which was originally founded in 1881. At the Cambridge Group of Clubs, its membership retention efforts revolve around three core fundamentals—properly introducing new members to its clubs, providing a socially supportive and interactive club environment, and focusing on the development of member relationships.

Category	Adelaide Club	Cambridge Club	Montreal Athletic Club	Toronto Athletic Club
Members	3,700	1,400	2,700	2,400
Retention %	71%	82%	62%	81%
Approximate % members who participate daily	30%	29%	35%	29%
Monthly dues range (individual)	$79 - $99	$129 - $189	$90 - $125	$125 - $175

When a prospect makes the decision to join one of its four clubs, the first step that is taken, after the membership application is completed, is to have a professional staff member take the new member through an extensive discovery-and-welcoming process. This discovery-and-welcoming process begins with an interview, in which the staff member seeks to understand what the new member's personal interests and goals are, what their current level of fitness is, and finally, identifying what support and assistance they will need to be successful. Once this initial interview process is completed, a thorough orientation process is undertaken that includes introducing the new member to key staff and existing members, each of whom can provide assistance and support to the new member as the individual embarks on the club journey. The primary focus throughout this introduction is to demonstrate genuine care and concern. As such, whatever time is needed is taken to make sure that the new member feels welcome in the club.

Another key element behind the retention success of the Cambridge Group of Clubs is based on the company's approach to creating an engaging physical environment that promotes social interaction between the members.

Another key element behind the retention success of the Cambridge Group of Clubs is based on the company's approach to creating an engaging physical environment that promotes social interaction between the members. In that regard, the club's social stages (casual lounges, food and beverage areas, etc.) are fundamental to bringing members together in a non-intimidating atmosphere. When members are able to engage with each other in a non-intimidating physical environment, the development of personal relationships is promoted. This element moves a Cambridge Group of Clubs' facility from being a gym to being more of a club. As a consequence, its members develop an emotional tie to their clubs.

Yet another underlying focus of the Cambridge group of Clubs is to encourage its staff to be matchmakers of sorts. In that regard, an essential element of everyone's job is to introduce members to each other, as well as to staff. The organization preaches that it is the responsibility of every employee to make sure that no member ever goes without a welcome and greeting, nor do they ever go without being introduced to another member of staff person. This attitude is a further effort on its part to bond members to each other and eventually to the club.

Reflections and Insights About the Cambridge Group of Clubs

- The Cambridge Group of Clubs, like many of the other clubs and club companies highlighted in this book, is fully aware of the fact that first impressions matter, especially when it comes to how a new member is initially enrolled in the club life. Similar to many of the great clubs, the Cambridge Club Group seeks to understand the underlying emotional and behavioural context of what will connect the new member to the club. In addition, they go one step further and make sure that new members are immediately introduced to existing members and staff, and in particular, to other members and staff who have interests that are similar to those of the new member. This sense of urgency behind creating immediate bonds between members is unique. As such, it is quite likely that is a key factor in creating an environment of which members want to be a part.

- The Cambridge Group of Clubs defines a club as more than just a place to exercise. It believes that it is also a place that offers great social ambience. This focus on creating an inviting and non-intimidating social ambiance allows members to "socially connect" without fear. While most operators might see a lounge as a waste of exercise space, the Cambridge Club sees it as glue that can help connect members with each other. To most operators, food and beverage are a nightmare, or at best a source of incremental revenue. At the Cambridge Group of Clubs, food and beverage are critical drivers of member relationships and social connectivity. It is interesting to note that because their food and beverage concept is socially driven, it manages to generate significant incremental revenue.
- The employees at the Cambridge Group of Clubs have a role that goes far beyond the mere performance of basic job duties, such as answering phones, providing exercise instruction, serving food, selling memberships, etc. rather, staff at the Cambridge Group of Clubs have a higher calling so to speak, which is simply to make sure that everyone knows everyone else. It could be argued that employees are asked to serve as hosts and hostesses, which means that they are present to make sure that no member is a stranger.

Using Statistics to Forecast Member Retention Behavior in Clubs
Bodytech Clubs
Bogota, Colombia
Executive Vice-President: Gigliola Aycardi
Average dues: $70 U.S. monthly
Retention rate: 52%

Bodytech is the largest health club chain in Latin America, with 40 sites in Colombia, as well as five additional locations in Peru. Recently, it announced a merger with the Chilean chain SportLife, which adds 37 more clubs to the organization.

For over 50 years, statistics have been used in the financial sector to predict the future behavior of customers and prospects. So much so, that this particular forecasting tool can estimate the probability of a lead or prospect becoming a good customer. Forecasting can help companies to make decisions, even with regard to approving or rejecting clients. For example, tools can predict payment manner, service consumption, attrition rate, employee performance, and related behavior (useful information in call centers and companies with high turnover). In fact, a methodology that is widely employed in the financial sector, telecommunications, and insurance, can also be used in fitness and sports clubs.

Forecasting can help companies to make decisions, even with regard to approving or rejecting clients.

As such, Bodytech has developed an instrument that uses the knowledge that it obtains about its members to predict their future behavior, especially as it pertains to detecting the possibility of membership cancelations and the development of proactive retention strategies. At Bodytech, the history and features of each member's defined parameters of behavior are collected. By initially collecting the appropriate data, and then analyzing it, Bodytech is able to obtain a complete profile of the members that reveals which clients may not use the club's services. In turn, this information can help identify which members are most likely to not be a person who actively uses the club.

Statistical tools allow each fitness center to recognize the member's behavior and to reply in a preventive way with better service, thereby avoiding member dissatisfaction and the end of the club's relationship with a particular individual.

Several demographic and behavioral parameters can help guide the attrition rate of sports club members, including the following:

- The socio-demographic information of members (age, marital status, gender, etc.)
- Members' use of complementary club services
- The existence of member requests, complains and claims (RCC), and their resolution
- Trends in how a member uses club services or assistance (permanence times, schedules, etc.)
- The motivations of members for using the club
- The profile of the headquarters of use, among others

The Value of the Forecasting Instruments for Members

The members who express concern are expecting the club to understand them, hear them, and respond to their complaints. Statistical tools allow each fitness center to recognize the member's behavior and to reply in a preventive way with better service, thereby avoiding member dissatisfaction and the end of the club's relationship with a particular individual.

The Impact of Using Forecasting Instruments by Bodytech

Statistical tools enable fitness centers to focus their retention campaigns on members with the highest probability of dropping out. These statistical measures also afford the club an opportunity to remove resources from reactive campaigns and funnel them into proactive ones (before the member exhibits a desire to stop using the club), which will help generate customer loyalty.

Bodytech collects information on the members starting with the day they join, and continues to do so throughout their tenure as a member, a step it hopes to prolong indefinitely through the use of its statistical tools. Figures 10-1 to 10-3 provide a simple visual representation of Bodytech's process. Figure 10-1 depicts the impact of perceived customer value on the probability of an individual dropping their club membership. The matrix illustrated in Figures 10-2 and 10-3 enables the club to segment the population in order to define strategies, actions, and ongoing feedback.

Impact (customer value)				
Probability of dropping out		High	Medium	Low
	High			
	Medium			
	Low			

Figure 10-1. The impact of perceived customer value on the probability of an individual dropping their club membership

Segment	Strategy	Action	Monitoring Results
	Proactive retention priority 1	How?	Measurement reports (segments, strategies and actions) and feedback
	Proactive retention priority 2	When?	
	Loyalty	Who?	

Figure 10-2. Segmenting the membership of the club in order to define strategies, actions, and ongoing feedback

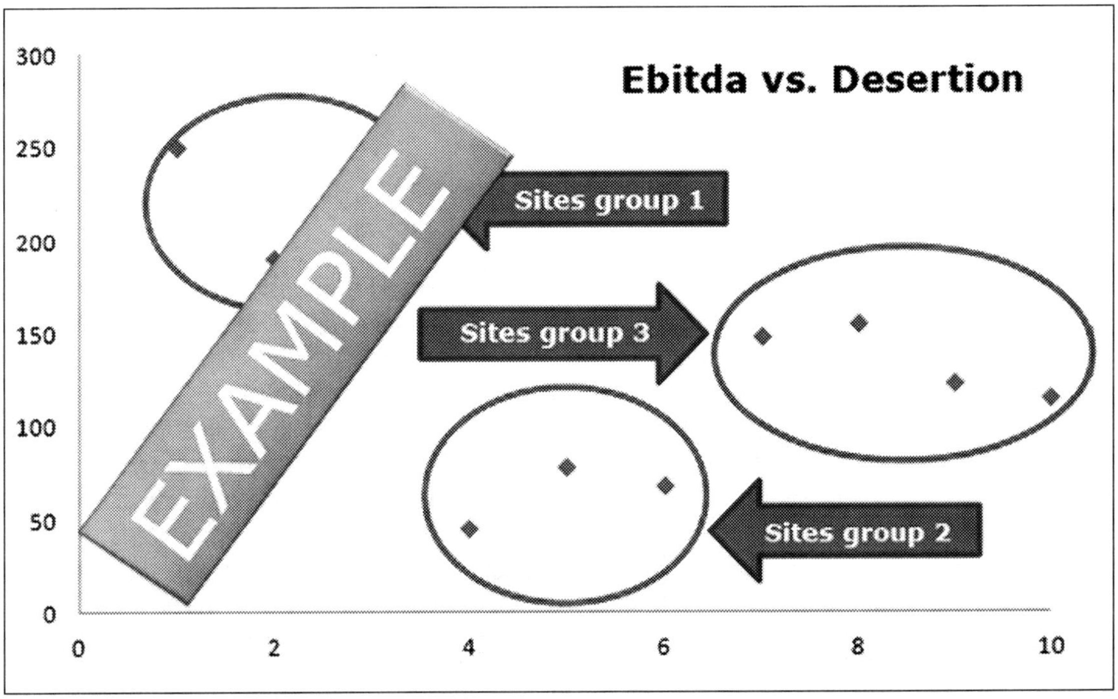

Figure 10-3. EBITDA vs. desertion

With this knowledge, Bodytech has been able to make more informed decisions concerning retention that collectively have had a positive impact on its finances. In terms of profitability and EBITDA, this tool helps Bodytech to invest time and resources in each client in accordance with their probability of dropping out.

Research shows that member loyalty and retention are driven by an emotional engagement.

Bodytech continues to develop new statistical tools in order to strengthen relations with its members. Understanding its members helps Bodytech to develop a more effective connection with them, so that their experience in the clubs consistently exceeds their expectations. The Bodytech promise of value is to delight each and every customer.

Reflections and Insights on Bodytech's Approach to Retention

The owners and management of Bodytech realize that in order to change people's behaviors, they first need to understand what influences those behaviors. The approach that the company has taken provides a means to record, as well as analyze, both the characteristics of each member and the behaviors that they exhibit. By using this data, Bodytech has been able to create a probability matrix that allows them to focus their efforts on those members whose characteristics and behaviors indicate that they are the most likely to resign their membership in the club. By identifying these individuals, as well as their characteristics and behaviors, the club can not only focus on implementing strategies to recover them, they can also create long-term proactive strategies that address similar members going forward.

Research shows that member loyalty and retention are driven by an emotional engagement. What Bodytech has realized is that through the collection and analysis of date, based on measurable characteristics and behaviors, they can ultimately influence each member's emotional attachment with the club. It is a merger of the right and left brains, a blending of science with emotion, the outcome being that they are able to more fully engage their members in the club experience.

Strategies for Getting Members Involved

- *Think clans and niches.*

  According to market research, the world's population has become a community of clans and tribes, otherwise defined as sub-populations or special-interest groups. This trend exists within the populations of health/fitness clubs and can be a powerful influence in driving member participation. For example, at World Class in Russia, a dance studio has been established that offers a membership within a membership for members of all its clubs in Moscow. The primary objective is to provide a niche experience for those members who enjoy sport (e.g., ballroom) dancing. As World Class discovered, and later leveraged with its dance studio, and in its other internal interest clubs, such as the combat club, when a club offers programs or services for special interests, overall member participation and profitability is actually increased. The key point is that clubs that want to increase member participation and involvement should consider serving special interest groups or tribes. Among the suggested steps that could facilitate this undertaking are the following:

✓ Create clubs within a club. These entities should be special groups whose interests lie within one area. At the present time, many club operators currently have begun to leverage this concept of clubs within a club by establishing special member groups in specific areas, such as yoga, Pilates, group exercise, swimming, jogging, biking, tennis, golf, etc.

✓ Organize special activities inside and outside the club for special interest groups. For example, monthly events could be offered for special interest groups, such as having a team to run a local 5K race (Fitness First in the U.K. has each of its clubs put together a team to participate in a special London-based charity run through the city). Other clubs host three-day ski trips with training, one-week adventure outings, and a "green club" for members who want to assist the local community in going green. For example, at World Class in Russia, fitness tours are offered that are essentially special, one-week trips that are targeted to the specific interests of members, such as Nordic walking, biking, skiing, etc. At the Atrium Club in New York back in the mid-1980s, the club created the "A-Team," a group of individuals that was comprised of over 100 members who trained regularly in Central Park and competed as a group in various New York running events.

✓ Make sure that if "clubs within a club" are created, that the members are accountable for the activities and that staff serve more as administrators. Practical evidence suggests that these small interest groups function significantly better when led by the members rather than the staff.

- *Keep your eye on the target; identify and monitor KPIs of participation.*

  If a club is going to change the level of member participation in its facility, it first needs to understand what its participation levels are. Furthermore, once a club knows what its participation levels are, it has to establish specific targets concerning what it wants to achieve. A club also needs to monitor its performance so that it knows whether it is achieving its goals, or falling short of them. In addition, a club has to be prepared to reward outcomes when the club achieves or exceeds member-participation goals. As a result, clubs need to establish and monitor indexes or metrics, often referred to in business as key performance indicators (KPIs), measures that reflect member involvement in the club. In this regard, among the suggested steps that can help facilitate this objective are the following:

Once a club knows what its participation levels are, it has to establish specific targets concerning what it wants to achieve.

✓ Establish a few KPIs that reflect member involvement that can easily be monitored. Since the research is clear about the impact of weekly and monthly usage on retention, it is important to have KPIs that measure member participation on either a weekly or monthly basis. As such, clubs should adhere to the KISS principle (keep it simple stupid) when establishing the KPIs they intend to monitor. Examples of the leading KPIs include:

- ⇨ Percent of total membership using the club daily
- ⇨ Percent of members who use the club at least four times a week
- ⇨ Percent of members who use the club at least eight times a month
- ⇨ Average visits monthly or annually per member

Monitoring KPI performance can be a waste of time unless a club's staff understands how these measures reflect the goals that the company has established.

At the Russian Fitness Group (RFG), based in Moscow, Russia, the company focuses on a few key metrics. For example, the company's primary metric in this regard involves tracking the average percentage of members who use the club daily. A secondary KPI that the company uses involves tracking the percentage of members who use the club less than once, one-to-four times, five-to-eight times, and more than eight times a month. Club One, based in California, employs the "Net Promoter Score" as one of its key metrics for framing its retention goals.

- Track the KPIs on a regular basis, and then communicate the results to all employees. Monitoring KPI performance can be a waste of time unless a club's staff understands how these measures reflect the goals that the company has established. If everyone on the staff knows the goals, and is given clear information on the actual performance outcomes, they will be more likely to try to help the company achieve its desired outcomes. For example, in 2008, The Russian Fitness Group was experiencing average daily member participation levels across clubs equal to12 percent of the membership. Approximately 18 months after establishing its KPI on member participation, accompanied by the appropriate incentives and monitoring, the company was able to bring the average member participation levels to approximately 15 percent, with some clubs achieving member participation levels of 17 to 18 percent. Not surprisingly, these numbers had a positive impact on the company's overall membership retention and renewal rates.
- Have incentives tied to achieving the desired KPIs. Once a club establishes targets for its KPIs, it should make sure to monitor them, and communicate the results throughout the organization. Providing incentives that are tied to achieving the KPIs will further enhance the club's ability to see positive results. At the Russian Fitness Group, senior leaders, club managers, and frontline staff had the ability to earn bonuses if the club and/or the company achieved its desired member-participation KPIs.

- *Honor club members with appreciation days.*

  Research indicates that one of the more important elements in creating customer loyalty, as well as reinforcing behavior change in an audience, is by leveraging recognition and appreciation. One business practice that is currently being seen more frequently in businesses and in particular clubs, is the establishment of customer appreciation days. Of course, in the health/fitness club industry, the preference is to refer to these events as member appreciation days, since most successful club operators believe members are more than just customers. Member appreciation days are specific days that are set aside to recognize members who are involved in the club. Among the suggested steps for creating exceptional member appreciation days are the following:

✓ Determine how frequently these appreciation days should be conducted. Some clubs hold them annually, while others do it as frequently as monthly. Once annually is probably too infrequent, while monthly may be too often, at least for some clubs. All factors considered, appreciation days that are held on either a monthly or quarterly basis seem to provide the greatest return. They also help ensure that a blend of new and existing members is captured.

✓ Keep in mind that appreciation days can take many forms. For example, appreciation days can incorporate one-time pricing specials for that day, bringing in a guest in for free the day, coupons for discounts on club services, complimentary coffee for whomever visits that day, offering a unique specialty class for the day, etc. At the Heart Healthy Fitness Center, a club that operated during the 1990s in Dallas, Texas, the manager had quarterly member appreciation days. One example of what was offered during those member appreciation days was to provide a special treat for members throughout the day. For the members who worked out in the morning, the club offered complimentary juice and bagels; for those individuals who arrived in the afternoon, sandwiches were available; and for the evening crowd, a special food item was provided. At another time, members drew a card from a jar and received whatever was indicated on the card (e.g., 20 percent off a massage, a free beverage, etc.).

✓ Consider another approach to member appreciation days, one that involves throwing an annual member appreciation party, which honors the members for their support throughout the year. At World Class in Russia, they conduct annual club birthday parties that celebrate the anniversary date of the club's opening. Sometimes these parties are held at the club, and other times they are conducted at an outside venue.

- *Let members take ownership; establish member committees.*

The concept of allowing members to take ownership goes back to principles fostered by member-owned clubs. In member-owned clubs, the members actually have an ownership position. As a result, they want to be involved and to contribute to the decision-making that occurs. As a rule, these member-owned clubs tend to have significantly higher retention rates than most commercial clubs. A large part of this situation is due to the feeling of ownership that the members have. Although a commercial club can't afford to give its members an actual ownership position, they can establish systems and practices that can instill a degree of that ownership feeling. At ClubCorp, a Dallas, Texas-based private club and resort company, club leaders are encouraged to form member committees, including a board of governors, membership committees, tennis committees, etc. The boards, as well as the committees, while not actually owning the facility, provide leadership and input to the club, and in doing so, help shape the club experience. Concurrently, the members who serve on these boards and committees feel a sense of ownership and pride in their club, which in turn, has a very positive impact on the club's level of membership retention. Examples of how a fitness club or fitness facility can employ this approach to enhance their level of member involvement include the following:

The concept of allowing members to take ownership goes back to principles fostered by member-owned clubs.

According to research on exercise behavior, providing rewards and recognition for achievement of process and outcome goals can have a positive impact on member loyalty and member retention.

✓ Create committees that revolve around specific areas of interest. For example, a tennis or racquet sport committee could be established, if the club has racquet sports. If a facility has a strong group-exercise audience, it might want to put together a group-exercise committee or a yoga committee. In turn, a club that wanted to establish a stronger following in outside adventures could create an adventure committee. Truth be known, the possibilities are endless, just as long as the club staff is ready to allow members to get involved.

✓ Keep in mind that clubs with successful committee groups do not provide any financial remuneration for the members who participate. Instead, they make sure that members feel a sense of ownership in the process and that the input that they provide is duly considered and acted upon. At the ClubCorp clubs, the members who serve on boards and committees are recognized in several ways, including their involvement is noted in the club newsletter or on its website, they receive a special gift during the holidays, they are being consulted by management when specific issues arise, etc.

✓ Consider holding committee meetings over breakfast or lunch and sponsoring the meals. Members appreciate such gestures. Such an action reinforces the perception that the club cares and values the input and involvement of members.

✓ Remember that committee roles do not have to be complex. Typically, the committee has a chair, who, along with a designated staff person, leads and facilitates the functions and meetings of the committee. Conventionally, the standard responsibilities for committee members tend to involve attending a specific number of meetings annually (usually, two to four), contributing to discussions around the topics brought forth, co-hosting a club event, on occasion, if it is sponsored by a committee, and providing feedback to management on relevant topics related to the role of the committee (e.g., the group-exercise schedule, club rules and policies, equipment needs, etc.).

The key to this premise is to allow members to get involved in activities that impact the overall member experience, and for which their collective involvement and input will benefit the experience that each and every member receives.

• *Reward and recognize involvement and activity.*

A number of industries, including the airline industry (American, Lufthansa, Southwest, United, Singapore Airlines, etc.) and big-box retailers (Best Buy, Office Max, Staples, etc.) offer reward programs for their customers. The underlying principle for these reward programs is to garner a greater share of the business of their customers, based on rewarding them for their loyalty, usage, and spend.

According to research on exercise behavior, providing rewards and recognition for achievement of process and outcome goals can have a positive impact on member loyalty and member retention. As for how rewards and recognition impact these factors, very little data is available to either validate or dispute their use as part of a membership retention program. Nonetheless, several club companies throughout the world offer their members reward and recognition programs.

At World Class, based in Moscow, Russia, the organization offers its members a club bonus program that awards points for both member purchases and member participation in various club activities. Members can accumulate points and use them for a variety of purposes, including reducing the cost to renew their membership, purchase in-club services, etc. Management of the company indicates that the reward program has had a positive impact on member participation in various activities.

At Club One, based in California, an incentive program has been established entitled Club Rewards, which provides members with special discounts on club services, based on a member's level of participation in the club.

At ClubCorp in the 1990s, the company offered a program called Heartbeat, which allowed members to earn points for their participation in various club activities, including working out, receiving a massage, dining in the club, etc. These points could then be traded in for various prizes, including merchandise with the ClubCorps logo on it, in-club discounts, resort vacations, adventure trips, etc. All members were enrolled in the program when they joined the facility. Company research showed that although the program did not provide a significant impact when it came to increasing the participation of the least-active members, it did raise the overall level of activity in the club, as well as, more importantly, the spending level of active members. It did what all well-designed loyalty programs do—it influenced the loyal members of the facility to spend more time and money in the club. Among the suggested steps for facilitating the success achieved by a rewards and recognition program are the following:

✓ Establish a clear set of rules and guidelines for the program. The terms and conditions of the program should be clearly laid out. Because members will hold the club to every word and condition, it is very important that clear guidelines and rules for the program be established.

✓ Determine what member behaviors should be rewarded. At ClubCorp, the objective was to reward member participation in club activities, as well the amount of money members spent in the club.

✓ Determine what the rewards will be. For most clubs, these rewards can be connected to in-house services, such as personal training, massage, beverage purchases, guest passes, etc. The program should not be limited to just club services. As such, a club should consider establishing partner arrangements with retail and service industries in its community. For example, an award might be a dinner for two at a local restaurant or a discount with a local retailer. While the rewards don't have to be highly valuable, they should provide variety.

A club should consider establishing partner arrangements with retail and service industries in its community.

✓ Use other forms of recognition if the club can't afford or doesn't want to spend its money on items that involve an out-of-pocket expenditure. This option could include offerings such as a story in the club newsletter, putting a story and picture on the club's web page, placing the member's picture up in the club in a prominent place, etc.

Clubs should strongly consider the value of providing either an internally generated social media site as part of their internet strategy, or leverage an externally generated site, such as Facebook.

- *Create chat sites for members; establish a member blog.*

  In current high-tech social society, blogs, forums, and chat rooms have become extremely popular. Without question, the general population enjoys having the opportunity to connect and engage in discussion with others through the Internet. Social media sites, such as Facebook, Linked-In, My Space, as well as niche chat rooms and forums (sites dedicated to connecting people with specific interests), have literally changed the way people meet, communicate, interact, share information, and learn.

  In a special report on social media that was released in 2011 by Ray Algar, the managing director of Oxygen Consulting in the United Kingdom, he indicated that social media has evolved into an essential tool for establishing and sustaining an open dialogue with members. Members want a forum to share their thoughts about the club, and also would like to have a viable way to connect with others members who have similar interests as they do.

  Clubs should strongly consider the value of providing either an internally generated social media site as part of their internet strategy, or leverage an externally generated site, such as Facebook. These social media sites should allow the members to communicate with management, as well as with other members. Among the suggested steps in this regard are the following:

  ✓ Form a fitness blog that is written by a qualified member of the staff. This site can offer information on fitness and health, as well as encourage questions from the membership.

  ✓ Offer a social media site where members can sign-in and invite other members. This site can be either externally hosted, such as a Facebook page, or internally hosted. The undertaking can involve offering each member their own page, including a wall for posting pictures. Equinox has a special internally hosted section on its website called My Body. My Life, which allows members to share. Club One leverages the power of Facebook to provide an open forum for its members to communicate with management. For example, First Place Fitness of New Zealand, showcased in the previous chapter, makes effective use of Facebook to get its members involved.

  ✓ Offer a few niche pages that are targeted toward special interest groups. These niche pages should allow members to connect with those individuals, in particular, who have similar interests, an effort that can later carry over to doing activities together inside and outside the club.

  ✓ Make sure to have a page where members can have a two-way dialogue with management. Providing members with open access to management can be an extremely important issue, especially since research shows that unresponsive management is one of the primary reasons that members give for resigning their membership.

The club experience is not just about what happens within the four walls of the club. In today's world, clubs must become an integral part of the life of their members. As such, clubs must find ways to reach outside the four walls of their facility and touch their members on a daily basis.

11

Strategies for Staging Memorable Member Experiences and Delivering Great Member Service

Member retention is highly dependent on member loyalty, which in turn, is highly correlated with a member's overall emotional rating as a "net promoter" of the club. When members become net promoters (i.e., they rate their overall experience with a club as excellent), it reflects the emotional attachment they have made with the people, programs and services of the club (e.g., memorable experiences).

As was discussed in Chapter 8, member loyalty can be assessed by measuring the responses of the members to four queries–their level of love for the club; their rating of the overall club experience (e.g., accumulation of favorable memories); their likelihood of recommending others to the club; and their likelihood of remaining a member of the club. In nearly every instance, members who accord these areas the highest level of response are those individuals who have been the recipients of great member service, and who have fond memories of their club experience.

Member loyalty can be assessed by measuring the responses of the members to four queries–their level of love for the club; their rating of the overall club experience (e.g., accumulation of favorable memories); their likelihood of recommending others to the club; and their likelihood of remaining a member of the club.

Beyond the member loyalty issue are the simple truths that members share in various industry studies when they're asked about what factors affect their club experience. In this instance, a number of leading truths are detailed, including friendly staff, knowledgeable staff, readily available staff, responsive management, socially inviting ambiance, fitting-in and having friends, and having colleagues who are members.

Similar to previous chapters, this chapter also shares, discusses, and breaks down club stories from actual clubs, as well as details several invaluable strategies that club operators from around the globe have found beneficial in helping them stage memorable experiences that win the heart and soul of their members.

Real Stories About Staging Experiences and Delivering Great Service

Exceeding Member Expectations
East Bank Club
Chicago, Illinois

Manager:	Joe Rossie
Individual dues:	$175 per month
Retention %:	79%
Avg. daily usage:	30% to 35% of the member base

The primary business focus of the East Bank Club is to exceed the expectations of the members. This unrelenting focus on exceeding the anticipated outcomes of the members is built on a model that encompasses the following core elements:

- Delivering an extremely high level of service
- Offering an unsurpassed variety of programming, amenities and services
- Providing an engaging club environment that provides members a multitude of ways to interact socially
- Offering a club environment that is energetic and exciting

Eastbank Club, Chicago, IL

Exterior, Eastbank Club, Chicago, IL

Employees—the Key to Great Member Service

Since the East Bank Club opened on December 15, 1980, the club's owners and management have been passionate about delivering exceptional member service. It has a staff of 650, more than 50 percent of whom have worked at the club for five years or more and 30 percent of whom have worked at the club for 10 years or more; while just over 10 percent of the staff have worked at the club for two decades or more.

The club recently implemented an extensive service-training program that each staff member undertakes (new hires and current employees). The service-training program ensures that all employees receive the tools that they need to professionally interact with members; resolve member service challenges or situations to the satisfaction of members; and provide members with a memorable experience. In addition, the program is designed to provide staff with an enhanced level of pride about where they work and the job that they perform.

Programs and Services of the East Bank Club

The club offers more than 200 complimentary group-exercise classes each week, including courses, such as yoga, Pilates, dance, strength conditioning, and aerobic conditioning. In addition, a host of other unique classes are tailored to the specific desires and interests of its members. Furthermore, the club offers an extensive array of "niche programs" for members, including tennis, aquatics, golf, triathlon, running, children's programs, and even kayaking on the Chicago River. The club has programs suited for a wide array of interests and needs, ranging from new members and individuals just starting a fitness regimen to programs tailored for the most experienced athletes. Collectively, the club runs more than 450 programs and classes each week, with an annual instructor payroll of more than $500,000.

The club generates approximately $3 million in revenue annually from personal training, personal Pilates, GYROTONICs, and personal performance-training sessions. These sessions are priced very reasonably in order to encourage member involvement.

In addition to group classes, niche programs, and private training, the club offers programs and services that include a full-service salon and women's spa that generates approximately $3 million in revenue annually; a pro shop that doubles as a boutique fashion store, which generates approximately $2 million annually; a gourmet deli with take-out items; and several unique specialty services, such as a car wash, dry cleaners, and physical therapy. Similar to its personal-training program, these services are priced reasonably in order to encourage member involvement.

The more members interact and socialize with other members, the more likely they are to remain members.

Social Interaction and Building Relationships

The more members interact and socialize with other members, the more likely they are to remain members. The club works hard to create an environment that encourages and supports the development of relationships between members.

Members befriend other members through the classes and programs that the club offers, as well as through casual interactions in the various social spaces in the club. The club also offers social networking on the club's website, which further enhances the ability of the members to connect with each other.

Building member relationships lies at the heart of what makes East Bank special.

The club holds regular social functions, ranging from small intimate events, such as Friday night tennis socials, to much larger functions, such as wine tastings that attract 300 or more people. The club's most attended social event and a club tradition is the annual Summer Sun Deck Party, which brings in more than 1,000 people.

The club's social environment is further enriched through a thriving food and beverage operation, with annual revenues exceeding $10 million. The food and beverage operations include Maxwell's at the Club, a sophisticated-but-casual upscale restaurant; a casual grill; a juice bar; a gourmet deli; and the Sun Deck Café, a restaurant located on the roof of the club (adjacent to two outdoor pools, a pool bar, and 20,000 square feet of lounge chairs and tables). The Sun Deck Café does approximately $500,000 in revenue annually between Memorial Day and Labor Day.

Quality in Everything the Club Does

The club's owners and management are passionate about providing a five-star experience. This focus is targeted around an unrelenting commitment to quality—quality staff, quality services, quality equipment, and quality facilities. East Bank is a single-facility operation, which has meant that quality control is inherent. It is, in fact, the club's sole focus.

Reflections and Insights on East Bank's Passion for Exceeding Member Expectations

- The first thing anyone notices when you read about the East Bank Club is its goal of exceeding member expectations. This singular focus on quality and service from the owners down to the frontline staff is a key element of the club's success. In fact, such a singular focus is critical for any business that expects to deliver great service and memorable experiences. If the owners, management, and frontline staff don't have the same focus, and therefore the same commitment to a well-defined goal, then achieving it becomes virtually impossible. In the case of the East Bank Club, everyone has bought into the same vision.
- Building member relationships lies at the heart of what makes East Bank special. The club provides an incredible variety of programs, events, and social areas, each of which is intended to bring members together. The East Bank Club understands that members don't leave relationships, they leave facilities. As a result, the club has made sure to offer the spaces (e.g., food and beverage, pools, lounges, etc.), the programs (e.g., group classes, personal programs, special events, regular social events, etc.), and the social ambiance that encourages members to interact with each other.

- The club's management understands that the key to success in this regard lies in the employees. The club is well aware of the fact that by providing an environment that enriches employees, the employees will, in turn, provide an exceptionally positive experience for the members. The club's level of employee tenure is incredibly high. As such, when employees have that type of tenure, it means they very likely have established strong relationships with the facility's members. As research shows, employee-member relationships are critical to driving membership retention. The simple fact that East Bank provides ongoing service training reinforces their resolute belief in the importance of the employee-member relationship.
- The club's management also understands that quality is not limited to just facilities or equipment, but also extends to the employees, the programs, and the fashion in which those factors are all brought together.
- East Bank's level of member participation is extremely high (30 to 35 percent of the members use the club daily). These levels of participation are part of the reason that the club's retention level is nearly 80 percent. When members are this involved, retention has to be exceptional.

Delivering an Authentic, Comfortable, Warm, Welcoming, and Supportive Club Environment

Club One (www.clubone.com)
San Francisco, California 94105

President and Chief Operating Officer:	Bill McBride
Average retention rate:	62% to 64%
Average individual dues:	$50 to $85 a month
Average daily club attendance:	560 per day

Club One, San Francisco, CA

Front desk, Club One, San Francisco, CA

Club One, San Francisco, CA

Pool, Club One, San Francisco, CA

Examples of monthly dues and retention rates at Club One facilities

Club Type	Avg. Monthly Dues	Retention %
Downtown urban club	$80	62%
Office/retail park club	$85	61%
Suburban family club w/pool	$50	69%
Suburban upscale adult club	$50	61%

The Club One mission of one body, one mind, and one life is based on engaging the emotions of each member.

Founded in 1991, Club One currently operates 18 facilities in California, with 14 Club One Fitness-branded clubs in Northern California and four Frog's Fitness-branded clubs in Southern California. In addition to its 18 commercial clubs, Club One also manages more than 60 corporate, community-based, multi-tenant business, municipality, and medical-based fitness centers that serve more than 140,000 members nationwide. Over the years, Club One facilities have garnered several awards for excellence in California, including: "Best Health Club," "Best Place to Work Out," and "Best Places to Work."

Club One's Goal Every Day

The Club One mission of one body, one mind, and one life is based on engaging the emotions of each member. The underlying premise is that engaging the emotions of each member can foster memorable experiences that will continue to bring that individual to the club. At the heart of this service philosophy are several phrases that Club One uses to reinforce with its team what its clubs are all about. A list of those phrases includes:

- We want our members to feel that our team is friendly and nice.
- We want our members to feel that our clubs and team provide a warm and accepting environment.
- We want our members to realize, sense, and experience comfort and social support.
- We want our members to know that we are always considerate of them and their circumstances.
- We want our members to have fun and be happy in our clubs and with our programs.
- We want our members to feel and be safe.
- We want our members to trust us, based on our authenticity—to realize that we are the "real deal."

The approach of the Club One team's to fitness involves personally getting to know its members so that they can be supported in achieving their goals. The Club One model encourages every member to utilize the club, an outcome to which the organization is firmly dedicated to achieving. Through care, knowledge, program efficacy, program specificity, and service, Club One works to retain its members and help each and everyone succeed.

Technology to Build Relationships and Engender Loyalty

Expanding on its underlying framework of authenticity, warmth, and social support, Club One created the WellPower program to further enhance its ability to drive member loyalty and retention. The WellPower program encompasses a database that tracks the "Net Promoter Score" of each member, as well as that individual's personality type, goals, interests, usage, spending patterns, and reward points earned. Currently, the company has over 20 percent of its member base enrolled, a number that continues to grow daily. Club One has found that members who are engaged in the WellPower program have a retention level that is three percentage points higher than its average member.

In addition to its WellPower program, Club One is a strong advocate of using social media (e.g., Facebook, Yelp) to spark conversation and build community with its members. By reaching out to its members through social media, it has created an even stronger sense of community among its members.

Reflections and Insights on Club One's Approach to Building Memorable Experiences

- Club One has done an excellent job in developing several core principles or standards around the type of environment it wants to create for its members. These core principles then form the foundation for its employee training efforts. It should be noted that these core principles are based primarily on the type of environment it wants to create for its members (e.g., inviting, authentic, warm, welcoming, comfortable), rather than on lots of equipment, fitness, programs, etc.
- The company has developed its member policies and systems to support an individualized approach to knowing the member. The WellPower program, for example, is based on this singular focus of knowing who the members are, how they feel, what their interests are, what their goals are, and how they are progressing toward achieving those goals and interests. Having this information on hand allows each employee, as well as management, to provide the best blend of facilities, equipment, programs, services, and personal attention.
- The company looks beyond the four walls of its facilities to engage members in open dialogue. Employing various social media, the company has been able to create open dialogue with its members, as well as provide each member with the opportunity to become a part of several online communities.
- The company makes sure it measures member satisfaction and loyalty through the use of the Net Promoter Score. As discussed previously, understanding how members feel about the club and how well the business is doing at creating business advocates (e.g., members with high Net Promoter Scores) are critical to providing an enriching club experience that drives member retention.

Club One is a strong advocate of using social media (e.g., Facebook, Yelp) to spark conversation and build community with its members.

In the club business, establishing a theme can go a long way toward creating member loyalty and driving retention.

Strategies for Staging Memorable Experiences and Delivering Great Service

- *Create a theme and then develop the proper stage, props, and script to bring it to life*

Walt Disney understood this concept better than anyone when he developed Disneyland. Over the past several decades, Disneyland has honed the experience model by formulating a distinct theme for each of its parks, and then making sure each has the right stage (facilities), right props (rides and people), and a script (the experiences it wants to generate and how each staff person fills a role).

All factors considered, Las Vegas took a page or two from the Disney model, and forged an entire city, based on various staged themes. The point is that when a business can establish a theme that appeals to people and that can be delivered flawlessly through the proper scripting, staging, and acting, people will turn out repeatedly to experience it. Not surprisingly, Disneyland and Vegas both profit considerably from the repeat business they generate.

In the club business, establishing a theme can go a long way toward creating member loyalty and driving retention. Over the past decade, the health/fitness club industry has seen several themed club models arise, for example:

✓ Crunch, New York. In the late 1980s and early 1990s, Crunch was the master at building an entire experience around its brand (theme). The Crunch brand was designed on a theme that encompassed certain characteristics, such as creativity, unusual, non-judgmental, and "eye-popping." The programs that resulted served as the script for the staff. In the end, a very unusual and themed experience was devised for the members of Crunch. From staff with tattoos and piercings to classes, such as cardio-striptease, Crunch was an experience, not a facility.

✓ Rochester Athletic Club, Rochester, Minnesota. In the early part of the 21st century, the Rochester Athletic Club converted a part of its facility into the "Neighborhood." The Neighborhood was designed to replicate the theme of old-town America, complete with a downtown that was comprised of shops, recreation areas, etc. The Neighborhood targeted families. As such, it provided a staged arena for the entire family to visit the club and simply enjoy being together. While there, individuals were encouraged to engage in activities that were reminiscent of small towns in the middle of the 20th century.

✓ Hillside City Club, Istanbul, Turkey. This club, located in the hills of Istanbul, has themed itself as a sport resort. The members and the public view the facility as more than just a club. Instead, it is seen as a destination and escape within the city. The club has an outdoor poolside movie theatre; saunas where individuals can actually lay down on a lounge, sip tea, and enjoy a personal viewing screen; a host of unique dining experiences; and much more. The facility is as much a resort as it is a club, and the staff is focused on delivering memorable moments, based on that resort theme.

✓ Ecofit, San Paulo, Brazil. At Ecofit, the owners have created a club that targets the environmentally conscious consumer. Toward this end, the club uses reclaimed rainwater to supply water for its pools and showers; solar energy to power many aspects of the club; recycled wood and glass products for the floor surfaces in the facility; and recycled paper products, as well as other environmentally friendly practices. The club also provides a means for members to recycle various products, such as cell phones, CDs, paper, aluminum, etc. In addition, the club offers an extensive array of programs (e.g., plant a tree) and services that allow members to get involved and engaged in contributing to the health of the local environment. Members not only see Ecofit as a club, they also view it as a part of their lifestyle and as part of their own personal commitment to the environment.

In fact, clubs can take any number of steps to create a unique theme and experience for their facility, including the following:

⇨ Identify an experience that can be created that will be different and unique from the competition. It does not have to be elaborate; it just has to be different (in a positive way). Just as importantly, it has to be deliverable.

⇨ Once a theme is selected, clubs have to determine what facilities and props they will need. For example, at Telos, a club located in Dallas, Texas, the club has been themed around ancient Athenian culture. To help bring this theme to life, the owners of Telos have designed the club's features to resemble ancient Greek and Roman structures. In addition, they have created programs, based on training philosophies from that period.

⇨ Establish a script to support the theme. A script refers to the policies, programs, and services a club offers. These elements must support the theme. For example, at Telos in Dallas, Spartan training and holistic balanced programs, both which support the aforementioned Athenian theme, are featured.

⇨ Make sure the staff can deliver on the theme. On a basic level, this factor requires that staff job descriptions lend themselves to the experience that the club wants to deliver. This element also necessitates that the club provides the proper education and training for its staff so that everyone can successfully fulfill their assigned roles. The Disney Institute, for example, hires cast members and then provides the appropriate education and training so that the cast members can deliver on the Disney script.

- *Is the club into traditions? If not, get started.*

One of the defining elements of any great culture is its traditions. Traditions serve as "glue" that binds people to the culture. In business, exceptional organizations understand that having long-held traditions can go a long way toward building outstanding customer loyalty.

One of the defining elements of any great culture is its traditions.

Customers tend to view traditions as not only providing memorable moments, but also security and stability as well. In addition, traditions can help bond people and customers of common interests. Harley Davidson and Airstream have several traditions, such as their annual rallies. In turn, Disney has a number of relatively well-known traditions, such as Mickey Mouse and Donald Duck roaming the theme park.

At Red's in Lafayette, Louisiana, the club has a tradition of doing one new thing for the membership each month.

World Class in Russia has numerous activities that are traditionally held, such as annual World Class Games, semi-annual sports dancing competitions, an annual fitness awards event, and annual club birthday parties. Each of these events or activities has been conducted by the company on a regular basis since its inception or shortly thereafter. As such, each event is important to its members. In fact, these events have become traditions that members and staff look forward to each year. Over the past decade, these traditions have been a great source of pride for the members, and have contributed significantly to member loyalty and retention. As such, many other clubs throughout the country have their own unique traditions, such as annual fun runs, charity events, parties, social events, and competitions.

At Red's in Lafayette, Louisiana, the club has a tradition of doing one new thing for the membership each month. This undertaking could involve any number of happenings, such as adding a class, introducing a new event, adding a piece of equipment, etc. Initiated by the club founder and owner, when he first started his business nearly 50 years ago, members have come to treasure this simple and time-honored tradition.

The New York Athletic Club, a member-owned club in New York City, has what could be called its "Hall of Fame," which is a time-honored tradition that goes back to the club's inception in the 1860s. When three of the club's original founding members (William Curtis, John Babcock, and Henry Buermeyer) formed the club, one of their primary goals was to bring order to the chaos of the times, by standardizing the rules for athletic endeavors and providing documentation of official records. From its earliest days as a facility on 200 Sixth Street in NYC, athletes from around the world migrated to the club to have their skills tested and their feats recorded. That humble beginning led to the creation of its "Hall of Fame," which houses the records of its members, including photographs, gold medals, etc. Many of history's greatest athletes have called the New York Athletic Club home. As such, many of their records and related historical documents are located in the club for anyone to observe in its "Hall of Fame." This particular tradition provides exceptional memories for its members, and is just one factor of many that help set the club apart in the private athletic club market of New York.

Abs Fitness, based in India, has established several traditions with events, such as its annual fashion show involving members and its annual talent show. Not only do these two events engage members in activities that they enjoy, they also give members the opportunity to showcase their talents. The real bonus is that the members are actively engaged in these events, which helps to strengthen their perceived value as honored club traditions.

Among the suggested steps that a club can consider for starting its own traditions are the following:

✓ Identify one or two events or activities that would have the greatest value to the local community of the club, as well as the members of the facility. Determine what the members find appealing and then develop a program or event around it.

✓ Once the club has identified the right event or practice, make it permanent. Traditions tend to be based on several factors, such as consistency over time, predictability (think cultural traditions, such as Halloween or Valentine's Day), and predictability concerning what can be expected. Whether it's the World Class Games, the ClubCorp Associate Club Golf Tournament or Red's new thing every month, each of these undertakings is consistent and predictable.

✓ Make sure the tradition has perceived value and provides positive memories. One key factor to keep in mind about traditions is that they stimulate memories. As a result, they generate perceived value in the mind of the individual. All factors considered, a club's traditions need to provide the opportunity to generate favorable memories for everyone who participates.

- *No sacrifices allowed ... eliminate the tolls.*

In the book, *The Experience Economy,* the authors, James Gilmore and Joseph Pine indicate that one of the keys to delivering memorable customer experiences involves lessening the gap between the sacrifices a customer makes and the expectations that they have. The authors identify a customer sacrifice as something the customer gives up to engage in the product, service, or experience that the business offers. Sacrifices can take many forms, e.g., time, energy, money, etc.

One common example of customer sacrifice in the retail world involves airlines. Airline customers who travel on a discount airline often voluntarily give up the ability to reserve a seat in advance. Instead, they put themselves in a position where they must arrive early and get in line to get their seat of choice. The sacrifice in this instance may be the extra time spent getting to the airport early just to get a preferred seat (i.e., leaving several hours early) or the time involved in standing in line.

One of the keys to delivering memorable customer experiences involves lessening the gap between the sacrifices a customer makes and the expectations that they have.

Another real world example of customer sacrifice involves cell-phone providers. If a cell-phone carrier does not provide coverage in a certain area or the service drops too many calls, then this sacrifice may be greater than the value received for a reduced monthly fee by a particular carrier. If the sacrifice is perceived as a negative by the customer, then the value of the purchase drops. In reality, customer sacrifices occur on a daily basis in the business world. All factors considered, when those sacrifices become a significant detractor in the customer's level of perceived value, the customer will typically choose to go with another provider.

The research previously discussed in this book clearly identifies some of the experiences that club members consider as sacrifices, such as not having equipment available when they want to use it, not having staff available to answer questions they have, not having friendly staff, not having peer support, having to pay to receive basic instruction, overcrowded facilities, etc. Far too often, member may buy the membership because the price is right, but once they start using the club, they are confronted by these sacrifices, which, in most cases, they never originally considered when deciding whether to purchase a membership. As a result, the value equation changes, because the resultant sacrifices are too costly.

Too many club operators fail to see the sacrifices that members must make in an effort to use its clubs.

Too many club operators fail to see the sacrifices that members must make in an effort to use its clubs. Collectively, these sacrifices provide members with a tangible reason to cancel their membership. Among the most common sacrifices that club members experience are the following:

- ✓ Waiting in line at the front desk to check-in
- ✓ Being placed on hold when calling the club, while a staff person talks to a friend
- ✓ Having the desired exercise equipment be in use when the member needs it
- ✓ Having no towels available when the member needs one
- ✓ Having all of the treadmills be occupied, since no time limit exists for how long a treadmill can be used by an individual
- ✓ Not being able to find a fitness instructor to assist the member in using a particular piece of exercise equipment
- ✓ Having one or more of the club's exercise machines be out of order and staying that way for an entire week
- ✓ Having the front desk person not know the member's name, even though they have interacted on numerous occasions over the past few months
- ✓ Having to "bump" bodies with another member in the locker room because the front desk gave a member a key for a locker right next to someone else, when other lockers were available
- ✓ Not having access to a group-exercise schedule in order to determine the most convenient class to take
- ✓ Having the soap dispenser in the shower be empty and having no way to find someone to fill the dispenser with soap to wash with
- ✓ Having a trainer state to a member who needs advice to sign-up for a personal-training session
- ✓ Having the nets on the tennis court be torn for an extended period
- ✓ Having to wait 45 minutes before being able to swim because other members are allowed to swim in a lane as long as they want
- ✓ Having to call a personal trainer to cancel an appointment, but then not being able to reach them because the club has no central hub for appointments
- ✓ Failing to communicate any change in the club's operating hours or specific policies to all members

As the aforementioned list suggests, members make a host of small sacrifices every day. Over time, these small sacrifices tend to become major sacrifices, which can eventually lead members to resign. Not surprisingly, it is highly recommended that member sacrifices and tolls be eliminated. Among the steps that a club can take in this regard are the following:

- ✓ Make sure that sufficient staff are on duty at the front desk so that members can easily enter the club.
- ✓ Know the club's usage patterns, and make sure to provide sufficient equipment to handle the expected load. If enough equipment is not available, establish policies regarding time limits so that members know what to expect from a time perspective. For example, at the Gym Group in London, members can go online to check out the club's busiest times.
- ✓ If equipment is broken down, let members know when it will be repaired and give them a time frame for the repair.
- ✓ If a particular class tends to have greater demand than supply, consider going to a class sign-up process. The club can even use its website or a smart phone application to accommodate this step.
- ✓ Make it relatively easy for members to sign-up for personal training so that they don't have to chase the trainers down. Centralize personal training appointments. In this regard, consider using a combination of tools, such as a concierge, website, etc. For example, at Telos Fitness Center in Dallas, management created a personal training desk and concierge service so that members only have to reach out once to schedule or change an appointment. At Equinox, members can sign-up for personal training online.
- ✓ Have fitness staff available on the fitness floor during peak usage periods so that members don't feel unattended. In addition, make sure that members can identify which staff is involved in personal training and which staff is present to assist. For example, at World Class Fitness in Russia, the fitness instructors who are present to help members wear one color shirt, while the trainers working with members wear another type of shirt. At the Gym Group clubs in London, the staff available to assist members wear a special uniform so that it's relatively easy for members to identify them.
- ✓ Establish a routine involving staff checking soap dispensers and towel supplies. Consider employing a system in which an effort is made to communicate to members that someone will go through the locker rooms periodically and make sure that towels and soap are in sufficient supply.
- ✓ Have a transparent communication system that enables members to easily learn about changes in club policies and practices.
- ✓ Ask members what they consider as essential sacrifices and then address them.

It is highly recommended that member sacrifices and tolls be eliminated.

The more staff listens, the more it learns, and the more it learns, the more it can do to improve the experience of the members of the club.

- *Two ears please ... listen to your members.*

  Robert Dedman, founder of ClubCorp, used to have a simple saying that makes a very cogent point: "We have two ears and one mouth for a reason. We should listen twice as hard as we talk." While a very simple phrase, its intended message was that managers and employees need to spend a significant amount of time listening to what their members say, rather than telling them what they think. The more staff listens, the more it learns, and the more it learns, the more it can do to improve the experience of the members of the club. When a club actively listens to its members, rather than waiting till they complain, it can build the club experience around what the members tell the club, rather than around what the club perceives that the members need.

  Among some suggestions on how a club can listen to its members more effectively and proactively are the following:

  ✓ Have an open-door policy. Management should communicate to the members that the door of the club is open and that anytime outstanding issues arise, the members are welcome to share their concerns.

  ✓ Have management walk the club as frequently as possible. Possibly, the best methodology for hearing what members have to say and observing what they are experiencing, is to get out in the club and listen to them. Management can learn more, as well as garner greater loyalty from the members, by making themselves accessible to the members.

  ✓ Conduct focus groups on a regular basis. Focus groups are a qualitative means of learning about the experiences and attitudes of the members. Holding focus groups throughout the year, possibly once a quarter or even once a month, can result in management learning a significant amount about what is important to the members.

  ✓ Conduct annual surveys. At least once annually, and preferably twice annually, clubs should conduct member-satisfaction surveys. If undertaken properly, these surveys can provide a wealth of information about what factors are valued by the members, what the club is doing well, and what it can do better.

  ✓ Establish a special page on the website of the club that allows members and management to have an open dialogue. With the advent of social media, more and more businesses are using their website and Facebook page to establish a two-way dialogue with their members. Clubs shouldn't be any different. In the previously discussed case study on Club One of California, it was indicated how important social media has become to its efforts to have an authentic and open dialogue with its members.

- *Recover with passion; implement a member-service recovery process.*

  One of the most frequently quoted reasons that members give for leaving a club is unresponsive management. This frequently mentioned rationale for resigning is the result of members perceiving that management doesn't care about the problems or sacrifices that the members experience. In fact, the annual member survey responses of one company looked at for background information for this book showed that nearly 30 percent of its members never took the time to report a problem, and for those members who did report a problem, less than 50 percent received a response from management. In other words, approximately one fourth of the members actually received a correspondence from management that addressed the negative experience that the member had. Obviously, the data from this company is not a good reflection of responsive management.

Research indicates that when a business responds quickly and professionally to the complaints of its customers, it can frequently turn a dissatisfied or even outraged customer into a contented customer. In other words, club operators can garner an incredible amount of "good will" and, eventually, member loyalty by having a system in place that ensures member issues and problems are addressed promptly.

Among the suggested steps that clubs can undertake to implement a "service recovery" system that is prompt and effective are the following:

✓ Create a system that allows members to communicate their issues easily, either anonymously or personally. This system should take advantage of the Internet so that members can submit their concerns through their computer or smart phone when they're not in the club, and while they're in the club, through either a computer or some other written tool. Virgin Active and Fitness First, which are both located in the U.K., as well as in other countries, have a standardized member-comment system involving comment cards.

✓ Make sure that the club has a policy in place that guarantees all concerns will be addressed within a specific time period. Research shows that a 24-hour response time is ideal, and that anything longer than 48 hours is unreasonable. In the current global environment, even 24 hours may be considered too slow. Whatever time frame is established, the club should make sure that all members know what it is.

✓ Make sure every comment or problem raised is addressed and a response is provided. If members leave their name, then the club needs to respond to them personally, either in-person, by phone, or by email. On the other hand, if the members submit their issue anonymously, a forum should be provided where the club can actually share the comment and the subsequent response from management. Some clubs undertake this step on their website, while others employ a bulletin board, where they post issues and responses. It should be noted that the response should always include an appropriate apology for the inconvenience and a clear description of the actions that management is ready to take.

✓ For issues that are significant, management should make an effort to meet personally with the member issuing the complaint. The situation should not be passed off to frontline staff. Members want to know that the club cares. All factors considered, nothing accomplishes that step better than having management meet with the member, apologize to them, show empathy and understanding, and finally to provide an honest and sincere response.

Research indicates that when a business responds quickly and professionally to the complaints of its customers, it can frequently turn a dissatisfied or even outraged customer into a contented customer.

✓ If more time is needed to respond to a particular issue, the club should communicate that it has received the complaint and will be finalizing a response in the near future (note: a time frame should always be given when the club responds). Although a club will not always be able to give the "right answer," it can provide an answer and let the member know what steps it will be taking going forward.

✓ Make sure that the members know what the club's system is and the steps involved for addressing their concerns.

Customer research shows that one of the most appreciated elements of great customer service is receiving a warm greeting and a sincere goodbye upon entering and departing the club, respectively.

Some clubs have a unique approach to their service-recovery system. For example, the system for one particular club was entitled "letters to the manager" (actually the program was identified by the manager's actual name). In that facility, if members had an issue, they would submit a comment on a specially designed card that was addressed to the manager. The members could submit the cards in one of several boxes that were placed throughout the club (in fact, the boxes were actually made to look like mailboxes). The program guaranteed that the manager would reply to a member's issue within 24 hours. If the members left their name, the manager would reach out to them within 24 hours, and if no name was provided, the manager would post the comment on a special bulletin board, along with the response. The members loved the program. As a result, the club had incredible loyalty among its members.

Another club called its program "Can the Comments"—an effort in which actual paint cans were used as collection points. The manager who created this program also made it a policy to respond within 24 hours.

- *Deliver warm hellos and sincere goodbyes.*

  While the precept seems easy, most clubs fail to deliver on this critical element of great service. Customer research shows that one of the most appreciated elements of great customer service is receiving a warm greeting and a sincere goodbye upon entering and departing the club, respectively. Warm welcomes involve smiles, name recognition, and an empathetic greeting. Fond farewells involve a smile, an invitation to return, and an empathetic expression of appreciation for the visit of each member.

  At Red's, a large multipurpose club in Lafayette, Louisiana, one of the club's core values is, "hellos and goodbyes". Red, who founded the club in 1963, believes that every member and every guest deserve to receive a hello when they enter the club and a goodbye when they depart. This simple value is endemic among the employees. As such, employees almost always utter hellos when members enter their area of the club and goodbyes when they depart. As a result, members tend to be greeted several times when they are in the club.

  One of the core values of ClubCorp is warm welcomes, magic moments, and fond farewells. This simple value carries significant weight among its employees. To most employees of the company, it is a mantra that was exemplified by the company's leaders, including the original founder and chairman. Even more than just warm welcomes and fond farewells, ClubCorp employees are encouraged to use the members' name whenever they greet them. At one time, the company had a standard that said, "We need to call a member by name at least four times while they are in the club." This core tenant was based on a phrase from Dale Carnegie's, How to Win Friends and Influence Others, which stated that the most precious word in any language is a person's name. Nothing says a person cares more than when an individual greets a member by using their name.

The value of this simple principle is reflected in this anecdotal recounting of a young woman's experience as a member at a large national multi-club operator. She had originally joined this particular club because of its convenience (open 24/7), large variety of equipment and programs, core amenities, great price, and the ability to occasionally bring a guest. Over a period of several months, she religiously used the club three and sometimes four times a week. Every time she visited the club, she would give her card to the front-desk person, and they would scan it and let her in. During this entire time (approximately 50 visits), not once did the staff person ever welcome her or use her name. Not by coincidence, this particular club chain has experienced annual retention levels of under 60 percent on several occasions.

Among the suggested steps that a club operator can do to create an environment of warm welcomes and ensure that employees apply this principle religiously are the following:

✓ Establish a core value or standard that dictates that every member should receive a greeting when they enter the club or any area of the club, and likewise, should be accorded they receive a sincere goodbye and an invitation to return.

✓ Make sure that employees understand that any greeting should be accompanied by a smile, eye contact, and personal name recognition—basic hallmarks of a warm greeting.

✓ As part of the club's employee training efforts, spend time on how employees can accomplish the aforementioned step, based on their own personal style.

✓ Recognize employees when they deliver on the value.

✓ Make sure that the club leaders model the value with employees and members, since the employees of the club will model what they witness, as opposed to what they are told.

Members want to know that the club values them as members.

- *Yes we have royalty … treat the members as honored guests and royalty.* Members want to know that the club values them as members. From the members' perspective, they have invested money and time into the club. In turn, they expect to be appreciated and valued. As such, clubs that build their service delivery process around the tenant of treating their members as royalty can reach new levels of member loyalty.

At ClubCorp, one of its core values proclaims that "the member/guest is king." This fundamental value was established when Robert Dedman founded the company in the late 1950s, and continues to this day, more than five decades later as a core tenant of the company's approach to members. Every employee understands that it is their responsibility to make each member and guest feel special and treat them accordingly. As the founder of ClubCorp, Robert Dedman, steadfastly declared, "Even when the member is wrong, they are right." While this phrase may seem unrealistic and unreasonable at face value, what Mr. Dedman meant by it was that when a problem arises due to a member's error, it needs to be handled in such a way as not to point blame or make an accusation. Instead, it needs to be acknowledged with humility that an error has occurred, and to communicate that the club will do its absolute best to address it. This approach makes club members feel valued and appreciated, and, in return, they enjoy coming to the club.

When problems arise, employees should look at it as an opportunity to exceed the member's expectations.

In fact, one personal story exemplifies this approach. In 1986, I was the fitness manager of the Atrium Club in New York. The club served a very affluent audience of business professionals, celebrities, and athletes, as well as citizens in the local market. One day, while standing in for the club's locker attendant, Victor, a member appeared before me and asked if I would be kind enough to rub lotion over his entire body. The member was 85 years old, wrinkled, and naked. At first, I was taken back by the request, but then the member told me that Victor, on a daily basis, rubbed his skin with lotion. Not wanting to disappoint him, I fulfilled the member's request. Later, I asked Victor why he did this for the member every day, since it was not part of his job description. Victor indicated to me that this particular member had skin problems and that by applying the lotion to the member, it made the member feel better for the remainder of the day. Victor then went on to say that his job was about finding out what a member needed, and doing his best to fulfill that need. In this case, rubbing lotion on the member was what was most important to him. As such, I learned from Victor what the real meaning of treating a member as a king is—in this instance, it is doing what no one else might do for a particular person, but which is incredibly important to that individual.

At Larry North Fitness, the founder and owner, Larry North, has as one of his company's basic values, "Happy to do it." This value is at the heart of everything the company does with respect to its members. By acting and reacting with this "Happy to do it" attitude, employees are able to treat the members as if they truly are royalty.

Among the possible actions that a club can undertake to support an environment in which the members are treated as royalty are the following:

✓ Communicate to employees the importance of treating every member as an honored guest or dignitary. All factors considered, this step can be as simple as making sure that members are greeted by name and treated respectfully. It can also involve making sure that members are not left having to ask for assistance in the club. Instead, the staff should be proactive in identifying what the member might need.

✓ Make sure that employees understand that when a member complains, it means they actually care. As a result, when problems arise, employees should look at it as an opportunity to exceed the member's expectations.

✓ Clarify that members are never to be blamed. When a problem is caused by a member, it is not the job of employees to point it out to the member. Instead, the employees' job is to apologize to the member for any inconvenience that has occurred and find a means to solve the issue in a mutually beneficial fashion.

✓ Focus on establishing policies and practices that make it enjoyable and easy for members to experience the offerings of the club. Try to avoid putting in place policies that treat the member as if they are an inconvenience in an employee's day. For example, a situation might arise when a member goes up to a fitness instructor and asks where a towel might be found to clean sweat off one of the resistance machines. If the attitude of the employees is centered on treating members as royalty, then the staff person would not just provide directions to the towels. Instead, while the staff member might indicate where the towels are located, the staff person would then proceed to get a towel and clean the machine on behalf of the member.

✓ Hire employees who have a servant's heart. Robert Dedman used to share with his employees that being in the service of others is a noble profession, that when people serve others, they are making a difference in their lives. One quote from his book, King of Clubs, epitomizes this principle of a servant's heart. In the book, Dedman shares a story about a discussion he had with one of the company's club managers. During the discussion, the manager said, "Bob, you were born to be an executive; I was born to be a maid." What the manager meant by this particular comment is that he was good at serving others, an attitude that is at the heart of the company's core value of treating every member as if they were a king.

- *Make sure that club staff interact with the members.*

In research conducted by Paul Bedford, Ph.D., of the United Kingdom, he looked at the importance of staff interactions on the likelihood of members visiting the club the following month. What he found was that if a staff person interacts with a member one time during a month, the likelihood of that member returning again the next month increases by 20 percent. On the other hand, if the staff interacted with a member on at least two to three occasions during a particular month, the likelihood of that member returning the next month jumps by 50 percent. As such, if more than four interactions take place, the likelihood of the member returning the next month increases by 80 percent. Bedford's research clearly confirms the importance of staff making contact with members, since the more interaction that takes place, the more frequently members return. Furthermore, the more frequently they return, the longer they remain members.

Among the possible steps that clubs do to make staff-member interactions occur are the following:

✓ Incorporate into the job description for each staff person accountability for interacting with the members.

✓ Create operating practices that support getting club staff to interact with the members. At one club, management expects the fitness staff to learn five new member names each week. At the end of the week, the fitness manager meets with the trainers, and they discuss the new members that each trainer met. The meeting reinforces the principle of getting out and making contact with the members. At another club, management

Clubs should try to avoid putting in place policies that treat the member as if they are an inconvenience in an employee's day.

asks the supervising trainer on the fitness floor to walk the floor every 30 minutes, sometimes with a tray of water, and other times with a tray of towels. The goal of this particular undertaking is to reduce the staff's anxiety about approaching members, and in turn, getting the staff to interact with members, an action they previously may have avoided.

The club should have at least one staff person whose sole role is to be an engager and networker on the fitness floor.

✓ Make sure that at least one staff person is always on the gym floor whose primary responsibility is to be a connector. More simply stated, the club should have at least one staff person whose sole role is to be an engager and networker on the fitness floor.

12

Design for Retention: Designing and Delivering a Facility That Promotes Retention

In two studies conducted in the U.K. nearly two decades ago—the Allied Dunbar National Fitness Survey and the Active for Life Campaign, researchers determined that among the many expressed barriers to exercise and physical activity, the physical environment represents one of the more significant hurdles to a situation in which people successfully embark on and maintain a physical activity program. In fact, this data is not isolated, having been born out in various studies on retention and physical activity that IHRSA has commissioned over the years.

It is interesting to note that these physical barriers are not always outwardly expressed by consumers and members. Instead, in many instances, they are intertwined with the general, physical, and emotional barriers that consumers and members frequently express about starting exercise, joining a club, remaining a member of that club, and of course, terminating their membership in that club. A list of examples of the most commonly expressed barriers to exercising and club membership, which carry with them either a direct or indirect connection to the physical environment of the club, includes:

- *Overcrowding.* When members and consumers express concern about overcrowding, it is directly related to the physical environment.
- *Waiting for equipment.* When members talk about having to wait, whether it's for a piece of equipment, waiting at the front desk, waiting for a swimming lane, etc., it also is referring to a barrier that relates to the physical environment.
- *Not fitting in.* While a number of reasons exist concerning why members may feel that they don't fit in, as shown in FIA research data that was discussed in previous chapters, one factor that often makes individuals feel uncomfortable involves not knowing how to navigate the environment of the club. This lack of confidence, emanating from being unable to successfully navigate the club environment, is very often tied to the physical design of the club.

While a number of reasons exist concerning why members may feel that they don't fit in, one factor that often makes individuals feel uncomfortable involves not knowing how to navigate the environment of the club.

- *Feeling intimidated.* Nearly all of the research pertaining to why members don't join a club, don't remain a member, or don't maintain their interest in the club is connected to the intimidation factor. The sense of intimidation is frequently related to the physical environment of the club.
- *Social ambiance.* Social ambiance is an important element in the value equation of consumers and members. As such, the physical environment of the club can either enhance or detract from the perceived level of social ambiance.
- *Losing motivation.* Members often indicate that one of their reasons for terminating their membership is related to their losing interest or motivation in being physically active. In fact, the physical composition of the club can play an important role in providing a more interesting and motivating environment for exercise.
- *Not enough time.* Time may be one of the most frequently cited reasons for ceasing to work out or participate in a club. Time is impacted by many factors, including the club's physical layout and how well it promotes or detracts from how well a member can complete their routine with a minimal loss of time. In the Allied Dunbar National Fitness Survey and the Active for Life Campaign, consumers rated not enough time as the leading barrier to participation, with 41 percent and 34 percent of men respectively and 43 percent and 39 percent of women respectively indicating this factor in the two studies.
- *Cleanliness and condition of the facility.* These two factors are often expressed by members as to why they resign from their club, or in the case of consumers who have never been members, why they choose not to join a particular club.

Club operators have a number of potential strategies that they can adopt that can contribute to providing a physical environment that is more conducive to membership retention.

Another variable that club owners should consider when it comes to how the physical environment of their facility impacts membership retention relates to the audience that they are targeting. As discussed previously in this book, every tribe or clan has certain expressed needs and wants that are directly and indirectly related to the physical environment in which they find themselves. For example, if the club is targeting a specific audience demographic (i.e., a particular demographic tribe), then how the physical environment is themed and delivered can have a significant impact on membership retention. As such, club operators need to be aware of how the physical environment of their club can create potential barriers for prospects and members, and how it can also become a key element in enhancing retention.

In reality, club operators have a number of potential strategies that they can adopt that can contribute to providing a physical environment that is more conducive to membership retention.

Strategies for Creating a Physical Environment That Contributes to Membership Retention

- *Design and build to lessen the intimidation factor.* Clubs often unknowingly design and construct their clubs in a fashion that is perceived by prospects, first-time exercisers, and new members as intimidating. Truth be known, many experienced fitness enthusiasts (the majority of club owners and operators) have a difficult time identifying what physical conditions can be intimidating to new members and beginning exercisers, possibly because they themselves are not intimidated by the fitness environment. In reality, nothing can be more intimidating to a new exerciser than walking into a club and immediately being overwhelmed by a vast ocean of equipment, having to perform exercises where everyone can see them, or having to change clothes in an open space where all members can view them. Among the approaches that club operators and designers should consider if they want to lessen the intimidation factor of the facility are the following:

✓ Remember that first impressions count; make the entry and reception environment of the club welcoming. Nothing scares a new prospect or member off more than entering a club and immediately having their senses bombarded by a number of potentially intimidating factors, such as lots of equipment, a row of sales cubicles, and a pro shop retail display. Instead, clubs should make sure that the entry experience of their facility provides the following:
  - A space that is open and inviting, rather than congested
  - A social space, such as a small lounge, that allows prospects to feel as if they are walking into their home
  - Soft lighting, rather than harsh lighting
  - An open view of the club, one that doesn't have views that remind members of a factory floor that has lots of intimidating equipment
  - A first impression that does not include a view of sales cubicles. While the sales staff must have access to the entry area, the sales offices should not dominate the entry experience.
  - Highlights, such as art work, water features, plants, or other elements that make the entry experience more inviting and welcoming
  - A welcoming and non-intimidating front desk. The front desk should not appear as if it's a sentry station, but rather a point of greeting for members.

Club H in the New York metropolitan area, body + soul in Munich, Germany, Sports Club/LA in New York, and Telos Fitness in Dallas, Texas are a few of the many clubs that provide an inviting and welcoming entry experience. The importance of having a positive entry experience in a club was reinforced to me recently when a group of colleagues and I had the opportunity to tour several budget clubs (high-volume, low-price) in Germany.

Nothing scares a new prospect or member off more than entering a club and immediately having their senses bombarded by a number of potentially intimidating factors, such as lots of equipment, a row of sales cubicles, and a pro shop retail display.

The first budget club we visited was Pure Fitness in Frankfurt that has four locations. Frankly, the club had an attractive, but not very open and inviting reception area. The second facility, Jumpers, which has locations in Bavaria, had an attractive and open entry that provided a very welcoming and non-intimidating experience. As such, it could easily been seen that for a first-time exerciser, the entry experience at Jumpers would be less intimidating and more welcoming. Furthermore, the exercise equipment at Jumpers was spaced appealingly behind the desk in a way that created a sense of openness. While these two budget clubs are both successful operations, from a first-impressions standpoint, Jumpers is far more inviting and appealing to a non-exerciser or a first-time member prospect.

Stephen Tharrett

Jumpers, Munich, Germany

Stephen Tharrett

Jumpers, Munich, Germany

Stephen Tharrett

Jumpers, Munich, Germany

Stephen Tharrett

Intenso, Darmstadt, Germany

- Create zones of comfort. When all of the equipment in a club is mashed together, such as rows and rows of cardiovascular equipment, or line after line of resistance equipment, the environment can become intimidating. One of the most common errors made in the health/fitness club fitness industry is to collectively place all of the cardiovascular equipment together in one direction and to do the same with resistance equipment. Furthermore, many clubs leave minimal, if any, transition space between workout areas, a practice that can result in the establishment of an intimidating physical environment, especially for first-time exercisers. Among the suggested steps that clubs can take to address this issue are the following:
  - ✓ *Create smaller, less-intimidating spaces for equipment.* Instead of one exercise area containing a hundred pieces of equipment, establish three or four smaller exercise zones that encompass fewer pieces. For example, a club might have one zone of 12 resistance pieces separated from another zone of 12 pieces of resistance equipment, with a small cardiovascular area in between. Clubs could also create exercise areas that target beginners, intermediate-level, and advanced-level exercisers, a practice that would allow members to congregate by experience level. Life Fitness, a leading manufacturer of fitness equipment, has developed a concept called Journey, which is based on laying out the exercise floor in specific zones that are separated by low wall partitions. Pure Fitness, a budget-gym operator in Frankfurt, Germany, has a small space set aside within its facility for women only. While the space is open to the main gym floor, it is still isolated by walls that are designed to provide privacy.

Stephen Tharrett

Fitness floor, body + soul, Munich, Germany

Research shows that first-time members often feel intimidated by having to work out with veteran members who know how to navigate the nuances of the exercise areas.

✓ *Separate exercise zones using low walls, opaque low barriers, or other material.* While the underlying premise is to have open energetic space, the use of low walls or similar moveable barriers creates a perception that the club offers multiple intimate spaces within the larger open space. All factors considered, this type of arrangement reduces the intimidation factor. A number of clubs understand the importance of this step. The East Bank Club in Chicago, for example, provides stretching areas that are on low platforms with low walls around them. At body + soul in Germany, a variety of partial walls and similar separation barriers are used to create a sense of intimacy, as well as openness. This approach provides individuals who are stretching with a sense of privacy within a cavernous gym area.

✓ *Offer zones geared toward new exercisers, as well as areas for more veteran club members.* Research shows that first-time members often feel intimidated by having to work out with veteran members who know how to navigate the nuances of the exercise areas. As such, clubs should consider establishing zones that focus on providing environments that are conducive for the inexperienced user who may be intimidated, as well as for those experienced exercisers who don't mind working out with other serious fitness members. New York Sports, which has over 90 clubs in the New York metropolitan area, features an approach where resistance lines of equipment are provided for three levels of exercisers.

✓ *Provide changing rooms or private changing areas.* For many members, especially women, undressing and changing in front of other individuals can be very intimidating. In that regard, clubs should consider providing private changing rooms or areas of the locker room that are at least partially protected from other areas of the locker room. Such a practice would provide those members who desire partial privacy to have it. One of the newest trends in clubs is to provide family-style changing areas, in which the lockers are in a common area, but the showers, sinks, and

Telos Fitness Center, Dallas, TX

Women's locker room, Telos Fitness Center, Dallas, TX

Ecofit, Sao Paulo, Brazil

Pool lounge, Ecofit, Sao Paulo, Brazil

water closets are in separate rooms for privacy. One interesting take-off of this approach to privacy in the locker rooms was adopted by Telos Fitness in Dallas, Texas. In its women's locker room, individual whirlpools with curtains are provided, instead of one large group whirlpool. This approach has proven far less intimidating than the whirlpools that typically exist in clubs.

✓ *Design in transition space.* One design flaw that often increases the intimidation factor is not providing transition space between exercise spaces and the locker room, or between different areas of the club. At Ecofit in Sao Paulo, Brazil, special relaxation spaces adjacent to each of their activity zones have been incorporated into the facility, a feature that allows members to wind down and transition before moving on to another area of the club. These areas also serve as a social space, a feature that further reduces the intimidation factor. Another example of this practice can be seen at Pfitzenmeir Wellness & Fitness Park in Schwetzingen, Germany, which has a wonderful waiting area outside its large group studio that serves as an excellent transition space between group exercise and other areas of the club.

✓ Utilize softer lighting and more neutral colors. While having bright colors and lights can help generate a feeling of energy in the club, it can also cause the space to be more intimidating for some members. As a result, clubs should consider the use of alternative lighting sources, such as indirect lighting, scones, and day lighting, to create a more-welcoming and less-intimidating environment. At Intenso, a small premium club located in Darmstadt, Germany, the facility has made excellent use of softer lighting and unique lighting fixtures to create a warm and inviting feeling. In addition, it should be remembered that the use of indirect lighting in locker rooms can help create a feeling of privacy in a space that typically isn't all that private.

- *Design in social space.* Consumers and members alike indicate that social ambiance is important to the overall club experience, as well as a key factor in their decision to remain a member. Research shows that a fundamental element of the club experience for many members is meeting other members and forming relationships. To foster relationship-building, clubs need to provide a physical environment that is conducive to social interaction. This observation does not mean that the clubs should abandon their primary focus—to engage members in physical activity and health-oriented programs and services. What it does mean, however, is that clubs should consider incorporating spaces or zones that are geared toward promoting social interaction in a non-intrusive fashion into the layout of their facility. Possible suggestions in this regard include the following:
  - ✓ Design in lounge or soft seating space into the entry or lobby area of the club. This area should provide comfortable seating that is arranged to promote social interaction, as well as the proper lighting and colors that indicate it is a gathering space. body + soul in Munich, Germany; the Harbour Club in London, England; Telos in Dallas, Texas; DMB Sports in Scottsdale, Arizona; Reebok Club in New York, NY; Pacific Athletic Club in San Diego, California; Virgin Active Classic in London, England; and Club H in New York, NY are all examples of clubs that offer lounge areas.
  - ✓ Incorporate social areas within the activity areas. At Ecofit in Sao Paulo, Brazil, the owners had small social spaces incorporated adjacent to the various activity areas in the club. As a result, whether members participate in group exercise, weight training, yoga, or aquatics, social spaces exist where they can relax and converse with other members who enjoy engaging in the same activities. As discussed previously, Pfizenmeir Wellness & Fitness Park in Germany has social spaces outside its group exercise studios. When Sports Club/LA redesigned its mind-body areas a few years ago, social spaces were incorporated as part of the design.

Stephen Tharrett

Cardiovascular area, Ocampo Wellness, Buenos Aires, Argentina

✓ Create social equipment zones. One new trend in clubs is to design part of the gym floor (e.g., fitness floor) to include a social aspect. At one club in Buenos Aires, Argentina, for example, the owners and management have arranged a portion of their cardiovascular equipment in an oval so that members using the equipment area are facing each other. This arrangement enables members to freely converse with each other while they exercise. It is also a set-up that is quite favorable for conducting group classes on equipment. In fact, numerous club operators are currently placing small social zones in where the equipment is laid out in a circular, oval, or curved fashion in order to promote social interaction.

- *Design space to reduce time barriers and the perception of overcrowding.* Members and non-members alike all seem to agree that the primary barrier to exercise is the individual not having enough time. Overcrowding is also a major obstacle to member participation. According to various IHRSA-supported studies, members, former members, and non-members all indicate that overcrowding is a serious problem. For members, it is one of the leading physical factors that influences their decision whether to terminate their membership, rather than choosing to rejoin. As a result, clubs can promote participation and continued membership by designing their facility in a manner that reduces potential time hurdlers, as well as lessens the perception of overcrowding and compaction. In this regard, possible steps that clubs can take include the following:

  ✓ Establish express zones on the gym floor. Consider having one or two areas of the gym floor dedicated to providing distinct express workout areas that allow the members to complete a circuit of cardiovascular, resistance, and flexibility exercise in 30 minutes or less. These areas should be clearly marked so that members who wish to expedite their workout can easily identify them.

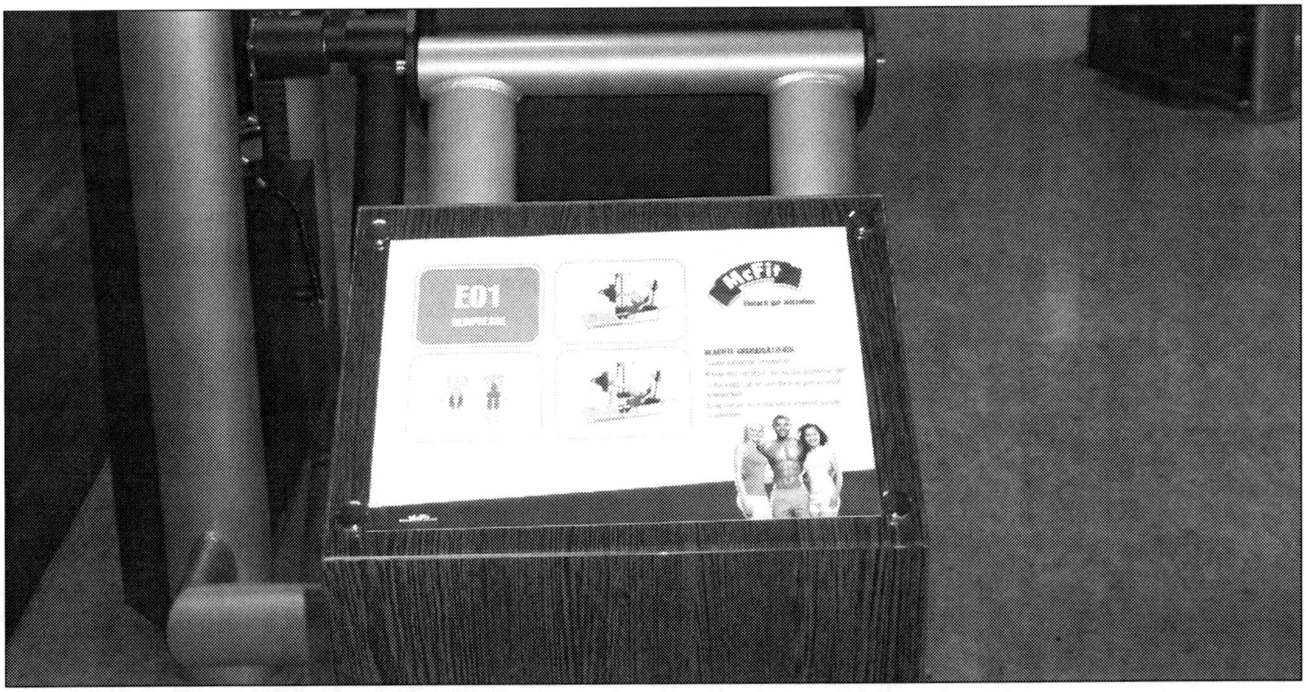

Stephen Tharrett

Equipment placard, McFit, Munich, Germany

Too many clubs design their gym floors and studios based on the expected overall level of membership, rather than on the number of users expected during the busiest peak periods of usage.

✓ Take steps to ensure that a measure of guidance exists on the gym floor. A one-time barrier that impacts most members involves having to find assistance when they don't understand how to use equipment. At Mcfit in Germany, the owner provides placards in front of the equipment that demonstrate the proper method for performing exercises on each particular piece of equipment. In addition, display areas are located on the gym floor that detail specific exercise routines. All factors considered, these two relatively simple design features make it much easier for members to navigate through their workout quickly.

✓ Design the club to have a logical flow that matches the usage patterns of members. One common error that is often repeated in the health/fitness club industry is designing a club in contradiction to how the members typically use a club. For example, most members, after checking-in, proceed to the locker room, and then from there to their favorite workout area. For women, this situation may mean going from the entry area to the locker room, and then to group exercise or the spa. For men, on the other hand, it might mean going from the entry area to the locker room, and then to the weight room or the resistance training area. As such, if the aforementioned usage patterns were taken into consideration, it would be logical to place the women's locker room near the group-fitness zones, near the entry, so that women would not have to trek across the entire club to get to the locker room. It would also avoid a situation in which after changing in the locker room, they would have to transverse the gym to get to the group-exercise studios.

✓ Design the gym floor and locker rooms to accommodate usage at peak periods. Too many clubs design their gym floors and studios based on the expected overall level of membership, rather than on the number of users expected during the busiest peak periods of usage. Statistics from various club operators throughout the world indicate that between 5 and 10 percent of the total membership of a club may use the club during a peak-usage period. For example, if a club has 3,000 members, it is likely to have 150 to 300 members appear in the club during the busiest peak period. In Russia and the U.S., it is typical to see approximately 10 percent of the member base during the busiest peak period. In Germany or England, on the other hand, that number may be closer to 5 percent of the members who are in the club during the busiest peak period. From a design perspective, the club should make sure that sufficient lockers, equipment, and space are provided to accommodate this flow.

✓ Design the area so that equipment is spaced appropriately. Many clubs literally stack equipment like bricks on a wall, with minimal space between units. Clubs that wish to reduce the perception of overcrowding should consider the following suggestions:

  ⇨ Provide more spacing between machines. Adding another foot between machines can go a long way toward reducing the perception of compaction and overcrowding.

- ⇨ Don't put all the same equipment together. Having 12 treadmills arranged side-by-side can make the area more compacted than if three treadmills, three elliptical trainers, three bikes, and three additional treadmills were arranged side-by-side.
- ⇨ Create equipment zones that are separated by physical barriers, such as low walls. Instead of arranging equipment all in one area, create zones or pockets for segments of equipment. For example, having four zones of 20 pieces of equipment will appear less crowded than having 80 pieces all together.

✓ Reduce the number of corridors and doors. The more corridors and doors the club has, the longer it takes for a member to transverse the club.

✓ Reduce corners in the locker rooms and provide wider corridors between lockers. A common mistake made in locker room design is to place lockers in sections where two lockers make contact with each other in a corner, thereby placing members in a very intimate physical situation. Furthermore, a number of locker rooms are designed such that the space between opposing lockers is so close that it is difficult for two bodies to pass. Most members can find this situation intimidating, as well as an intrusion of their personal space. To alleviate these two issues, clubs should design the bays for the lockers so that as few corners exist as possible. As such, the lockers should be arranged across from each other with a space of at least 10 feet provided between rows.

- *Theme the design to appeal to the tribes of the club and to create excitement.* According to industry-based research on membership retention, one of the leading reasons that members indicate is their basis for terminating their membership involves their loss of interest in using the club and/or a decline in their level of motivation. When this dynamic of a loss in interest and level of motivation is considered with the need to serve new tribes, it becomes imperative that clubs look at ways to invigorate their physical environment in order to appeal to these new tribal audiences. Concurrently, they also have to create a sense of excitement and interest for both new and veteran members. One way to achieve this outcome is to design the physical environment of the club around a specific theme, one that is not likely to be replicated by a competitor.

  At the Telos Fitness Center in Dallas, Texas, ownership designed the club around an Athenian theme (i.e., ancient Greek culture). As such, the club's reception area, locker rooms, and gym all incorporate design elements that portray the desired theme. As a result, members may find themselves among Greek columns or baths (whirlpools).

  At Amanusa, a women's-only club in Darmstadt, Germany, the owners established an Asian theme. This facility offers two outdoor Asian gardens for relaxing, bamboo partitions separating various exercise zones of the club, Asian paintings, and ceilings comprised of bamboo and fabrics. These themed-design elements are tied into program elements, resulting in a very unique experience.

Clubs should design the bays for the lockers so that as few corners exist as possible.

At Ecofit located in Sao Paulo, Brazil, the owners designed their club around an ecological theme. In this facility, members feel as if they are within a rain forest. It is also interesting to note that reclaimed rain water is used for the pools and rest rooms, solar power is employed for lighting and power generation, recycled and reclaimed woods are incorporated in the flooring, and similar reclaimed or recycled materials are utilized in other areas of the club.

As such, the members of each of the aforementioned clubs find the physical environment in their facility interesting, motivating, and possibly more importantly, appealing to their particular interests.

As briefly discussed in this chapter, how a club physically designs and builds its facility can have a notable direct or indirect impact on its ability to retain members. Similar to everything else concerning the club membership issue, no one element stands alone. As such, focusing just on design will not be the end-all solution to the retention challenge facing clubs. All factors considered, incorporating one or more of the design suggestions detailed in this chapter can help a club create an environment that is more conducive to enhancing retention. In combination with the strategies reviewed in the previous three chapters, these proposals can provide real-time solutions to the retention challenges facing every club.

13

Case Studies on Retention From the United Kingdom

Over the past decade, Paul Bedford, Ph.D., and Melvin Hillsdon, Ph.D. (partners in ReAim, now trading as RetentionGuru.com, a consulting and research company that focuses on retention and attrition management), have been conducting extensive research on membership attrition and retention. Their work has been featured in numerous articles that have appeared in industry publications, as well as included as part of presentations made at IHRSA and other related global industry meetings. In addition, their work has served as the foundation for several reports that have been released by the Fitness Industry Association of England, including:

- *Winning the Retention Battle series* (a six-part report released over a few years)
- *Fitness Industry Association National Retention Report*

As an integral part of their research and consulting services, they have studied the retention strategies that have been implemented by club operators throughout the United Kingdom. These case studies illustrate how specific clubs and club companies have approached the issue of attrition and retention management. The case studies detail each company's successes and missed opportunities, as well as provide a wealth of information and insights concerning the challenges and fortuitous circumstances inherent in addressing membership attrition and retention. As such, this chapter is designed to shed light on several factors, including the retention strategies that these club operators have implemented, the results that they were able to achieve, and what actions worked and which did not.

Case Studies

- Club Kingswood; Health, Fitness, and Spa, Basildon, England

  Club Kingswood (Figure 13-1) is a health and country club that was originally founded in 1967. The club offers its members a host of facilities and amenities, including seven racquet and squash courts, a tennis court, two group-exercise studios, a cycling studio, a fully equipped gym, a spa and salon, a licensed bar, and a restaurant. On several occasions, the club has been voted one of the top five health clubs in the United Kingdom and has twice been named club of the year in the U.K. The club's key metrics at the start of their retention efforts were as follows:

  ✓ 3,000 members

  ✓ Fifty percent of its members are 18 to 35 years old, 40 percent are 36 to 64 in age, and 10 percent are over the age of 65.

  ✓ Its retention rate in the year prior to working with the researchers was 55 percent.

  The club, aware of the fact that its membership retention performance was not satisfactory, pursued a retention strategy that was based on the research reflected in the FIA studies on member retention. Based on the results of Bedford and Hillsdon's research, Club Kingswood took the researcher's principles and developed their new induction process. Among the specific steps that they undertook in an effort to enhance the retention level of the club were the following:

Paul Bedford

Figure 13-1. Interior shots, Kingswood Health, Fitness, and Spa, U.K.

✓ Established clear financial and retention metrics that could be regularly monitored and shared with their team

✓ Provided a highly individualized induction (orientation) process for members over their first 12 weeks of membership. In essence, they asked the members of the club to commit to a 12-week induction process. During the first week of membership, they provided each member with a consultation that was conducted by the club's fitness staff, as well as an orientation to the cardiovascular equipment. In the second week, they provided each member with an orientation to both resistance training and flexibility training. In the third week, they provided members with an accountability program that was designed to help make sure that each member was headed in the right direction. In the fourth week, the club provided each member with a refresher orientation and reassessment program. In the fifth week, they introduced the members to other programs (e.g., group-exercise, racquet sports, aquatic, etc.), from which the members were asked to select the one that interested them the most. Finally, in the last week (week 12), the club did a reassessment and check-in with each member.

✓ Allowed each member, during their first month of membership, to bring a guest with them to work out.

✓ Followed up closely with each member on a regular basis.

✓ Coordinated the efforts of the entire staff of the club toward the successful implementation of the strategy. This step involved training and openly communicating on a consistent basis concerning both the process and the targeted metrics.

After the first year, the club's overall membership retention level had climbed from 55 to 65 percent, resulting in an additional $356,400 in profit.

After the first year, the club's overall membership retention level had climbed from 55 to 65 percent, resulting in an additional $356,400 in profit. The club's director, Georgina Jupp, was quoted as follows with regard to the club's experience when taking an entirely new approach to membership retention: "Members expectations are higher; however, we are now retaining people that would have previously left."

• Banana Fitness & Health, England

Banana Fitness & Health is the health and fitness brand of parent company Sports and Leisure Management (SLM), Ltd. SLM is a sport and leisure management company in the U.K. that operates 46 Banana Fitness Suites throughout the Midlands and southern England. Banana Fitness & Health provides its members with three unique ways to exercise—their bXP programs, comprised of eight different training programs, such as dash, punch, balance, etc.; their bGX group-exercise programs, which include the Les Mills suite of classes; and their bPT program, which offers members half-hour and full-hour personal training sessions. The company serves over 20,000 members. The company's vision is to promote and enhance the wellbeing of communities through exercise and sport.

Prior to implementing its new retention strategy, Banana Fitness & Health experienced the following metrics:

✓ 21 percent of members left in the first three months.

- ✓ 45 percent of members left within the first six months.
- ✓ 30 percent of members left after 12 months.

In an attempt to address the attrition issues facing its managed properties, the company developed a retention program, which it entitled *"Boomerang; keeping you coming back"* (Figure 13-2). The Boomerang Program concentrated on a few critical performance outcomes, while also narrowing the focus of the company at overcoming a few core challenges that it had encountered in previous efforts to manage its attrition and retention challenges. Quantitatively, the Boomerang Program attempted to address three key objectives:

- ✓ Decrease the percentage of leavers in the first three months by 10 percent
- ✓ Decrease the percentage of leavers in months four through six by 5 percent
- ✓ Focus on new members, infrequent users, and members who had lapsed for a long period of time (previously, management had focused its retention strategies on every member)

Paul Bedford

Figure 13-2. Retention program, Banana Fitness & Health

The *Boomerang Program* incorporated the following strategies:

- ✓ *Five Steps to Fitness* (Figure 13-3). This phase involved a series of five appointments for each new member, including an initial consultation with the new member to identify that individual's needs and interests, a second consultation that focused on providing a cardiovascular workout and program schedule, a third appointment built around providing a resistance training workout and an abs routine, a fourth appointment that updated the member's initial program, and finally, a fifth appointment to go over each member's results.
- ✓ *The Banana Program.* This multifaceted approach involved reinforcing the company's commitment to personal contact with each member on the gym floor, establishing targeted KPIs that were transparent to everyone on the team, establishing incentives that would encourage and reward employees to live the program values, holding employees and management accountable through monthly audits of the company's retention efforts, and finally, sharing of the program's KPIs on a daily basis.

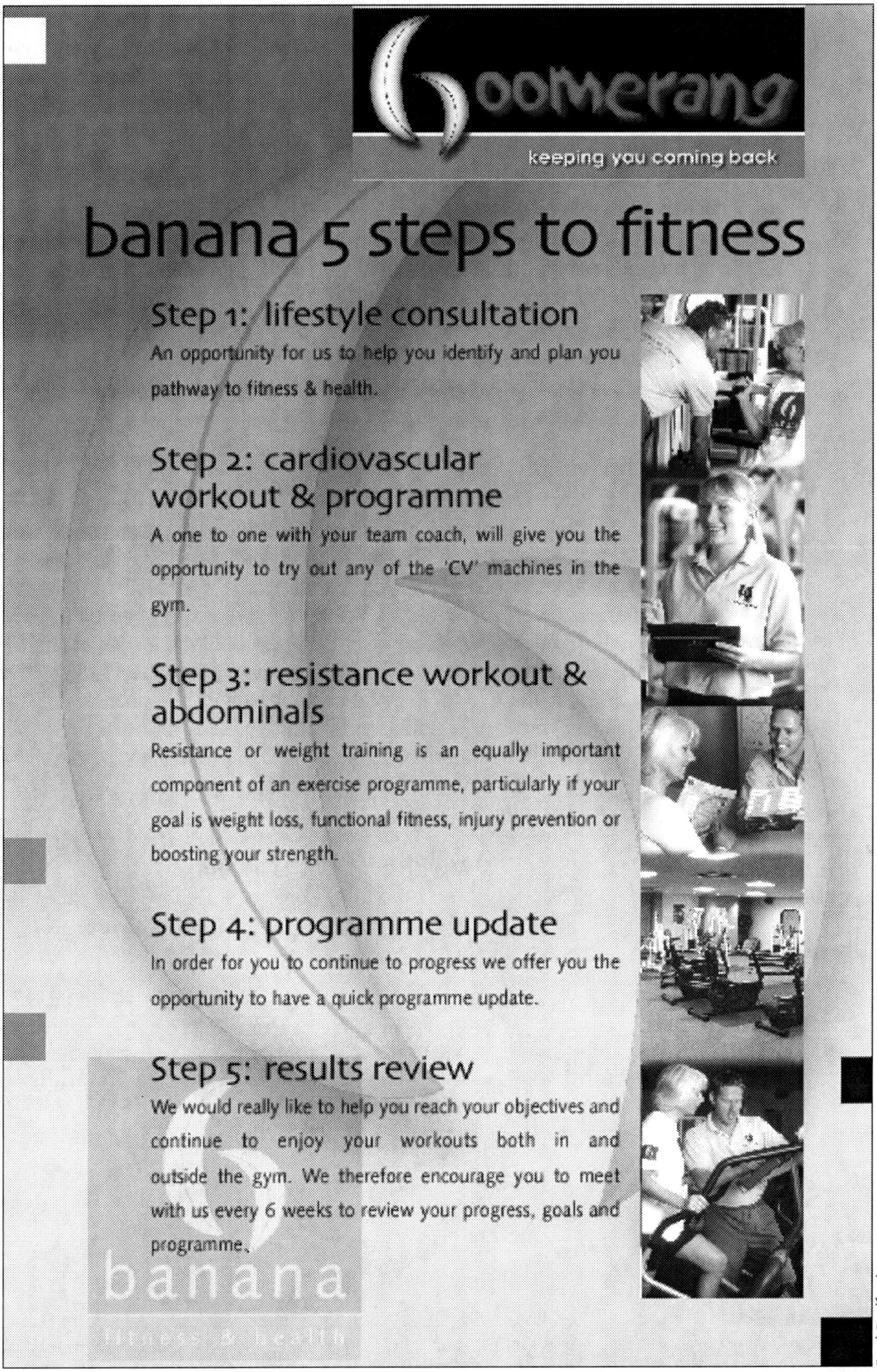

Paul Bedford

Figure 13-3. The series of five appointments in one of the phases of the Boomerang program of Banana Fitness & Health

✓ *Training.* The company made sure every employee was properly trained in how to deliver the five steps of fitness. As such, the employees were instructed in all facets of customer service, particularly concerning how to approach people, as well as how to counsel members on exercise and lifestyle behaviour.

As a result of the Boomerang Program, the company was able to achieve the following results:

✓ The percentage of members who left in the first six months dropped from 45 percent to 33 percent (a level of improvement that exceeded the goals of the company).

✓ The percentage of new members who participated in the initial consultation increased to 96 percent.

✓ The number of appointments scheduled throughout the five steps of fitness increased dramatically.

- David Lloyd Leisure Group, England

  David Lloyd Leisure was founded in 1983 as David Lloyd Leisure Ltd. At its inception, the company focused on operating a racquet sports club (squash and tennis, accompanied by food and beverage) that served an upscale audience. Over the years, the company moved into fitness, aquatics, and spa services. In 2007, the company was acquired by London & Regional Properties, owners of Next Generation Clubs, which created a new company, entitled the David Lloyd Leisure Group. The Group now operates 79 clubs throughout England and another 10 clubs in Europe. The company is recognized as a global leader in the premium club segment. As of 2011, the company had approximately 6,000 employees, who served

Figure 13-4. The title of the retention program established by David Lloyd Leisure

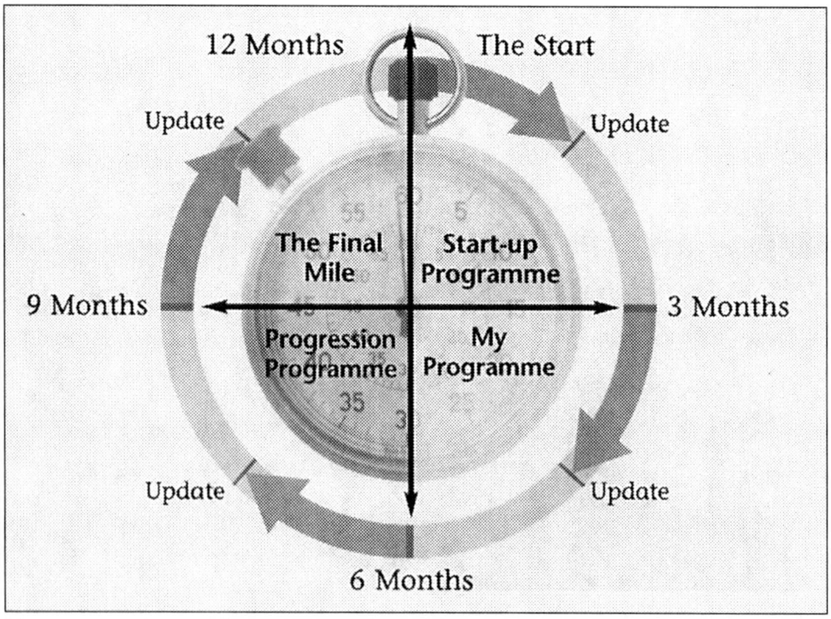

Figure 13-5. A graphic representation of the retention program of David Lloyd Leisure

a membership base of 450,000. At the time that this particular case study was undertaken, David Lloyd Leisure operated 57 racquet, health, and fitness clubs and had a membership base of 320,000.

Looking to positively impact its membership retention levels, and enhance member exercise adherence, David Lloyd Leisure established a retention program it entitled the *David Lloyd Health and Fitness Experience* (Figure 13-4), which was structured to support the social cognitive theory (self-efficacy model) of exercise behavior adoption. The program was initially piloted in eight clubs over a 12-month period, using a sample population of 400 members. The program incorporated four distinct phases, each of which was composed of a few key elements. Figure 13-5 provides a graphic representation of the program phases, which included the following:

- ✓ *Start-up Program.* During this phase, each member received an induction. A month later, a follow-up appointment was held. During this phase, the staff focused on assessing the needs of each member (personal-goal profile, self-motivation inventory, and exercise-feeling inventory). Based on the results of their initial assessment, each member then received an appropriate exercise program.
- ✓ *My Program.* During this phase, the staff of the club focused on providing the member with counseling, education, and support (the core elements of the social cognitive theory). At the half-way point of this phase, the member had an appointment with the staff to update their program and check on their progress.
- ✓ *Progression Program.* During this phase, the primary focus was to establish the proper program progressions so that each member would continue to experience progress toward achieving their results. This stage expands on the self-efficacy model of behavior adoption, which states that by mastering one phase, a person's level of self confidence improves, thereby enabling the individual to move on and master a more challenging program. During this phase, each member had an appointment with the staff.
- ✓ *The Final Mile.* During this final phase, the objective was to provide each member with the support and counseling that were necessary to help bring the member's goals to fruition. Similar to the other phases, each member had an appointment with the staff at the midway point of the phase.

Based on the results of their initial assessment, each member then received an appropriate exercise program.

As part of the program, the company made sure that the fitness staff was trained in the application of the social cognitive theory and behavioral counseling. In addition, the fitness staff was held accountable for membership-retention outcomes. Finally, the membership team and fitness team worked together to create a seamless transition for the members, as the members moved from enrollment to engagement.

As for results, Figure13-6 provides a comparative illustration of the exercise adherence results of the pilot group versus members not involved in the study. As can be seen, the participants in the *David Lloyd Leisure Health and Fitness Experience* had significantly higher exercise adherence than members who did not participate in the pilot program. Figure 13-7 compares the retention levels

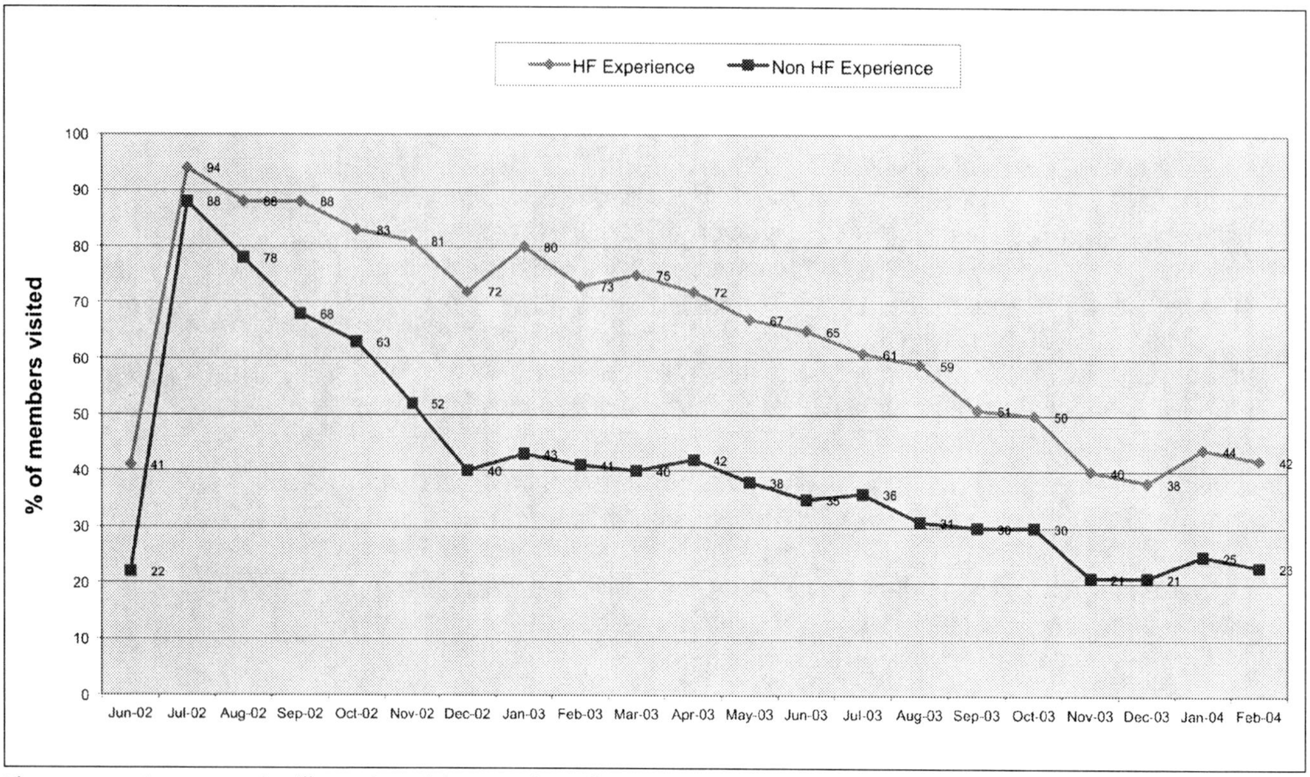

Figure 13-6. A comparative illustration of the exercise adherence results of pilot group participants vs. non-study participants

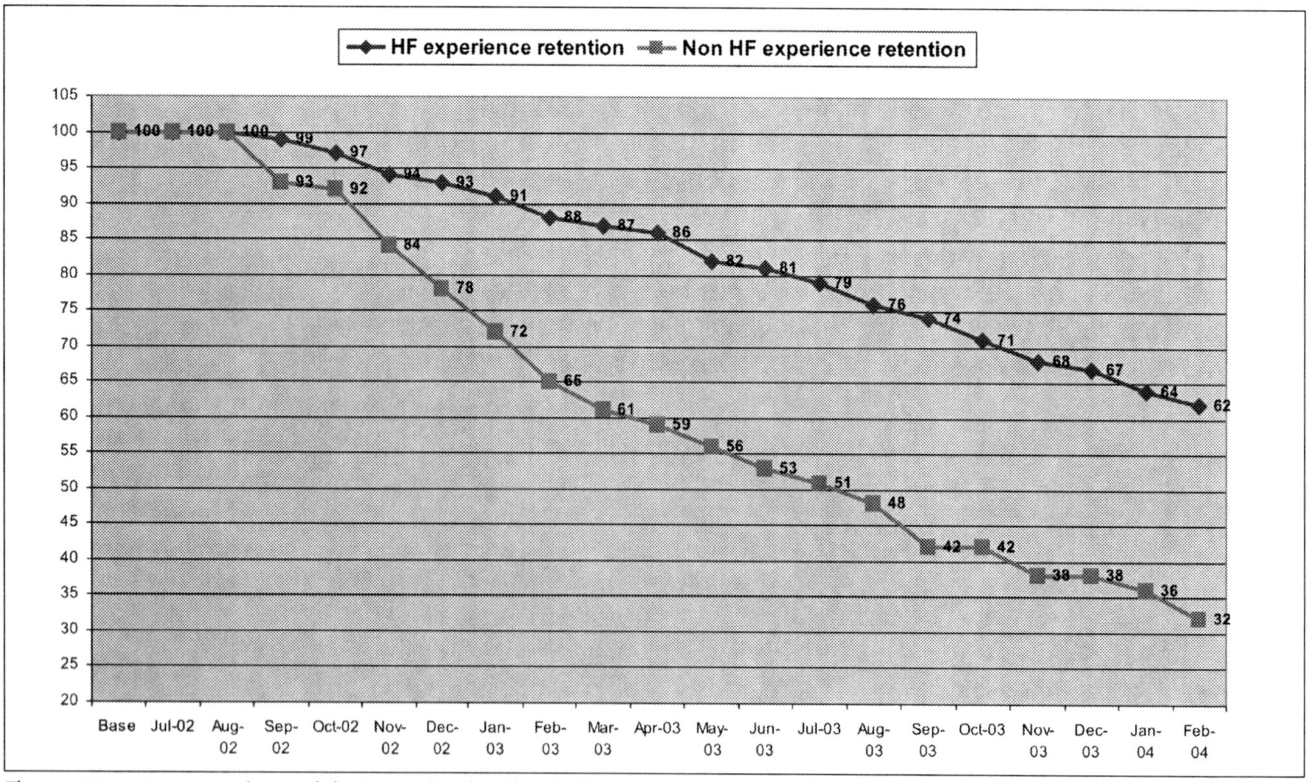

Figure 13-7. A comparison of the retention levels of pilot group participants vs. non-study participants

of program participants with those of non-participants. The data clearly shows that program participants had a significantly higher retention level than did non-participants. It should be noted that 68 percent of the eligible members participated in the pilot study.

- Reebok Sports Club, London, England

  The Reebok Club of London is a large, multipurpose sports club that offers a diverse array of services and programs for its members. Located in one of London's leading financial districts, Canary Wharf, the club provides its members with a comprehensive mix of programs and services. In 2006, the club approached Dr's Hillsdon and Bedford to assist it in identifying the underlying factors behind the club's existing retention challenges, as well as to assist the club in identifying a targeted strategy for improving retention.

  After considering the available research data, along with interviews of 1000 club members, Bedford and Hillsdon recommended several strategies to improve the club's membership retention performance. Among the several strategies recommended by these two renowned experts, the club chose to pursue a retention approach that relied on the club utilizing its fitness team to provide an individualized induction process. This strategy involved providing those new members who were most at risk of quitting, with a complimentary induction that utilized behavior change approaches, based on motivational interviewing and follow-up sessions. After the initial induction, new members were provided with extra support in their early weeks, in an effort to increase their self-efficacy, along with an option for program updates and reviews each month. Those new members who had previous experience with exercise were provided with the option of a fast-track induction. In order to deliver this level of service, it was essential that an efficient system existed that would enable members to easily schedule their appointments.

  The management and the researchers employed this approach to retention for two reasons. First, a personalized approach was the best fit for this particular group of members (the club experienced 73,000 member visits in January 2012), since it was positioned as an upscale club. Second, it avoided requiring those members who had previous exercise experience with having to go through the same induction process as first-time exercisers.

  Figure 13-8 depicts the results of the impact of the program on the retention level of the club, compared to the same time periods for prior years. For example, Figure 13-8 shows that when compared to the three proceeding years (2004, 2005, and 2006), new member retention was already higher after the first three months. Figure 13-9 delineates the pre- and post-program results concerning retention five months into the program. The overall impact on retention was significant, with an absolute improvement of 8 percent (91 percent retention versus 83 percent), after a member's first five months of membership.

The club chose to pursue a retention approach that relied on the club utilizing its fitness team to provide an individualized induction process.

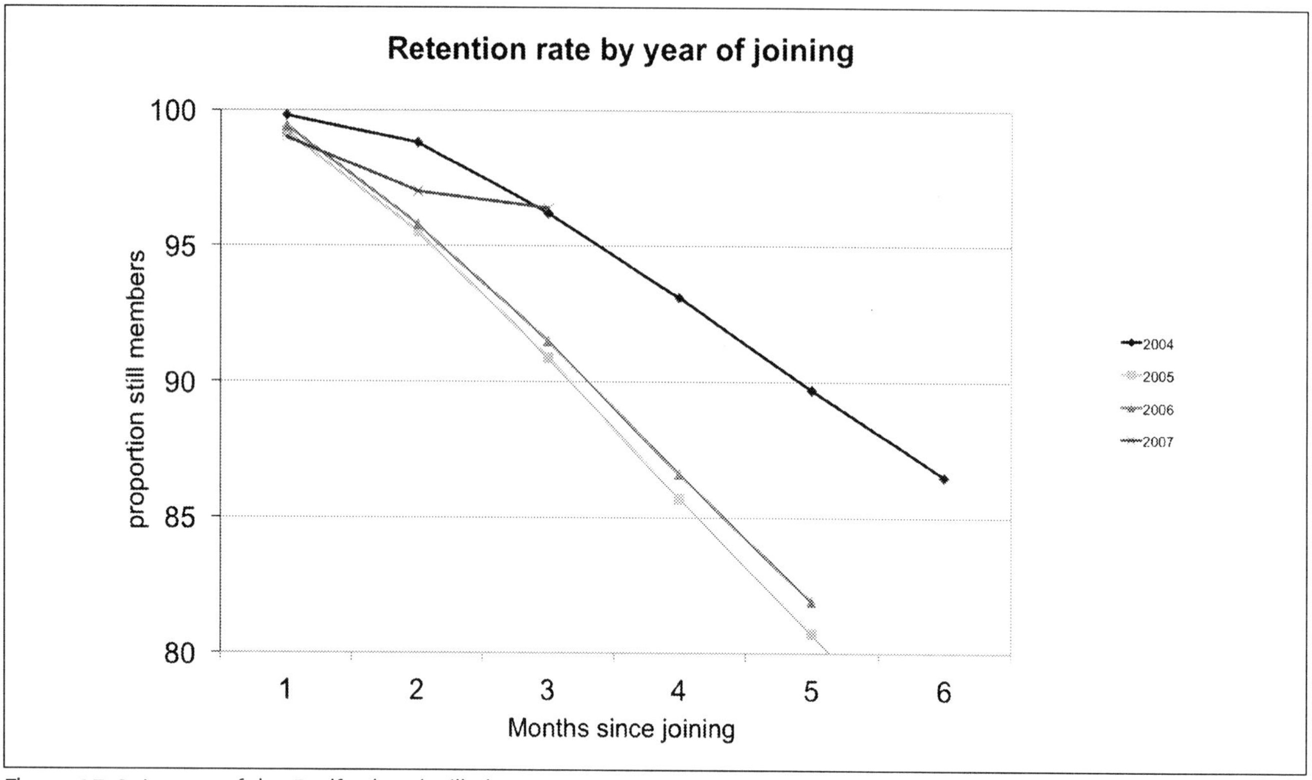

Figure 13-8. Impact of the Bedford and Hillsdon program on retention level

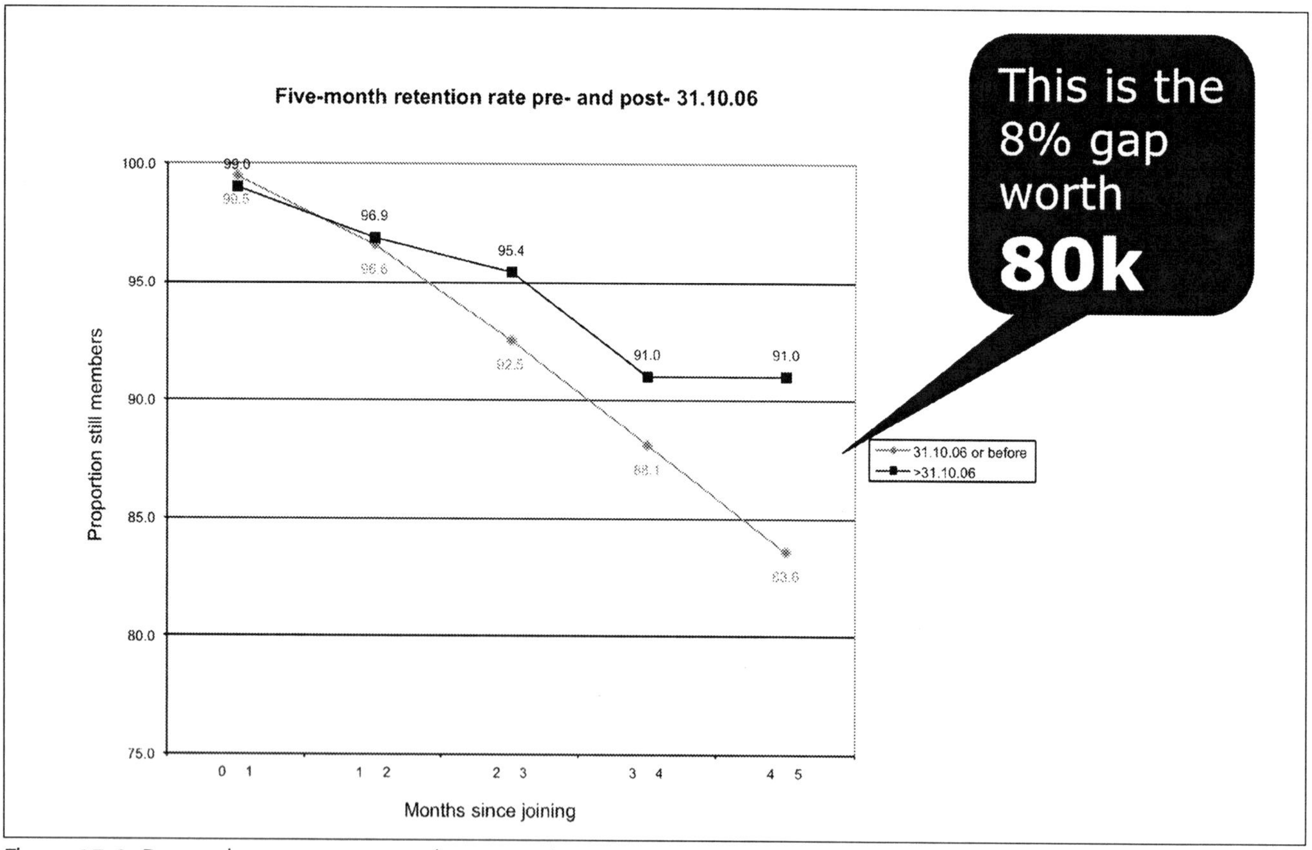

Figure 13-9. Pre- and post-program results concerning retention

Insights From the Case Studies

Retention success requires a plan, as well as disciplined adherence to the plan.

- Retention success requires a plan, as well as disciplined adherence to the plan. Each of the clubs reviewed in this chapter had a retention plan that included the following:
  - ✓ Specific and measurable retention metrics or KPIs
  - ✓ Focused strategies and action steps that were tied to approved performance metrics
  - ✓ Staff training in the principles and practices necessary to successfully implement the approved strategies
  - ✓ Staff accountability. Each of the aforementioned club companies made sure that management and frontline staff were held accountable for implementing the strategies and achieving the desired outcomes.
  - ✓ Regular inspections or audits of the action steps, strategies, and outcomes. These inspections were designed to support each company's focus on accountability.
  - ✓ Efforts to communicate the results to everyone on a regular basis. Management made sure that everyone involved in the process understood how the outcomes aligned with the goals.
- Different strokes for different folks. While each club discussed in this chapter relied on specific research-proven principles and theories concerning exercise adherence and membership retention, each organization chose a separate path to achieve its goals. David Lloyd Leisure, for example, created an experience based on the social cognitive theory of exercise adoption. Reebok, on the other hand, leveraged one of its strengths, personal training, to drive retention. In contrast, Banana employed a case-management approach to managing retention, while Club Kingswood focused on the member-induction process.

  As such, primary takeaways from the information presented in this chapter are the following:
  - ✓ Clubs should build their plan around proven principles concerning either exercise adherence or membership retention.
  - ✓ Clubs should narrow their focus and avoid trying to pursue too many goals or implement too many strategies. In other words, clubs should keep their efforts simple, focused, and disciplined.
  - ✓ Clubs should understand their strengths and limitations before proceeding. The key for clubs is to leverage their strengths as an integral part of their retention efforts.
  - ✓ Clubs should understand their members so that they can tailor their programs to the personality of their membership and the culture of the club.
  - ✓ Clubs should be flexible. If a particular approach doesn't work, they should refocus on another strategy.
  - ✓ Clubs should commit to whatever they decide to do and be relentless about it.

Supplemental Form A

Club Name

Annual Personal Physical Activity and Health Promotion Agreement

Member Name: ______________________________

Member Contact #: W) ____________ H) ____________ C) ____________

Member Email: ______________________________

Staff Liaison/Trainer: ______________________________

Staff Contact #: W) ____________ H) ____________ C) ____________

Staff Email: ______________________________

My primary goal of the next year is to:

____

____

____

____

To achieve my primary goal, I am committed to the following short term goals and actions:
30 Day – Goal and agreed to actions

____

____

____

90 Day – Goal and agreed to actions

____

____

____

180 Day – Goal and agreed to actions

____

____

____

On behalf of the club, I/we agree to provide the following support to assist you in achieving your goals!

____

____

____

____

Are there any challenges or obstacles that you feel might arise that could hinder your ability to achieve your goals and which we could be of assistance in working together to help overcome?

____

____

____

____

It is hereby agreed that for each goal you achieve, that you will be entitled to receive from the club:

____

____

____

____

It is hereby agreed that in the event that the club does not fulfill its portion of this agreement that you will be entitled to receive:

____

____

____

____

We hereby agreed to the terms set forth in this physical activity and health promotion agreement.

Member Signature: ________________________________

Staff Signature: __________________________ Date: __________

Supplemental Form B
Club Name
New Member Profile

The information provided on this profile will help us to get to know you better and create a foundation for personalizing your club experience.

Name: ____________________

Address: ____________________

Contact Phone #: ____________________ Email (optional): ____________________

Please place a check mark by the appropriate response.

Interests and Hobbies

1. Which types of fitness activities/health promotion programs interest you?
   - ☐ Personal training
   - ☐ Pilates
   - ☐ Yoga
   - ☐ Martial arts
   - ☐ Group exercise classes
   - ☐ Spinning
   - ☐ Weight management
   - ☐ Back fitness
   - ☐ Racquetball
   - ☐ Health promotion programs
   - ☐ Nutrition programs

2. What kinds of club services might offer interest you?
   - ☐ Massage
   - ☐ Day spa services
   - ☐ Alternative health care
   - ☐ Café
   - ☐ Nursery service
   - ☐ Youth programs and camps
   - ☐ Basketball leagues and events
   - ☐ Racquet sport leagues and programs
   - ☐ Tennis leagues and programs
   - ☐ Other: ____________________

3. What kinds of adventure and social activities if made available would interest you?
   - ☐ Networking events
   - ☐ Skiing trips
   - ☐ Golf outings
   - ☐ Whitewater rafting
   - ☐ Rock climbing
   - ☐ Scuba diving/snorkeling
   - ☐ Sporting event outings
   - ☐ Social events (e.g. wine tasting, book club, etc.)
   - ☐ Other: ____________________

4. What goal(s) would you like to achieve during your first 30 days, 90 days and 360 days as a result of your membership at the club?

   30 Day Goals

   a. ____________________ b. ____________________

   90 Day Goals

   a. ____________________ b. ____________________

   360 Day Goals

   a. ____________________ b. ____________________

5. Please describe your **top three expectations** are for your membership experience?

   a. ____________________

   b. ____________________

   c. ____________________

Membership Communication

1. What are your preferences in regards to receiving prompt information and communication from the club (please check all responses that are appropriate)?

   ☐ Cell phone. If checked, please provide number: ______________________

   ☐ Text message. If checked, please provide number: ______________________

   ☐ email message. If checked, please provide email address: ______________________

   ☐ Other. If checked, please provide information for reaching you: ______________________

2. Which social media outlet would be one you would most likely use to obtain information about what is happening at the club?

   ☐ Facebook page ☐ Member blog ☐ Web site ☐ Other: ______________________

3. Are you likely to reference the club's web site for information? ☐ Yes ☐ No

   If yes, can you describe the type of information you would like to be able to access through the web site?

   ____

4. What services could the club offer through its web site or the intranet that would make your membership experience more enjoyable and productive?

   ☐ Post class schedules ☐ Ability to check account status ☐ Sign-up for events

   ☐ Schedule personal training appointments ☐ Schedule spa appointments

   ☐ Submit complaints and suggestions to management

General Demographic Information

1. Gender ☐ Male ☐ Female

2. Age segment ☐ Under 18 ☐ 18 – 34 ☐ 35 – 54 ☐ 55 +

3. Marital status ☐ Single ☐ Married

4. Number of children (if applicable):

5. Household income category (annual)

   ☐ Under $50,000 ☐ $50,000 – $74,999 ☐ $75,000 – $99,999

   ☐ $100,000 – $149,999 ☐ $150,000 – $199,999 ☐ $200,000 +

6. Highest level of education earned?

   ☐ High school ☐ Undergraduate ☐ Graduate ☐ Post graduate

Member Signature: ______________________

Staff Signature: ______________________ Date: __________

Supplemental Form C
MY Personal Profile

The professional wellness team at the club greatly appreciates your completing this personal profile. The information obtained through this profile will help our team identify the best strategies for insuring that your membership experience at the club is an enjoyable and rewarding one.

Name: ______________________________ Date joined: ______________________

Contact Phone #'s: (w) ______________________ (c) ______________________

Email: ____

I. Club Experience

1. Prior to joining the club, have you ever been a member of another health and fitness club? ☐ Yes (0) ☐ No (5)
   If you answered yes to question 1, please continue with question 2 and if you answered no to question 1, please proceed on to question 3.

2. How many other clubs have you previously been a member of? ☐ 1 (0) ☐ 2 – 4 (1) ☐ 5 or greater (2)

3. In your last club, how long were you a member?
   ☐ less than 6 months (3) ☐ 6 months to a year (2) ☐ 1 year to 3 years (1) ☐ 3 years or greater (0)

   Total Points: ________

II. Fitness Experience

4. Do you currently exercise on a regular basis (at least twice a week for at least 30 minutes) or have you exercised on a regular basis at any time in the last 6 months? ☐ Yes (0) ☐ No (5)
   If you answered no to question 4, please continue with question 5 and if you answered yes, please proceed on to question 6.

5. Please indicate your primary reason for not engaging in a regular exercise program?
   ☐ no place to conveniently exercise (1)
   ☐ did not have the time to exercise or continue exercising (2)
   ☐ did not have the motivation to exercise or continue exercising (3)
   ☐ do not enjoy exercising (4)
   ☐ did not feel I needed to exercise (5)

6. Have you ever exercised or participated in a sport activity in the past? ☐ Yes (0) ☐ No (5)

   Total Points: ________

III. Tell us About Yourself

7. When learning a new skill you are most likely to?
   - ☐ jump right in and try it (0)
   - ☐ read up on it first then try it (1)
   - ☐ observe someone else a few times then proceed to try it (2)
   - ☐ seek advice and get training before trying it (3)

8. When confronted with a new situation, such as a new work environment, new community or new social environment you are most likely to?
   - ☐ stay to myself and only introduce myself to those I need to. (0)
   - ☐ take the time to observe and explore before introducing myself (1)
   - ☐ immediately introduce myself and get connected (2)

9. When you need to relieve stress you are most likely to:
   - ☐ escape by myself and read a good book. (0)
   - ☐ escape by myself and either watch TV or play computer games. (1)
   - ☐ get together with a close friend and do something (e.g., play a game, shop, etc.) (2)
   - ☐ get together with a group of friends and do something (3)

10. Which of the following tend to bring you the greatest enjoyment?
    - ☐ being alone for a quiet evening (0)
    - ☐ getting together with a few close friends for dinner or conversation (1)
    - ☐ attending a sporting competition, theatre or related event (2)
    - ☐ throwing a party or attending a party with lots of people. (3)

11. If you currently exercise, do you prefer exercising?
    ☐ alone (0) ☐ with a close friend or associate (1) ☐ as part of a group (2)

Total Points: ________

IV. Challenges, Goals and Preferences

12. Please indicate the top two challenges or barriers you foresee arising over the next six months to a year that could make it difficult for you to effectively achieve your fitness goals. Please indicate the most likely challenge/barrier with a 1and the second most likely challenge/barrier with a 2.
    - ☐ family obligations (child care, household chores, etc.)
    - ☐ work obligations (travel, weekend work, etc.)
    - ☐ not achieving my desired results or desired goals
    - ☐ losing motivation
    - ☐ not finding someone to exercise with
    - ☐ financial considerations
    - ☐ having the time to fit using the club into my schedule

13. Please indicate the top two general goals you want to achieve as the result of your membership at the club. Use 1 to represent your first goal and 2 to represent your second goal.
    - ☐ too lose weight
    - ☐ to prevent health problems
    - ☐ to get fit
    - ☐ to assist with a medical condition
    - ☐ to remain fit
    - ☐ for relaxation and to reduce stress
    - ☐ to improve health
    - ☐ for competition and challenge
    - ☐ to feel better
    - ☐ to look better
    - ☐ perform better at work
    - ☐ performing better at a sport

14. What single expectation/goal do you have, that if met during your first 6 months as a club member, would represent a milestone achievement?
    - ☐ lose weight
    - ☐ perform better at work
    - ☐ feel better
    - ☐ recover from a health problem
    - ☐ look better
    - ☐ get more fit
    - ☐ perform better at desired sport

15. Please rank the following exercise related activities based on either your level of interest or your current participation practice using a scale of 1 to 5, with 1 representing your top choice/practiced activity and 5 your least acceptable choice/ practiced activity.
    - ☐ jogging/running
    - ☐ playing tennis
    - ☐ walking
    - ☐ swimming
    - ☐ bicycling
    - ☐ exercise classes
    - ☐ lifting weights
    - ☐ martial arts (e.g., karate, etc,)
    - ☐ Yoga
    - ☐ Pilates
    - ☐ basketball
    - ☐ indoor racquet sports

V. General Information (optional)

16. Age range: ☐ under 18 (5) ☐ 18 – 24 (4) ☐ 25 – 34 (3) ☐ 35 – 44 (2) ☐ 45 – 54 (1) ☐ 55 – 64 (0) ☐ 65 + (0)

17. Please indicated your estimated HH income during the most recent 12-month period?
    - ☐ under $25,000 (5)
    - ☐ $25,000 – $49,999 (4)
    - ☐ $50,000 – $74,999 (3)
    - ☐ $75,000 – $99,999 (2)
    - ☐ $100,000 – $149,999 (1)
    - ☐ $150,000 + (0)

18. Please indicate your highest level of educational attainment?
    - ☐ Some high school, no diploma (4)
    - ☐ High School Graduate (or GED) (3)
    - ☐ Some College (2)
    - ☐ Undergraduate Degree (B.A., B.S., etc.) (1)
    - ☐ Graduate/Professional Degree (0)

19. Please indicate your household type and presence of children?
    - ☐ Single, no kids (1)
    - ☐ Married (2)
    - ☐ Single w/kids (3)
    - ☐ Married w/kids (4)

Total Points: ________

Supplemental Form D

Guidelines for Using the MY Profile to Recommend a Plan of Engagement for New Members

Section I: General Information

Purpose

This section is intended to solicit demographic information that has been shown to have the highest correlation to an individual's use of a club membership and/or an individual's likelihood of starting and staying with an exercise program. Those variables include age, gender, household income, level of education and family status.

The Score and Interpretation

Range of Scores: 2 to 19

The more points an individual attains, the more likely they are to understand the value of exercise and the more likely they are to begin and stay with an exercise program at a club. The two most significant determinants in this category that impact maintaining a club membership and adopting a program of physical activity are having a college degree or higher and having a household income over $75,000 annually.

Score	*Interpretation*
2 – 7 points	This individual will be the most receptive and most likely to leverage their membership if we get them engaged properly. The first appointment with a professional is the key.
8 – 14 points	This individual may require educational support in addition to an initial appointment with a professional. Be prepared to "teach" them about the benefits and provide validation of the outcomes and the work that will go into achieving those outcomes. This individual will also have some hurdles related to balancing exercise with the rest of their life that are more difficult for them to overcome since they are less likely to accept the exercise value equation. The professional that works with them should be a good coach and teacher.
15 – 19 points	This individual will probably require extra effort if you intend to have them adopt an exercise program. They will need to be educated about the benefits of exercise, provided evidence that it works and encouraged along the way. This individual should be assigned to your best coach and educator.

Section II: Club Experience

Purpose

This section is focused on uncovering the individual's prior experience with club membership, a valuable predictor of their likelihood to remaining a member.

Score and Interpretation

Range of Scores: 0 to 11

Empirical research shows that individual's who have never used a club before will be the most intimidated by the club experience and the most likely to drop their membership if a challenge arises.

Score	*Interpretation*
0 - 1	This person is very familiar with the club experience and will not require as much education about how to use a club. You definitely want to make sure that they receive an appointment, but they are most likely to be comfortable using the club.

2 – 3 This individual is someone who has used a club previously, but not for a long period of time or may have been a member of several clubs for short periods of time. This individual has probably had a poor club experience and as a result will be jaded. The professional who works with this individual should be prepared to provide a great introduction, but also be prepared to provide follow-up appointments or contact.

4 – 5 This individual is either new to the club experience or has had an unfavorable club experience. The professional who works with them must provide a greater level of attention in regards to providing them with a good club experience. It may help to introduce them to another member who has had a great club experience.

Section III: Fitness Experience

Purpose

This section is focused on uncovering the individual's prior exercise experience. Research shows that individual's who currently exercise or who have experience with exercise and sports are more likely to adopt an exercise routine.

Score and Interpretation

Range of Scores: 0 to 15

Research clearly shows that individuals who have never exercised or participated in a sports activity are much less likely to adopt a regular program of physical activity. Furthermore, if the individual sees no value to exercise, then it is even less likely they will adopt the exercise "habit".

Score *Interpretation*

0 - 5 This individual already exercises at least twice a week and may or may not have been active in a sport activity. They will not require much education or reinforcement to stay with exercise, but should receive a personal program from the staff. The goal is to make sure these individual's know were things are so they can take advantage of them. Give them the option of private instruction, but realize they may benefit more by receiving a general orientation.

6 – 15 This individual will require initial instruction and a custom exercise/fitness program. In addition, they will most likely need at least one follow-up session before being left on their own. Some additional suggestions based on their answer to question 10 include;

a. If they indicate they do not have time, then make sure you develop a behavioral contract and set a schedule with the member. These people are excellent candidates for personal training at set times or group classes held at the same time each week.

b. If they indicate they lack motivation, then make sure that you offer them some form of ongoing support. Personal training, whether it's weekly or monthly would be a great recommendation. This individual will also need a program that is changed regularly.

c. If they indicate they do not enjoy exercise, and then have them work with a professional who can develop an entertaining program. Furthermore, this individual is going to find exercise a chore, so don't make the program too challenging and, make sure to prescribe activities that they show some interest in (see sections IV and V).

d. If the individual indicates they did not feel they need to exercise, then the challenge to get them to adopt exercise will be the most challenging. The key is to find out what goals they have and then connect those goals to exercise. A behavioral contract will be very helpful with this individual. This individual should be assigned to a professional who meets with them regularly and provides feedback and support. Sometimes introducing them to another member who had the same attitude in the past and has now adopted exercise can help.

Section IV: Tell Us about Yourself

Purpose

This section is designed to identify the individual's social preference as it pertains to engaging in a new experience. The goal is to uncover the social structure that will be the least intimidating to the individual and, the most motivating for their general personality.

Score and Interpretation

Range of Scores: 0 to 13

While every individual's personality is unique, there are some common tendencies among all individuals when it comes to the level of social interaction that they feel most comfortable in. For example, we know that certain individual's thrive in a highly social environment, while others thrive in a more solitude environment. The goal of this section is to determine the most suitable social environment to introduce the new member to so they can be successful.

Score	*Interpretation*
0 – 2	This individual is the type of person who prefers to do things on their own. Once this individual has learned how to exercise and use the club, they will prefer to work out at times when the club is not as busy. These individuals will also prefer a minimal level of contact with staff or other members.
3 – 5	This individual is the type of person who would prefer to have some interaction with a small group of people who have common interests. Once this individual has learned how to exercise and use the club, they would benefit from being introduced to a small group of members who have similar interests. For example, they might value being part of a small morning workout group. They key is to make sure they are introduced to a few members of like interest. In addition, these individual's will value regular recognition and contact from the staff.
6 to 13	This individual prefers a more social environment. They will prefer group oriented programs that allow them to socialize. This individual will also value being introduced to other members or volunteering to lead club activities. This individual will benefit from having a trusting relationship with several staff members.

Question 12 is critically important in regards to how to actually introduce the new member to their program at the club. Recommendations based on their response are as follows:

a. *Jump right in.* for this individual, all you really need to do is provide a general program orientation. They will likely have no problem trying new activities at the club. **It is important to let them know they can ask staff questions whenever they need to.**

b. *Read up first and then try.* In addition to providing this person with an orientation and possibly a personal session. **Consider providing them with handouts, audio tapes or video that can help them learn more about what they are doing.**

c. *Observe someone else a few times then proceed to try it.* This individual may benefit from multiple sessions with a trainer or professional before they feel comfortable on their own. They will benefit from having the trainer/professional demonstrate exercises several times. **Group training might be an excellent alternative since this individual will learn from observing others perform an exercise.**

d. *Seek advice and get training before trying it.* This individual will want professional guidance and instruction. This individual will not try something new unless they are taught by a professional before hand. As a result, the staff will need to stay in touch regularly to provide instruction on new exercises or activities. **This individual will require personal instruction before they start anything new.**

Section V: Challenges, Goals and Preferences

Purpose

This section is intended to uncover the specific goals the new member has, as well as the types of activities/exercises they are interested in. This section is also designed to determine what barriers may arise that could impact their ability to continue with exercise.

Interpretation

This section has no scoring as each question is intended to solicit answers specific to the individual. Rather than interpret a score, the answers to these questions will prepare the staff on how to individualize the program based on the new member's goals, interests and potential hurdles.

a. *Barriers.* Once you know the two primary challenges that the individual believes they will face, then you can develop a program that will help them deal with those challenges when they arise. To accomplish this, the professional should consider drawing up a behavioral contract with the member that identifies specific strategies for dealing with the hurdles, but also identifies rewards for overcoming them. Finally, it's important that we incorporate into the individual's program room for mistakes. They need to know its okay to fall short on occasion. Ultimately, you want to eliminate opportunities for the individual to feel guilty for temporarily succumbing to a barrier and provide easy strategies for overcoming those challenges.

b. *Goals & Expectations.* Once you know what the member's general goals are you need to work with them to establish reasonable and attainable targets and timelines for those goals. A behavioral contract that identifies the goals in easily measurable terms and identifies rewards for reaching those goals is important. The staff should be focused on creating a plan that both they and the member can agree to. The staff must provide the support to make sure the member achieves those goals. Consider having a way that the member can check in with the staff regarding the progress of their goals.

c. *Interest.* This question will help you identify the specific activities that are most likely to be interesting to the individual. The key is to prescribe a program that incorporates the top two or three interests into the program. Don't give them a program that involves an activity that they don't rate in their top five or you are likely to create an additional barrier to their participation.

Supplemental Form E
Share Your Experience
Member & Guest Comment Card

Date: ______________ Time: ______________

Experience you would like to share:

____

____

____

____

____

____

____

____

Overall how did you feel about your experience in the club today? Please indicate by checking of the appropriate response!

☐ 1 = definitely unsatisfactory

☐ 2 = Partially Unsatisfactory (did not meet your expectations)

☐ 3 = Not sure, neither satisfactory or unsatisfactory

☐ 4 = partially satisfactory

☐ 5 = Completely Satisfactory (wow)

Would you like us to follow-up directly with you? ☐ Yes ☐ No
If yes, please provide us with your name and contact information.

Name (optional): ____

Contact phone #: ____

Contact email: ____

Thank you for sharing your feelings about your experience today.

Supplemental Form F
Physical Activity Readiness Questionnaire

I. General Information (Please check the appropriate box)

Gender: ☐ Male ☐ Female Age: ☐ <45 ☐ 45 to 54 ☐ >55

II. Predisposing Coronary Risk Factors (Please check yes or no for each of the questions in this section)

Yes	No	Has your physician or other healthcare professional ever indicated that you have one of the following?
☐	☐	a. High blood pressure (e.g., systolic equal to or over 140 and/or diastolic equal to or over 90)
☐	☐	b. Elevated or abnormal blood lipids (e.g., cholesterol, triglycerides, LDL, HDL, etc.)
☐	☐	c. Smoke cigarettes or former smoker who has quit in the last six months.
☐	☐	d. Overweight (e.g., waist circumference over 40 inches for men and 35 inches for women)
☐	☐	e. Sedentary (e.g., do not exercise at all or perform less than 150 minutes of moderate activity weekly)
☐	☐	f. Elevated blood sugar (e.g., levels greater than 100 mg.dl)
☐	☐	g. History of heart disease (e.g., father/ first degree male relative under age 55 or mother/first degree female relative under age 65.

Total number of Yes checks If you are male and over the age of 45 or female and over the age of 55 and have checked of at least one yes in this section it is recommended that you consult with your physician or healthcare professional before engaging in a program of regular physical activity.

III. Signs and Symptoms (Please check yes or no for each of the questions below)

Yes	No	
☐	☐	1. Has your physician ever told you that you have a heart condition and that you should only do physical activity recommended by a physician?
☐	☐	2. Do you experience pain in your chest or radiating into your jaw, neck or arms when you are physically active?
☐	☐	3. In the past three month, have you experienced chest pain at rest or when asleep?
☐	☐	4. Do you lose balance because of dizziness or do you ever lose consciousness?
☐	☐	5. Do you experience shortness of breath at rest or with mild exertion?
☐	☐	6. Is your physician currently prescribing medications for your blood pressure, blood lipids or a heart condition?
☐	☐	7. Do you or have you experienced recently swelling in the ankles or other extremities?
☐	☐	8. Do you experience pain or severe discomfort in your lower extremities when walking that subsides within 1 to 2 minutes after you stop?
☐	☐	9. Do you have diabetes?
☐	☐	10. Do you have asthma or another respiratory condition that causes difficulty with breathing?
☐	☐	11. Do you currently or have you experienced within the past 6 months back pain/discomfort or other joint related problem that prevented you from carrying out normal daily activities?
☐	☐	12. Are you pregnant?

Total number of Yes checks. If you answered yes to any of the questions in this section you will need to consult with your physician prior to becoming physically active and/or before the club can prescribe an exercise program for you. The club does provide a form that your physician can complete and forward to us indicating how best to prepare your exercise program.

Supplemental Form G
Pre-activity Screening

Name: ______________________ Member Number: ______________

Address: ______________________

Telephone: (W) ______________ (H) ______________

Fax: ______________ E-mail: ______________

Gender: ______________ Birthdate: ______________

Regular physical activity is enjoyable, safe and healthy for most people. However, some individuals may have health related risks that might be aggravated by participation in a program of physical activity and as a result might require them to check with their physician prior to embarking on a program of physical activity. To help determine if there is a need for you to see your physician before beginning an exercise program, please answer the following questions carefully. All information will be kept in the strictest confidentiality.

I. Pre-activity Screening Questions

Yes	No	
☐	☐	1. Has your physician ever told you that you have a heart condition?
☐	☐	2. Do you experience pain in your chest when you are physically active?
☐	☐	3. In the past month, have you experienced chest pain when not performing physical activity?
☐	☐	4. Do you lose balance because of dizziness or do you ever lose consciousness?
☐	☐	5. Do you have a bone or joint problem that could be aggravated by a change in your level of physical activity?
☐	☐	6. Is your physician currently prescribing medications for your blood pressure or heart condition?
☐	☐	7. Do you know of any other reason why you should not participate in a program of physical activity?

If you answered yes to any of the above questions, it is recommended that you consult with your physician, by phone or in person, before having a fitness test or participating in physical activity program.

Suggested Resources

- *101 Programming Strategies for Engaging Members in Health/Fitness Clubs.* Stephen J. Tharrett and Teresa J. Thomason. Healthy Learning: Monterey, CA. 2012.
- *101 Strategies for Improving Member Retention in Health/Fitness Clubs.* Stephen J. Tharrett and Patricia C. Amend. Healthy Learning: Monterey, CA, 2012.
- *ACSMs Health/Fitness Facilities Standards and Guidelines,* 4th edition. Stephen J. Tharrett and James A. Peterson, editors. Human Kinetics: Champaign, IL. 2012.
- *American Attitudes Toward Healthy Lifestyle Incentives.* IHRSA Study conducted by American Sports Data. Boston, MA.1995.
- *Facility Design and Impact on Retention.* Bedford, Ph.D. and Hillsdon, Ph.D.
- *Fitness American Style: A Look at How and Why Americans Exercise.* Prepared for IHRSA by Roper Starch Worldwide. 2001.
- *Fitness American Style III: Major Consumer Forces Shaping the Health Club Industry.* IHRSA study conducted by Ketchum, Boston, MA. 2007.
- *Fitness Industry Association 2008 National Retention Report.* Dr. Melvyn Hillsdon and Dr. Paul Bedford. ReAIM.
- *Fitness Management, 3rd Edition.* Stephen J. Tharrett and James. A. Peterson. Healthy Learning: Monterey, California. 2012.
- *How Consumers View Health and Sports Clubs.* IHRSA study by the Center for Research on Active Lifestyle Behavior, University of Michigan, Ann Arbor, Michigan. 1994.
- *The IHRSA Asia Pacific Market Report: The Size and Scope of the Industry.* IHRSA in cooperation with Deloitte, Boston, MA. 2008, 2006.
- *The IHRSA European Market Report: The Size and Scope of the Industry.* IHRSA in cooperation with Deloitte. Boston, MA. 2010, 2008, 2007, 2006.
- *The IHRSA Global Report; The State of the Health Club Industry.* IHRSA, Boston, MA. 2010, 2009, 2008, 2007, 2006, 2005
- *IHRSA's Guide to Membership Retention.* John McCarthy. IHRSA, Boston, MA. 2007.
- *The IHRSA Health Club Consumer Report; 2010 Health Club Activity: Usage, Trends and Analysis.* IHRSA, Boston, MA. 2010.
- *IHRSA Profiles of Success: The Annual Industry Data Survey of the Health and Fitness Club Industry.* IHRSA, Boston, MA. 2010, 2009, 2008, 2007, 2006, 2005, 2004, 2003, 2002, 2001, 2000.

- *Inductions for Retention.* Hillsdon, Ph.D. and Bedford, Ph.D. Health Club Management and Cybertrack. 2009.
- *King of Clubs.* Robert H. Dedman with Debbie DeLoach. Taylor Publishing: Dallas, Texas. 1999.
- *Retention and the Induction Process.* Bedford, Ph.D. and Hillsdon, Ph.D.
- *The American Health Club Experience.* An IHRSA Study conducted by American Sports Data. Boston, MA. 1997.
- *The Deconditioned Market.* Christine Brooks, Ph.D., Fitness Research Center, University of Michigan, Ann Arbor, Michigan. 1991.
- *Understanding Exercise Adoption Behavior.* University of Michigan, Ann Arbor, Michigan. 1996.
- *Why People Join; A Look at the Behavioral Barriers That Inhibit Health Club Membership.* Conducted by IHRSA, Boston, MA. 2006.
- *Why People Quit.* An IHRSA Study conducted by American Sports Data. 1998.
- *Why People Stay: Health Club Retention Research and Best Practices.* IHRSA. 2000.
- *Why and Where People Exercise.* An IHRSA Study conducted by American Sports Data. Boston, MA. 1995.
- *Winning the Retention Battle; Reviewing Key Issues of United Kingdom Health and Fitness Club Membership Retention,* volumes I-VI. Fitness Industry Association in cooperation with Leisure Industry Week. England. 2001 and 2002.

About the Authors

Stephen Tharrett is currently the owner and president of Club Industry Consulting, a global consulting business established in 2006 and based in the U.S. Stephen is also a partner in Club Intel, a recently formed company that is focused on providing the global club industry with insight, inspiration, and impact revolving around the emotional power of a brand and its ability to establish a powerful base of advocates and fans. From 2008 to 2010, Stephen served as the chief executive officer for the Russian Fitness Group, a privately held health/fitness club company that was, at the time, the largest in Russia. Prior to forming Club Industry Consulting, Stephen had a 20 plus year career with ClubCorp, a billion dollar private club company based in Dallas, Texas, where he served in several roles, ranging from director of athletics to senior vice-president for athletics, golf, and tennis, as well as serving on the company's leadership cabinet and business planning committee.

Stephen has authored or co-authored several management textbooks: *Fitness Management, 3rd Edition; The Health/Fitness Operator's Guide to Recruiting and Retaining Great Employees; ACE's Fitness and Business Forms Handbook; Legends of the Trade: A History of the Artisans, Influencers, and Innovators of Fitness; 101 Programming Strategies for Engaging Members in Health/Fitness Clubs;* and *101 Strategies for Improving Member Retention in Health/Fitness Clubs.* Stephen is also the co-editor of the 2nd, 3rd, and 4th editions of *ACSM's Health and Fitness Facility Standards and Guidelines.*

A former president of IHRSA, having served as president of the international association from 1996 to 1997, Stephen is widely respected for his knowledge of the health/fitness club industry. Stephen and his wife, Denise, reside in Highland Village, Texas. They have two grown children, Travis and Alyssa.

Paul Bedford, Ph.D., is a renowned authority on the management of retention, attrition, and the customer experience in the health/fitness club industry. Paul's company, retentionguru.com, works with clients to improve customer experience, loyalty, and, as a result, profitability for club operators. He frequently presents on the topics of retention and attrition at conferences on the international stage (Austria, Finland, Germany, Holland, India, Italy, Ireland, Norway, Spain, Sweden, Switzerland, Turkey & USA), as well as serves as a regular speaker at the annual IHRSA conference.

Paul has been working in the fitness industry for the past two decades. He holds masters degrees in both exercise and health behaviors and social science research. During his tenure in the industry, he has held various positions, ranging from gym instructor to club general manager, which collectively provide him with insight concerning what is applicable to the industry. He currently divides his time between conducting fitness-related research and developing and delivering training courses that provide practical approaches to retention, attrition, and customer service.

Working with the Central Club (London) in 2006/7 and as part of his PhD. research, Paul has applied his behavioral change strategies to the club-induction process. The multiple- appointment process that he subsequently defined has resulted in increases in average membership length in many facilities, ranging from seven months to 13 months, and in reduction in cancellations from an average of 77 per 1000 members per month to 23 per 1000 per month. He has also directed an extensive effort involving brief interviews of nearly 23,000 fitness facility members that examined the relationship between the various levels of customer service and whether individuals maintain their club membership. In addition, Paul was the lead facilitator on the development and application of a bespoke behavior-change model as part of "Activate England"—a national physical activity project aimed at engaging hard-to-reach groups. As a result, Activate England was able to successfully encourage over 8,000 people to become involved in physical activity, a total of which, 30% were from areas of deprivation, 46% were new to exercise, and over 80% were not participating sufficiently enough to benefit their health.

Paul also has significant expertise in the education sector, where he currently lectures at Middlesex University on physical activity and exercise psychology as part of the institution's master's degree program, and at Bath University, where he tutors GPs (MDs) on brief health behavior-change interventions. Previously, he served as a senior lecturer with YMCA Fitness Industry Training for 14 years, during which time he trained over 3,000 personal trainers.

At the present time, Paul is working with private (hotel groups, small and large chains) and public-sector operators of various groups, as well as several national governing bodies in the U.K. for sport.